Fixing Language

Fixing Language

An Essay on Conceptual Engineering

Herman Cappelen

OXFORD
UNIVERSITY PRESS

Great Clarendon Street, Oxford, OX2 6DP,
United Kingdom

Oxford University Press is a department of the University of Oxford.
It furthers the University's objective of excellence in research, scholarship,
and education by publishing worldwide. Oxford is a registered trade mark of
Oxford University Press in the UK and in certain other countries

First Edition published in 2018

Impression: 1

Published in the United States of America by Oxford University Press
198 Madison Avenue, New York, NY 10016, United States of America

British Library Cataloguing in Publication Data
Data available

Library of Congress Control Number: 2017955744

ISBN 978–0–19–881471–9

Printed in Great Britain by
Clays Ltd, St Ives plc

Contents

Part IV. Towards a General Theory 3: Worldliness and the Varieties of Conceptual Engineering

Part V. Compare and Contrast: Alternative Accounts of Conceptual Engineering

Acknowledgments

I've worked on this material for many years and have received more feedback than on any work I have done. Very many people read the manuscript at various stages and there have been reading groups and workshops on the material at several institutions. Too many have given feedback over that period for me to remember and list all of them. Suffice it to say that I'm very grateful for all those discussions, comments, and suggestions. They have helped me improve the book immensely (and also convinced me that philosophers come to this topic with such divergent background assumptions that it's impossible to write a book on it that won't strike many as deeply misguided).

There are a few people whose work and input have been particularly helpful at various stages. These include Derek Ball, Josh Dever, Matti Eklund, Olav Gjelsvik, Patrick Greenough, Sally Haslanger, Peter Ludlow, Tristram McPherson, Robert Pasnau, David Plunkett, Peter Railton, Mark Richard, Jennifer Saul, Kevin Scharp, Rachel Sterken, Tim Sundell, Amie Thomasson, and Brian Weatherson. Many thanks to all of them.

In 2015 Camilla Serck-Hanssen, Øystein Linnebo, and I started a center called ConceptLab at the University of Oslo. Our collaboration in ConceptLab has been a great source of help and inspiration for work on this book.

I got tons of help from three research assistants: Lea Schroeder, Matt McKeever, and Joshua Habgood-Coote. They did an almost unbelievable job helping to improve the manuscript.

Three detailed referee reports from readers for Oxford University Press also improved the manuscript.

Finally, thanks to Peter Momtchiloff for his support and for suggesting a title for another book that made me think of the title for this one.

Herman Cappelen

Oslo, April 2017

Preface

One goal of this book is to identify and advocate for its topic. Conceptual engineering isn't a recognized field within philosophy. I think that's unfortunate. It should be considered one of the central topics of philosophy, or perhaps even *the* central topic of philosophy. This book is an attempt to make a case for this claim.

Another aim of what follows is to articulate some of the central questions and challenges for the field and thereby provide a structure to it. I will develop a theory of conceptual engineering, but I care as much about identifying and making a case for the field as I do for my own theory.

One way to focus in on the topic of this book is to think about revisionist projects in philosophy. In all parts of philosophy—e.g., metaphysics, philosophy of mind, epistemology, logic, theories of race and gender and other social categories—there are philosophers who criticize the concepts we have and propose ways to improve them. Once one notices this about philosophy, it's easy to see that revisionist projects occur in a range of other intellectual disciplines and in ordinary life. That fact gives rise to a cluster of questions: How does the process of conceptual amelioration work? What are the limits of revision (how much revision is too much)? How does the process of revision fit into an overall theory of language and communication?

This book is an effort to answer those questions. In so doing, it is also an attempt to draw attention to a tradition in twentieth- and twenty-first-century philosophy that isn't sufficiently recognized as a unified tradition. Roughly, there's a pretty straight intellectual line from Frege (e.g., of the *Begriffsschrift*) and Carnap, on the one hand, to a cluster of contemporary work that isn't typically seen as closely related: much work on gender and race, revisionism about truth, revisionists about moral language, and revisionists in metaphysics and philosophy of mind. These views all have common core commitments: revision is possible and important. They also face common challenges: how is amelioration done and what are its limits? Unfortunately practitioners don't tend to see themselves as engaged in a common project.

My own path into this topic came from two directions: First, an interest in ways language can become meaningless. The thought that large swaths of language can appear meaningful, but nonetheless be nonsensical, is familiar from the history of philosophy from Kant through Carnap and the logical positivists (and I defend a version of it in Cappelen 2013). That way of thinking is still alive, but is now articulated somewhat differently: we find frequent claims to the effect that certain of our concepts are *incoherent* or *inconsistent*. *Freedom, truth, knowledge,* and *race* have all been so described. A second and in my mind related path into the topic was through Sally Haslanger's work on what she calls 'ameliorative projects': I think the kind of project she advocates is of massive significance throughout philosophy and beyond. We should therefore try to develop a range of competing frameworks to implement that project, but we're still just starting to understand the range of possible implementations. This book is a progress report on one way to do it.

This is a progress report *from a certain perspective.* Once one delves into this field, one very soon notices (and gets told) that literature from an extremely broad range of sources is relevant. It would be good to engage with literature from law (and philosophy of law), socio-linguistics, developmental psychology, history of ideas, and sociology. I've been told that I have to engage with the work of Bruno Latour and Deleuze, and Heidegger and Foucault. Some insist that detailed case studies are required to say anything important about the topic. I'm sympathetic to many of these suggestions: It would be a very good thing to write a book that synthesized all these varied perspectives and put them into a readable and unified whole. That, however, is not something I know how to do and so here is what I have done: I've written a book that provides *one way* into what I think of as one of the richest and most important fields in philosophy. I've tried to create a narrative that is relatively easy to follow and that engages with topics and debates that are familiar from recent Anglo-American philosophy. That said, I invite the reader to think of this book also as an invitation to develop competing narratives.

PART I

Introduction to Conceptual Engineering

PART I

Introduction to Conceptual Engineering

1

Introduction to Conceptual Engineering

1.1 Introduction

This book is about the process of assessing and improving our representational devices.[1] If you like describing representational devices as 'concepts',[2] then one way to characterize the topic of the book is: how can we assess and improve our concepts? One of the central questions will be whether our representational devices can be defective. I think the answer is 'yes', and that this defectiveness opens up a rich field of inquiry, involving questions such as:

- What kinds of representational deficiencies are there?
- How can we assess the adequacy of our representational devices?
- Once we have found deficiencies, what strategies are available for amelioration?
- What are the roles of this kind of assessment and improvement in philosophy and other intellectual disciplines?
- What are the roles for this kind of assessment and improvement in political and social life?
- What are the roles for this kind of assessment and improvement in our individual lives?

I will use the term 'conceptual engineering' for this critical/constructive enterprise of assessing and improving our representational devices. I think of *a theory*

---

[1] And also expressive devices. See chapter 6, section 6.7.

[2] As will become clear along the way, and in particular in Part II, I don't think concepts play a role in conceptual engineering, but that (apparently) paradoxical view will be bracketed these first few chapters: I speak the language of those whose views I present. Throughout this book I will call the activity that I am interested in 'conceptual engineering' (rather than meaning change) in order to make clear that my topic is the activity that self-described conceptual engineers are engaged in. Throughout this book I need to refer to concepts (in a way that's neutral between theories of concepts). There are many and varied conventions for how to do that. I have settled on the following (non-ideal) convention: to talk about the concept expressed by 'horse', I use the location: 'the concept "horse"'.

of conceptual engineering as one that tries to answer (some of) the questions just outlined. The aim of this book is to develop a theory of conceptual engineering.

This book is in part about the significance of terminological choices and so it's fitting that the terminology for talking about this field itself presents us with difficult choices. The term 'conceptual engineering' is used by Simon Blackburn (1999) and also Matti Eklund (2014, 2015). Sally Haslanger sometimes talks about 'ameliorative projects', sometimes about 'analytical projects' when she describes her work on race and gender (Haslanger 1999, 2000, 2006). Others use the term 'revisionary project' (Railton 1989, 1993, Scharp 2007, 2013a). Some use Carnap's term 'explication' for a sub-version of this kind of project. Others again prefer 'conceptual ethics' over 'conceptual engineering' (Burgess and Plunkett 2013a, 2013b). I've settled on 'conceptual engineering' though it is far from ideal. It's important that readers don't take that name as a description: on the view I defend in this book, the project isn't about concepts and there isn't really any engineering. Despite the descriptive inadequacy of the terms, my experience is that the label directs people's attention in the right direction and that's why I've chosen to go with the Blackburn/Eklund terminology.[3]

The book has five parts:

- Part I is an effort to identify the phenomenon I want to theorize about. I do this in two ways: through discussion of a number of examples (chapter 2), and through some general remarks about the nature of conceptual engineering (chapter 3).
- Parts II, III, and IV develop my positive theory, which I will call the *Austerity Framework*.
- Part II turns to the metasemantic foundations of conceptual engineering. The metasemantic theory that I endorse is externalist (chapter 6) and I claim that conceptual change is inscrutable, beyond our control, and non-luminous (chapter 7). I also explain why some philosophers might have thought that there were *inconsistent* or *incoherent* concepts (chapter 8).
- Part III is about the limits of revision (or amelioration). What's the difference between changing the topic and engaging in conceptual engineering? Why aren't all instances of conceptual engineering just a way to change the topic? Chapter 9 outlines these challenges and chapters 10 and 11 respond to them.

---

[3] For all those who think there are concepts and that they can be engineered, this terminological choice is also descriptively adequate.

- Part IV completes the presentation of the Austerity Framework, arguing that conceptual engineering involves changing the world (chapter 12), offering a typology of conceptual engineering (chapter 13), and responding to some objections (chapter 14).
- Part V considers some alternative approaches to theorizing about conceptual engineering, focusing primarily on: i) proposals by Ludlow (2014) and Plunkett and Sundell (2013) that focus on *metasemantic negotiation* (chapter 15); ii) proposals by Haslanger (1999, 2000, 2006), Brigandt (2010), Thomasson (forthcoming), and Richard (forthcoming) that focus on conceptual *functions* (chapter 16); and iii) Chalmers's method of elimination (Chalmers 2011) (chapter 17). I describe the relevance of these views to conceptual engineering and explain why I think that the Austerity Framework is a better approach than what they propose. In closing, I discuss whether there are any limits to conceptual engineering, discussing Chalmers's and Eklund's arguments for thinking that there are (Chalmers 2011, Eklund 2015) (chapter 18).

1.2 A Heuristic: Representational Complacency vs. Representational Skepticism

Conceptual engineering is an activity that many people—not just philosophers—engage in. In later chapters I will provide many illustrations and consider various theories about the nature of this activity, but I want to start by describing an intellectual attitude—or cognitive disposition—that I see as underlying this activity. As a rough but useful heuristic, we can divide those of us who think and speak into two broad categories:

The representationally complacent: The representationally complacent uncritically take over the representational devices that are handed to them. They do their thinking and talking with whatever concepts they have inherited from their peers, teachers, and community. Someone who is representationally complacent can be a skeptic in the traditional epistemic sense: when she hears an assertion, she can be disposed to provide counterevidence and opposition, but she does so using only inherited concepts. More generally, the representationally complacent think and speak without a great deal of meta-reflection on the tools of their thinking and speaking.

The representational skeptics: Representational skeptics do *not* uncritically take over the representational devices handed to them. A significant part of their intellectual efforts consists in questioning and trying to improve the concepts of their peers, teachers, and community. When a representational skeptic starts reflecting on an issue, the first question she asks herself is whether the language used to articulate the key questions is good enough. The representational skeptic does not throw herself headlong into efforts to answer questions; rather, she first questions the concepts used to articulate the questions.

Of course, these groups represent a continuum, and the same person might be complacent in some domains, but skeptical in others, but at least in intellectual work the distinction is significant. I'll use myself as an illustration of what characterizes a representational skeptic: I've spent my professional life doing philosophy, and what I've found, over and over again, is that important debates in my field are plagued by defective language: questions are asked in the wrong way and core concepts are defective. I've written one book on intuitions (Cappelen 2012) and one on the so-called de se (Cappelen and Dever 2013). A central thesis in both works is that the debates are fundamentally flawed by the use of defective concepts; in particular, both 'intuition' and 'de se' are fundamentally defective pieces of terminology, or so I argue (Cappelen 2012: C3, Cappelen and Dever 2013: 3). When I look beyond philosophy to debates about social and political issues in non-academic contexts, I find these debates very hard to engage with because the issues are often framed using what I take to be flawed terminology. And so it goes across the board: my own thinking about any question whatsoever is in large part meta-reflection on how to frame the question at hand.

Life is not easy for us representational skeptics. Communication with others is hard, because we refuse to take their language for granted. We also lack any solid resting point: we representational skeptics need a language in order to engage in critical reflection about representations. But what about *that* language? Shouldn't we be critical about that as well? The answer is 'yes': we should be skeptics throughout, and this makes our project exhausting. Or perhaps worse than exhausting, for in its most extreme form it will seem internally inconsistent. After all, the question 'Is X a defective representational device?' is just another question. If the representational skeptic is disposed to be skeptical about the way questions are framed, how can she ever start inquiry? She would have to be skeptical of the very question she is asking about representational devices. But then what is left of representational skepticism?

I don't have answers to all these questions, but this book is a kind of progress report on my effort to make sense of and practice representational skepticism. The next chapter provides many illustrations of representational skepticism. One way to start reflecting on conceptual engineering is to look at *local* examples of representational skepticism, that is, *local* efforts to show that particular concepts (or other representational devices) are defective and *local* efforts to ameliorate them. I've italicized 'local' in the previous sentence because many of the worries about representational skepticism result from describing it as a universal attitude. The kind of self-referential worries that arise as a result are analogous to those that face relativists (see MacFarlane 2014: C2). A way around this for the relativist is to be a *local* relativist—about, say, epistemic modals, or about predicates of personal taste. Similarly, one can be a local representational skeptic, say, about vague language, generic language, gender terms, or specific concepts like 'belief' or 'intuition'. Some of the examples in the next chapter are of local representational skepticism, while others are expressions of very general representational skepticism.

1.3 Central Themes of This Book

This book is about a very BIG topic and there are many avenues into it. One natural entry point into this topic is from a field you already care about and central concepts in that field. So a psychiatrist can get into this topic by thinking about DSM classifications; a lawyer by thinking about legitimate interpretations of laws and regulations; someone engaged in thinking about race can focus on concepts used in that domain; someone working on ethics can get into the topic by thinking about revisionism in ethics. And so on. That's not the path into the field that I provide. This book is to a certain extent 'from above': The first chapter provides a host of specific illustrations, but then the details of these examples are left behind and the rest of the book is focused on general issues that face anyone engaging in conceptual engineering.

It might facilitate understanding and help readers to keep track of what's happening to highlight some central themes already at this stage:

Theme 1: At the foundation of a theory of conceptual engineering is a theory of metasemantics: The first theme is that at the center of any theory of conceptual engineering is a metasemantic theory, i.e., a theory of that which makes it the case that expressions have the meanings they have. There's no agreement about what the correct theory of metasemantics is. As a corollary we're likely to have a plethora of theories about conceptual engineering. This book—Part II in particular—provides an externalist metasemantics for conceptual engineering. Along the way I argue that much of what I say generalizes to alternative frameworks.

Theme 2: Conceptual engineering and externalism: How is conceptual engineering compatible with externalism in the philosophy of language and mind?

The term 'engineering' naturally leads to an image of someone sitting around fiddling with their concepts, but if even moderate versions of externalism are true, we speakers are not in a position to do any such thing. This issue is particularly urgent for me, because the theory I propose in Part II builds externalism into the very core of what conceptual engineering is. This has wide-reaching effects on how to think about the topic.

Theme 3: In or out of control? To what extent are we *in control* of the process of conceptual engineering? I think we're *not* in control. In that respect my view contrasts sharply with most of those who theorize about conceptual engineering. An important challenge for me is to explain how we should react to the fact that conceptual engineering is a process we are not in control of. (My view, very roughly, is: being in control is overrated and for the most part an illusion anyway.)

Theme 4: No systematic theory—contestation throughout: If you expect a theory that provides necessary and sufficient conditions for when successful conceptual engineering has happened, or an instruction manual for how to do it, this book will disappoint. I argue that no such theory can be given: even the success conditions for conceptual engineering are up for grabs. On my view revisionism is also pervasive at the meta-level, meaning that the rules for conceptual engineering are constantly being engineered.

Theme 5: Conceptual engineering and continuity of inquiry: The central theme of Part III of the book concerns a cluster of related issues: How is conceptual revision (or amelioration or evolution) compatible with continuity of inquiry, continuity of interpretation, diachronic agreement and disagreement, and how does the activity avoid generating massive amounts of verbal disputes? In chapter 9 I trace this concern back to Strawson's objection to Carnap's account of explication. This worry is also found in many contemporary revisionists (e.g., Haslanger and Railton). Much of this book is an effort to respond to that worry.

Theme 6: Conceptual engineering is not only about concepts and words, but also about the world: Finally, even though I follow others in calling the process I'm interested in 'conceptual engineering', I do not think that the kind of change involved is merely conceptual. For example, the process is not about the concepts of 'race' or 'gender' or 'freedom' or 'belief'. It is about race, gender, freedom, and beliefs. Conceptual amelioration is better understood as amelioration of the world.

2

Illustrations
Conceptual Engineering in Philosophy and Beyond

This chapter introduces conceptual engineering through a series of examples. It has three sections: Section I provides illustrations from philosophy. Section II presents instances of conceptual engineering from other intellectual disciplines, and from political and social discourse. Section II also relates conceptual engineering to the phenomenon of gradual semantic drift (and non-intentional conceptual evolution). Section III of this chapter is called 'The Logical Space of Conceptual Engineering: A Taxonomy'. The aim of this section is to systematize the illustrations given in the first two sections.

Section I

2.1 Conceptual Engineering in Philosophy

I start with philosophy not because it's the only (or most important) domain where conceptual engineering takes place, but because it provides some good examples of explicit and theoretically self-aware instances of conceptual engineering. If you have a hard time identifying just what the phenomenon under investigation is, here is an initial answer: it is the kind of activity instantiated by the examples in this chapter. The rest of the book then tries to answer questions such as:

- What do these examples have in common?
- Do those activities constitute an interesting, unified category?

I should emphasize right away that the answers to these questions are entirely non-obvious. There is a reason why not a single book has been written that is focused exclusively on questions related to conceptual engineering:[1] *it is hard to see that there is a unified topic here.* I think there is a unified topic—a rich field of research, even—but it takes work to clear the ground for it to become salient. That's one of the goals of this book: even if you end up disagreeing with the theory I propose, I hope that you will at least end up agreeing that conceptual engineering is an important topic for philosophers.

One more preliminary. In this chapter, I use various instances of philosophizing as *data points*. I do so to draw the reader's attention to a kind of activity that many philosophers take themselves to be engaged in: a form of conceptual engineering, a form of revisionism, or an effort to ameliorate our concepts. Now, many of those philosophers will also have a theory of what that activity is. This is *not* my focus at this point. For now, my take on the issue is this: there is a kind of activity that all of these philosophers are engaged in, and their preferred description or understanding of that activity can be mistaken. Since philosophers tend to mix object and meta-level discussions quite freely, the examples below will involve ~~both~~ both philosophers engaging in conceptual engineering and their descriptions of what they think this activity is like (descriptions that I will argue, in later chapters, are all wrong).

Note that these philosophers will each have a preferred terminology for talking about the activity, and in this chapter I will adopt those terminologies uncritically. In later chapters, however, I will try to develop an improved framework for understanding what it is that these philosophers are doing. My use of these philosophers' terminology for describing the activity of conceptual engineering does not indicate an endorsement of it.

2.1.1 Clark and Chalmers on 'belief' and the extended mind

In their paper 'The Extended Mind', Clark and Chalmers propose, among other things, that 'A believes that p' be used in a way that makes it true even when p is a proposition that A has access to only with the assistance of various 'external' devices (Clark and Chalmers 1998). In connection with that proposal, they consider various objections of the form: *Well, that's just not how we use 'belief' in English.* In response they say:

We do not intend to debate what is standard usage; our broader point is that the notion of belief *ought* to be used so that Otto qualifies as having the belief in question. In all *important* respects, Otto's case is similar to a standard case of (non-occurrent) belief . . .

---

[1] At least not as I construe the questions in this book—as this first part of the book will make clear, there's an extensive literature on specific instances of conceptual engineering. What's lacking is literature on *general* frameworks that those specific efforts can be embedded in.

By using the 'belief' notion in a wider way, it picks out something more akin to a natural kind. The notion becomes deeper and more unified, and is more useful in explanation.

(Clark and Chalmers 1998: 14)

Clark and Chalmers' goal is not to describe our current concept of 'belief'—they want us to *revise* our current concept (if it turns out not to be their proposed concept). Note two particularly important features of the proposal. (i) Their revision changes both the extension and the intension of the concept 'belief'. (ii) They briefly provide a justification for the revision: it is, they say, more useful in explanations. Their new revised concept is also 'deeper' and 'more unified'. So our current notion is defective, as it is not sufficiently unified, not sufficiently deep, and not sufficiently useful in explanations.

2.1.2 Explication: from Carnap and Quine to Gupta

According to Carnap, philosophers should engage in what he calls 'explication'. He describes this activity as follows: "The task of *explication* consists in transforming a given more or less inexact concept into an exact one or, rather, in replacing the first by the second" (Carnap 1950: 3). In a very broad sense, this entire book is about explication, i.e., the idea that we take a term that has a certain deficiency and then transform it into a better concept.

Carnap's notion of explication, however, is narrower than the activity I'm interested in. He recognizes only one kind of deficiency, 'inexactness'. Similarly, improvements for Carnap are also of a specific kind. An explication should be assessed along four dimensions:

1. The explicatum is to be similar to the explicandum in such a way that, in most cases in which the explicandum has so far been used, the explicatum can be used; however, close similarity is not required, and considerable differences are permitted.
2. The characterization of the explicatum, that is, the rules of its use (for instance, in the form of a definition), is to be given in an exact form, so as to introduce the explicatum into a well-connected system of scientific concepts.
3. The explicatum is to be a fruitful concept, that is, useful for the formulation of many universal statements (empirical laws in the case of a nonlogical concept, logical theorems in the case of a logical concept).
4. The explicatum should be as simple as possible; this means as simple as the more important requirements (1), (2), and (3) permit. (Carnap 1950: 7)

Carnap does not *argue* for restricting the relevant deficiencies to inexactness and the relevant virtues to dimensions (1)–(4); he simply *states* this without argument. It is natural to try to expand on the idea, as Anil Gupta does in his SEP entry on definitions. Gupta says.

Conditional

An explication aims to respect some central uses of a term but is stipulative on others. The explication may be offered as an absolute improvement of an existing, imperfect concept. Or, it may be offered as a 'good thing to mean' by the term in a specific context for a particular purpose.   (Gupta 2015 §1.5)[2]

I'd like to focus on idea that an explication is a 'good thing to mean' by the term in a specific context for a particular purpose. Here is an illustration from Gupta:

The truth-functional conditional provides another illustration of explication. This conditional differs from the ordinary conditional in some essential respects. Nevertheless, the truth-functional conditional can be put forward as an explication of the ordinary conditional *for certain purposes in certain contexts.* Whether the proposal is adequate depends crucially on the purposes and contexts in question. That the two conditionals differ in important, even essential, respects does not automatically disqualify the proposal.

(Gupta 2015 §1.5)

Much the same idea of explication can be found in Quine's *Word and Object*, where Quine writes on explication:

We do not claim synonymy. We do not claim to make clear and explicit what the users of the unclear expression had unconsciously in mind all along. We do not expose hidden meanings, as the words 'analysis' and 'explication' would suggest; *we supply lacks*. We fix on the particular functions of the unclear expression that make it worth troubling about, and then devise a substitute, clear and couched in terms to our liking, that fills those functions. Beyond those conditions of partial agreement, dictated by our interests and purposes, any traits of the explicans come under the head of 'don't-cares' (§38). Under this head we are free to allow the explicans.   (Quine 1960: 258–9)

On this more general understanding of explication, there is no unique correct explication of any term. Carnap was clear about this:

. . . if a solution for a problem of explication is proposed, we cannot decide in an exact way whether it is right or wrong. Strictly speaking, the question whether the solution is right or wrong makes no good sense because there is no clear-cut answer. The question should rather be whether the proposed solution is satisfactory, whether it is more satisfactory than another one, and the like.   (Carnap 1950: 4)

2.1.3 Haslanger on amelioration in general and of gender and race terms in particular

In a number of papers, Sally Haslanger argues for the importance of what she (in some papers) calls 'ameliorative projects'. According to Haslanger, the goal

---

[2] According to Gupta (in SEP), the quoted phrase is due to Alan Ross Anderson; see Belnap 1993: 117.

of an ameliorative project is not to describe our concepts or their extensions. Instead,

... we begin by considering more fully the pragmatics of our talk employing the terms in question. What is the point of having these concepts? What cognitive or practical task do they (or should they) enable us to accomplish? Are they effective tools to accomplish our (legitimate) purposes; if not, what concepts would serve these purposes better?

(Haslanger 2000: 33)

For example, the question 'What is knowledge?' might be construed in several ways. One might be asking: What is *our* concept of knowledge? ... On a more naturalistic reading one might be asking: What (natural) kind, (if any) does our epistemic vocabulary track? Or one might be undertaking a more revisionary project: What is the point of having a concept of knowledge? What concept, (if any) would do that work best?   (Haslanger 2000: 32)

These last questions are starting points for what she calls 'ameliorative' projects.[3]

Haslanger not only talks in general terms about ameliorative projects, she has *practiced* amelioration. In a series of papers spanning thirty years, she has proposed that we revise our ordinary concepts of race and gender (Haslanger 1999, 2000, 2004, 2006, 2008, 2009, 2010).[4] One of Haslanger's most influential proposals is the proposal that we change the meaning of the word 'man' and 'woman' so that their meanings accord with the following definitions:

S is a woman iff$_{def}$
(i)   S is regularly and for the most part observed or imagined to have certain bodily features presumed to be evidence of a female's biological role in reproduction;
(ii)   that S has these features marks S within the dominant ideology of S's society as someone who ought to occupy certain kinds of social position that are in fact subordinate (and so motivates and justifies S's occupying such a position!); and
(iii)   the fact that S satisfies (i) and (ii) plays a role in S's systematic subordination, i.e., along some dimension, S's social position is oppressive, and S's satisfying (i) and (ii) plays a role in that dimension of subordination.

S is a man iff$_{def}$
(i)   S is regularly and for the most part observed or imagined to have certain bodily features presumed to be evidence of a male's biological role in reproduction;

---

[3] Note that this version (or interpretation) of Haslanger is different from the one I object to in chapter 7, section 6. I think Haslanger changed her mind (without telling us) somewhere between Haslanger 2000 and Haslanger 2006. As I argue in chapter 7, section 7.6.2, Haslanger 2006 in effect gives up the ameliorative project.

[4] Many of these papers are collected in Haslanger 2012.

(ii)   that S has these features marks S within the dominant ideology of S's society as someone who ought to occupy certain kinds of social position that are in fact privileged (and so motivates and justifies S's occupying such a position); and

(iii)   the fact that S satisfies (i) and (ii) plays a role in S's systematic privilege, i.e., along some dimension, S's social position is privileged, and S's satisfying (i) and (ii) plays a role in that dimension of privilege. (Haslanger 2000: 39)

It is worth highlighting two features of her proposal:

- The ameliorative proposal is revisionary: according to the proposal, there cannot be a woman that is not subordinated. It is true by definition that those falling under 'woman' are subordinated. As a result, Haslanger changes the intension of the term 'woman', since the ordinary language term 'woman' is used in such a way that it is *possible* for a woman not to be subordinated.
- The justification for this revisionary project is broadly political: the justificatory claim is that this new usage would be good for various political reasons. More specifically, Haslanger's stated political goal is the elimination of what she calls women. She says: 'I believe it is part of the project of feminism to bring about a day when there are no more women (though, of course, we should not aim to do away with females!)' (Haslanger 2000: 46).

Even prior to a more systematic theory of conceptual engineering, it should be easy to see the difference between Haslanger's project and a descriptivist project. A descriptivist would be interested in describing (some features of) the extension of 'woman', the mechanism through which that extension is picked out, or the concept of 'woman' that we currently have. Haslanger's project might be constrained by these descriptive issues in various ways (more on that in later chapters), but its central goal is normative: to ask what our concepts ought to be or what extensions our terms ought to have.

2.1.4 Revisionism about moral language

Moral philosophy is a good illustration of a theoretical domain in which many of the leading theories are revisionary. These theories generally take this form: (a) they hold that moral language is flawed, and (b) they offer a proposal for how to improve it. Two examples of such theories are Peter Railton's naturalism (Railton 1989) and Richard Joyce's revolutionary fictionalism (Joyce 2005).

2.1.4.1 RAILTON'S REVISIONISM

Railton proposes a naturalistic account of moral terms, such as 'right', but, crucially, does not claim that his proposed account coincides in extension with the relevant natural language terms. The project is explicitly revisionary: Railton is a naturalist who thinks that moral language as is fails to be naturalistically acceptable, and his aim is to provide a naturalistically amenable revision of our moral language. Moreover, Railton thinks that this form of revision is required *throughout* philosophy:

Since almost any notion P found in natural language will draw its meaning from multiple sources, and will have taken on diverse functions—and possessed diverse relations to other concepts—at various points in its evolution, it is to be expected that any rendering of that concept intended to make it sufficiently clear to suit purposes of theory-construction will be, to some degree, revisionist. . . . It lies among the tasks of a philosophical theory to shed light upon the ways in which a discourse has functioned and evolved, and to motivate the particular rectification of discourse effected by theory. To accomplish these tasks, a theory must explain how those features upon which it fixes afford the most compelling understanding of the discourse.

. . . Revisionism may reach a point where it becomes more perspicacious to say that a concept has been abandoned, rather than revised. No sharp line separates tolerable revisionism and outright abandonment, but if our naturalist wishes to make his case compelling, he must show that his account of a person's good is a rather clear case of tolerable revision, at worst.   (Railton 1989: 158–9)

Central to Railton's project is making clear the difference between tolerable revision and abandonment. This is a theme that I devote Part III to—and there I return to Railton's proposed solution.

2.1.4.2 RICHARD JOYCE'S REVOLUTIONARY FICTIONALISM: MORAL DISCOURSE IS HOPELESSLY FLAWED

Revolutionary fictionalists about moral language, such as Richard Joyce (2005), argue (a) that moral language is fundamentally flawed (in that moral assertions fail to state truths), and (b) that we should continue to use moral language despite these flaws by using this language *in an improved way*. For Joyce, this improvement involves a form of non-cognitivism. What makes this an important instance of what I call 'conceptual engineering' is that fictionalism is not claimed to be an accurate description of actual usage, but rather a suggestion for an improved way of talking about morality.

2.1.5 *Revisionism about truth*

Many authors (Tarski 1933, Chihara 1979, Eklund 2002, Scharp 2007, 2013a, 2013b) think that various paradoxes show us that our notion of truth is broken: the concept 'truth' is defective. Note that this view is different from the kind of dialetheism proposed, for example by Graham Priest (2005, 2006):

It is crucial to distinguish between inconsistency approaches to the liar and *dialetheism*, which is the view that some contradictions are true. Although a dialetheist accepts all the premises and inference rules used to derive the contradiction, he or she also accepts the conclusion (i.e., that the liar sentence is both true and false).... from the point of view of an inconsistency theorist, the dialetheist is no better off than someone who advocates a traditional approach—neither of them realizes that our conceptual competence leads us to both accept the premises and inferences of the liar reasoning and reject its conclusion. The challenge for the inconsistency theorist is to provide a theory that avoids the problems with traditional approaches without falling into dialetheism.

(Scharp 2007: 607)

Scharp (2007, 2013a, 2013b) argues that the inconsistency theorist has to take on a constructive task: the task of finding an improved version of the concept of 'truth'. Note that there is a somewhat important difference here from the examples above: Scharp says explicitly that he is not trying to improve our truth concept. Instead, he tries to develop *replacement concepts*.

According to Scharp, a revisionist project generally has four stages:

1. *Pre-revolution*: people possess and use concept X and theory T in which X serves an explanatory role (e.g., mass and Newtonian mechanics).

2. *Early revolution*: people discover that X is an inconsistent concept; they have some idea of which situations cause problems for those who use X; because of these problems, doubt is cast on the explanatory force of X and the acceptability of T as fundamental theory; however, without an alternative, people still use T and X.

3. *Late revolution*: new concepts (say, $Y_1, \ldots, Y_n$) are proposed and a new theory (say, U) is proposed in which the Ys serve an explanatory role (e.g., relativistic mass and proper mass and relativistic mechanics); U reduces to T in familiar cases, and the Ys agree with X on familiar cases; U is used to determine the cases in which it is acceptable to use T; at this point, the conceptual repertoire and language have been extended.

4. *Post-revolution*: U has replaced T as the accepted fundamental theory, and the Y concepts have replaced X as the accepted fundamental concepts; people might or might not still use T (and thus X) in certain cases (e.g., phlogiston theory has been totally superseded, but Newtonian mechanics is still indispensable for everyday situations). (Scharp 2013a: 137)

It is worth noting already at this stage that Scharp has a theory of what inconsistency consists in: he thinks that concepts have constitutive rules and that they can be inconsistent (2013a: C2). This proposal is one I discuss (and reject) in chapter 8.

2.1.6 More on inconsistent or incoherent concepts: Weiner and van Inwagen

Scharp's 2013 book is about the inconsistency of truth, but in it he also makes the intriguing suggestion that *all* philosophical concepts are inconsistent:

My view is that philosophy is, for the most part, the study of inconsistent concepts... Once enough progress has been made to arrive at a set of relatively consistent concepts for some subject matter, it gets outsourced as a science.   (Scharp 2013a: 3).

Less extreme versions of this view are often suggested. For example, Matt Weiner (2009) argues that the concept 'knowledge' is inconsistent, while van Inwagen argues that our concept 'freedom' is inconsistent. Here is the argument for the latter claim:

There are seemingly unanswerable arguments that... demonstrate that free will is incompatible with determinism—and there are seemingly unanswerable arguments that... demonstrate that free will is incompatible with indeterminism. But if free will is incompatible both with determinism and indeterminism, the concept 'free will' is incoherent, and the thing free will does not exist.   (van Inwagen 2008: 327–8)

Van Inwagen goes on to suggest that we should reject our concept of freedom.

2.1.7 Engineering the concept of race

The literature on the concept of race exhibits a very wide range of views on how and whether that concept should be engineered. Kwame Anthony Appiah is an eliminativist about race. According to Appiah, "the truth is that there are no races: there is nothing in the world that can do all we ask 'race' to do for us" (1992: 75). As Appiah sees it, our concept 'race' presupposes what he calls 'racialism', the view that "we could divide human beings into a small number of groups, called 'races,' in such a way that the members of these groups shared certain fundamental, heritable, physical, moral, intellectual, and cultural characteristics with one another that they did not share with members of any other race" (Appiah 1996: 80). Since racialism is empirically false, there are no races and so the term 'race' has an empty extension. Some eliminativists about race use the falsity of racialism as motivation for a normative claim: we should get rid of the concept 'race' (see Mallon 2004 and 2006 for an overview of this literature). Others see it as motivation for improving our concept of race: the concept that we have is defective, but it could be improved. Haslanger (2000, 2004, 2005, 2006, 2008, 2009, 2010) is an advocate of amelioration about racial concepts. She describes herself as developing a new concept of race that aims to be an improvement on the defective concept we actually have (see especially Haslanger 2009). It's important to note, however, that the eliminativist is also making normative claims: the eliminativist thinks we would be better off not using the term 'race' anymore. It's unclear exactly what it is to eliminate a concept, but here is one interpretation: no natural language terms should denote that concept.

2.1.8 Leslie on generics and social prejudice

Recently, Sarah Jane Leslie has proposed a form of conceptual engineering that is interestingly different from those considered so far. The basic structure of her argument is the following: *she presents empirical evidence that the use of certain linguistic constructions leads those using them to make cognitive mistakes.* The expressions in question are so-called generics,[5] and the mistake in question is that of essentializing[6] social kinds. In the light of this empirical evidence, she proposes that we consider a large-scale linguistic revision:

> The foregoing discussion suggests that we might consider altering our ways of speaking about race, ethnicity, religion, and so on. Instead of labeling a person as a Muslim, we might instead describe the person—if needed—as, say, *a person who follows Islam*, thus emphasizing that *person* is the relevant kind sortal, and that *following Islam* is a particular property that the individual happens to possess. Instead of speaking of *Blacks and African Americans* we might instead adopt locutions such as *people with darker skin*.
>
> (Leslie forthcoming: italics in original)

The 'we' who should consider this revision is the entirety of humankind (or at least those who speak languages with generics). Leslie has no concrete proposals for how to go about implementing this revision, but she speculates that it would have a range of positive effects:

> Adopting such a way of speaking and thinking may have some immediate benefits; the results of Carnaghi and colleagues suggest that hearing a member of a familiar social kind described by an adjective rather than a noun can reduce the extent to which adults expect the individual to conform to a stereotype. It is possible, though, that the real benefits would not lie just in the alteration of the attitudes of adults; the really intriguing possibility would be to decrease the extent to which children in our society grow up essentializing social kinds.   (Leslie 2017)

---

[5] These are expressions of the form 'tigers are striped', 'a duck lays eggs', 'the dodo is extinct', and 'ticks carry Lyme disease'. For an introduction to generics, see Leslie and Lerner (2016).

[6] Her view of essentializing is this: 'We essentialize a kind if we form the (tacit) belief that there is some hidden, non-obvious, and persistent property or underlying nature shared by members of that kind, which causally grounds their common properties and dispositions' (Leslie forthcoming).

[handwritten margin notes:] Why is this not always worth changing

[handwritten note at bottom:] Generics are fine for other purposes.

What makes Leslie's foray into conceptual engineering distinctive[7] is that it is based on empirical data about the effects of using specific linguistic expressions. It is not an armchair exercise of any kind.

2.1.9 Epistemology: 'what is knowledge?' or 'what should knowledge be?'

Large chunks of epistemology are concerned with what exactly the English word 'know' is used to pick out. Gettier's 1963 paper 'Is Justified True Belief Knowledge?' triggered an enormous amount of literature aimed at figuring out the conditions under which a justified true belief becomes knowledge. This goal is primarily what Robert Pasnau calls 'lexicography': to describe our concept of knowledge or the extension of the term 'knows'. That is, the goal is purely descriptive. Since Timothy Williamson's *Knowledge and its Limits*, there has been an upsurge in the so-called 'knowledge first' tradition in philosophy (Williamson 2000). This tradition treats knowledge as a primitive, using it to define other concepts rather than trying to figure out how knowledge is build up from other, more primitive parts. But note that this tradition is just as descriptive: it takes our actual concept of knowledge and uses it for various purposes. For Williamson, the goal is not to improve on our concept of knowledge: it is primitive and untouchable.

This contrasts sharply with the revisionary tradition. Those engaged in conceptual engineering would ask: what *should* our concept of knowledge be? Can we improve on what we have? Why should we be intellectually complacent and stick with the concept that we have if we could have a better concept of knowledge? Recall Haslanger expressing just that attitude:

. . . the question 'What is knowledge?' might be construed in several ways . . . One might be asking: What is *our* concept of knowledge? . . . On a more naturalistic reading one might be asking: What (natural) kind (if any) does our epistemic vocabulary track? Or one might be undertaking a more revisionary project: What is the point of having a concept of knowledge? What concept, (if any) would do that work best?

(Haslanger 2000: 32; see also Haslanger 1999)

A more recent defense of revisionary epistemology can be found in Fassio and McKenna (2015), who say:

What is knowledge? What should knowledge be like? Call an epistemological project that sets out to answer the first question 'descriptive' and a project that sets out to answer the second question 'normative'. If the answers to these two questions don't coincide—if what

---

[7] The uniqueness claim might seem like hyperbole, but I mean it literally: I don't think any other philosophical work on concept revision has been based on work in psychology.

Need to determine function/purpose first. Purpose is what matters.

knowledge should be like differs from what knowledge is like—there is room for a third project we call 'revisionary'. A revisionary project starts by arguing that what knowledge should be differs from what knowledge is. It then proposes that we revise our account of knowledge accordingly.   (Fassio and McKenna 2015: 755–6)

2.1.10 Carnap on nonsense

I end this list of illustrations with what might be the most radical claim about conceptual deficiency. Wittgenstein, Carnap, and other logical positivists suggested that many important domains of discourse lack a semantic foundation: they are meaningless. This may be the ultimate form of conceptual defect.

The first half of the twentieth century was the heyday of the great theorists of nonsense, Wittgenstein and Carnap in particular. They argued that large swaths of discourse (and of philosophy in particular) were nonsensical and that many of those we consider great thinkers were not thinking at all. According to Carnap, some of the discourses that were considered by some to be the high points of human intellectual achievement amounted to nothing more than a bunch of people making noises and marks on paper. Those who read, commented on, and developed such work suffered from the same illusion. They had what appear to be discussions; they wrote books and papers apparently responding to each other. But none of it was anything other than the most fundamental kind of failure. Their discourse was neither true nor false, it expressed no thoughts, and there was no agreement or disagreement. It was all just a complete waste of time, energy, ink, and paper.

Just like the examined examples 'principle' and 'God,' most of the other specifically metaphysical terms are devoid of meaning, e.g. 'the Idea,' 'the Absolute,' 'the Unconditioned,' 'the Infinite,' 'the being of being,' 'nonbeing,' 'thing in itself,' 'absolute spirit,' 'objective spirit,' 'essence,' 'being-in-itself,' 'being-in-and-for-itself,' 'emanation,' 'manifestation,' 'articulation,' 'the Ego,' 'the non-Ego,' etc.   (Carnap 1959: 67)

Carnap concludes that '[t]he alleged statements of metaphysics which contain such words have no sense, assert nothing, are mere pseudo-statements' (67). He goes further, arguing that all normative speech is nonsense as well:

. . . the same judgment must be passed on all philosophy of norms, or philosophy of value, on any ethics or esthetics as a normative discipline. For the objective validity of a value or norm is (even on the view of the philosophers of value) not empirically verifiable nor deducible from empirical statements; hence it cannot be asserted (in a meaningful statement) at all. In other words: either empirical criteria are indicated for the use of 'good' and 'beautiful' and the rest of the predicates that are employed in the normative sciences, or they are not. In the first case, a statement containing such a predicate turns into a factual judgment, but not a value judgment; in the second case, it becomes a pseudo-statement. It is altogether impossible to make a statement that expresses a value judgment.   (Carnap 1959: 77)

In earlier work (Cappelen 2013), I defended a version of Carnap's view—a version that doesn't rely on Carnap's verification theory of meaning, but applies no matter what meaning happens to be. The version I defend is more local and not as wide ranging as Carnap's. I summarize the view as Pocket Nonsense:

> *Pocket Nonsense.*   A version of Carnap's claim can be defended, but its scope is very different from Carnap's. It is not that specific subject matters (e.g., ethics, religion, aesthetics, or metaphysics) are nonsensical, but rather that when language is introduced and used in defective and irresponsible ways, it can lead to pockets of nonsensical speech and nonsensical cognitive events. When this happens, the individual is not to blame, nor is it easy for the individual to avoid being engulfed in nonsense. It can happen as a result of participation in a defective linguistic practice where individual speakers are unable to make the relevant correction on their own.   (Cappelen 2013: 34)

2.1.11 Is all of philosophy conceptual engineering?

Above I gave many examples of philosophers who explicitly engage in what I call conceptual engineering. Some philosophers think that's what philosophers *should* do *all* the time. Here is Matti Eklund's normative version of the view (elaborating on a point he takes from David Chalmers):

> ... while philosophers often have been concerned with our actual concepts or the prop- erties or relations they stand for, philosophers should also be asking themselves whether these really are the best tools for understanding the relevant aspects of reality, and in many cases consider what preferable replacements might be. Philosophers should be engaged in *conceptual engineering.* Compare: when physicists study reality they do not hold on to the concepts of folk physics but use concepts better suited to their theoretical purposes. Why should things stand differently with what philosophers study?   (Eklund 2014: 293)[8]

Some philosophers think this actually takes place in philosophy all the time (even when it is not explicitly described as such). In the introduction to *Think*, Simon Blackburn describes his work as follows:

> I would prefer to introduce myself as doing conceptual engineering. For just as the engineer studies the structure of material things, so the philosopher studies the structure of thought. Understanding the structure involves seeing how parts function and how they interconnect. It means knowing what would happen for better or worse if changes were made. This is what we aim at when we investigate the structures that shape our view of the

---

[8] This is in effect an endorsement of Haslanger's ameliorative project. See chapter 2, section 2.1.3.

Improper analogy.

world. Our concepts or ideas form the mental housing in which we live. We may end up proud of the structures we have built. Or we may believe that they need dismantling and starting afresh.   (Blackburn 1999: 1)

Think of this as the descriptive version of Eklund's normative claim—Richard, for example, thinks that we actually are doing what Eklund thinks we should be doing:

Conceptual analysis is generally not just descriptive but normative. In interesting cases— the analysis of knowledge, of free action, of truth—what we tend to find is evidence not of a single underlying albeit vague concept, but a profusion of more or less mutual, not altogether consistent, presuppositions and patterns of application that (with a bit of the philosopher's art) can be resolved into a collection of articulations of candidates for what we might mean by the terms we use. To arbitrate amongst them is at least in part a matter of asking, not what natural or gerrymandered kind we are trying to pick out, but asking what the point or points of having and applying the concept under study is.

(Richard forthcoming)

Elsewhere, Richard uses 'freedom' as an illustration:

Some philosophers tell us that to act freely would be to perform an act, the performance of which was not determined by conditions over which one has no control. Others tell us that to act freely is, roughly put, to perform an act such that one could have decided not to perform it (and would not have performed it, had one so decided). Yet other accounts are on offer.... Why should we think that when we use the phrase 'free action' in speech or token it in thought, it is determinate that we are picking out the property isolated by one as opposed to another of these candidate analyses of free action?...it is not at all implausible that 'free action' does not determinately denote.... I do not say that all or even most of the notions philosophy investigates suffer from the kind of indeterminacy I've suggested may infect the notion of free action. But I do say that it is very probable that some, and not improbable that many, do.   (Richard 2014: 8)

2.1.12 Chalmers on conceptual pluralism and pointless verbal disputes

According to David Chalmers, philosophers should endorse a form of *conceptual pluralism*. According to this view, "there are *many* interesting concepts in the vicinity of philosophical terms such as 'semantic', 'justified', 'free', and very little depends on which one goes with the term." According to Chalmers, it might be that a term like 'free' denotes a particular concept, but even if it does, that's not particularly significant: there's a range of concepts in the vicinity of all (non-basic) philosophical concepts:

The model also leads to a sort of pluralism about the properties that these concepts pick out. For example, it naturally leads to semantic pluralism: there are many interesting sorts of quasi-semantic properties of expressions, playing different roles.

(Chalmers 2011: 539–40)

None of these is privileged. Many of them are equally interesting and philosophically significant. So, Chalmers concludes, this view leads to a kind of philosophical pluralism:

> It leads to epistemic pluralism: there are many different epistemic relations, playing different roles. It leads to gene pluralism: there are many different things that deserve to be called 'genes', playing different roles. The same goes for confirmation pluralism, color pluralism, and so on. In fact, I am inclined to think that pluralism should be the default view for almost any philosophical concept. It may be that, as it happens, usage of a term such as 'gene' or 'confirmation' or whatever in our community is uniform enough that it has a single referent. But even so, there will be nearby possible communities, and probably numerous speakers within a community, who use the term in a different way, with equally interesting referents.
>
> (Chalmers 2011: 540)

One corollary of this way of thinking about philosophical concepts is that we should give up the goal of merely describing the concepts that happen to be expressed by our words. What we refer to by 'freedom' or 'meaning' or 'knowledge' is arbitrary and relatively insignificant. There is an important constructive project here: the project of identifying all relevant concepts in the vicinity of a particular term and seeing to what use they can be put. This is a form of conceptual engineering.

The other illustrations in this chapter have all started by identifying a defect and have then, at least in some cases, suggested an improvement. This is true about Chalmers as well. We have just seen his positive proposal, but this positive view springs from a deep skepticism about philosophy as it has been practiced throughout its history. Chalmers thinks that because we have not been aware of conceptual pluralism and haven't engaged in the kind of conceptual engineering that he advocates, very many philosophical debates have been pointless wastes of time. They have been exercises in what he calls 'verbal disputes'. This is a different kind of defect from those considered above: think of it as a *communicative defect*. When we are not aware of conceptual pluralism, the following will often happen. One speaker will take, say, 'freedom' to express a property, P, while another speaker takes 'freedom' to express another property, P*. Since they both continue to use the expression 'freedom', they give the appearance of disagreeing with each other. One might say 'Freedom is F', and the other might say 'Freedom is not F'. It certainly looks like they are disagreeing. According to Chalmers, this form of pointless verbal dispute has characterized most of philosophy, and so he concludes philosophy is mostly 'pointless'. The way to fix it is to engage in a form of conceptual engineering.

2.1.13 Brief historical digression: analytic philosophy, Strawson, Soames, and contemporary semantics and epistemology

I wish someone would write a history of philosophy as in large part a battle between descriptivists and revisionists. The distinction will not be simple or clear cut and the battle lines have been drawn in different ways in different time periods. But in each time period and in all parts of philosophy, we find these two fundamentally conflicting attitudes. For some, success is measured by a true description of, for example, what knowledge, belief, morality, representation, justice, or beauty is. For others, the aim is figuring out how we improve on what there is: how can we improve on knowledge, justice, belief, beauty, etc.? Those with the former aim tend to find the latter unintelligible (or naive) and those with the latter aim tend to find the former complacent, uninspired, and lazy. Maybe Strawson thought about the history of philosophy a bit like this.[9] At the beginning of *Individuals* he distinguishes between *descriptive* and *revisionary* metaphysics: "Descriptive metaphysics is content to describe the actual structure of our thought about the world, revisionary metaphysics is concerned to produce a better structure" (1959: 9). One of his characterizations of the revisionists' objection to descriptivists is acute. He imagines the revisionist insisting that metaphysics is "essentially an instrument of conceptual change, a means of furthering or registering new directions or styles of thought" (1959: 10). In that brief introduction Strawson also gestures at a way of writing a history of the kind I imagined above. He says, "Perhaps no actual metaphysician has ever been, both in intention and effect, wholly the one thing or the other. But we can distinguish broadly: Descartes, Leibniz, Berkeley are revisionary, Aristotle and Kant descriptive. Hume, the ironist of philosophy, is more difficult to place. He appears now under one aspect, now under another" (1959: 9).

At the time of writing this book, this contrast is again salient in many philosophical domains. Philosophy of language provides a particularly striking illustration of this tension. Philosophy of language (and more generally the tradition that is often described as 'analytic') has its origin in the early twentieth century. The founders of that tradition were all focused on normative questions and on projects of engineering and amelioration. Frege, Wittgenstein, and Carnap did not see their central goals as that of describing the semantic or conceptual structures of specific languages. Their approach was critical and constructive. Frege wanted an *improved* language. In the *Begriffsschrift* he writes: 'If the task of

---

[9] I should note that Strawson would not be on board with the particular theory of revision that I propose later in this book. His construal of the revisionist vs. descriptivist distinction is focused on concepts, mine is not.

philosophy is to break the domination of words over the human mind . . . then my concept notation, being developed for these purposes, can be a useful instrument for philosophers' (Frege 1879, Preface to the *Begriffsschrift*). Frege's *Begriffsschrift* is a paradigm of conceptual engineering (more on this below). Or consider the Wittgenstein of the *Tractatus Logico-Philosophicus*, who aimed to draw a line between what could be said and what could only be shown. You *shouldn't*, according to Wittgenstein, try to say what can only be shown. The aim of telling philosophers (and others) about the legitimate and illegitimate uses of language is a *normative* aim. Without getting bogged down in Wittgenstein exegesis, it's fair to say that most interpreters have taken his later work to be motivated by a related concern. According to the *Philosophical Investigations*, the aim of philosophy is 'to show the fly the way out of the fly-bottle' (*PI* 309)—the fly-bottle of language, that is. And so the aim of philosophy is a therapeutic one: to improve the condition of those that Wittgenstein saw as deceived by a lack of understanding of their own use of language. Finally, consider the following three aspects of Carnap's work that are related to engineering:

- First, the process he calls 'explication' is an effort to *improve* our conceptual apparatus. The idea is to take a term that suffers from various deficiencies— Carnap focuses on what he calls 'vagueness' and 'indeterminacy'—and then improve them along various dimensions.

- Second, according to Carnap, a great deal of speech is deficient because it isn't verifiable in the way he thought language should be. The most famous expression of this is in his paper "The Overcoming of Metaphysics through the Logical Analysis of Language." There, Carnap tries to show that most of Western philosophy is, literally, meaningless: it is nonsense. And nonsense is bad, he thinks, and should be avoided. So the goal of his paper is normative: philosophers should start speaking in new and improved ways.

- Third, and more controversially, we can understand Carnap's proposed theory of meaning—the verification theory—as a normative suggestion. That is, it is a theory we should adopt not because it is adequately descriptive of how we use language (or the word 'meaning'), but because doing so would have good effects. It would improve our language if we adopted it. So, on this view, the verification theory is a theory of what meaning *should be*.

The so-called 'ordinary language' movement that dominated much of philosophy in the second half of the twentieth century also had an important normative engineering related component. In '"A Plea for Excuses," Austin says that "ordinary language . . . embodies . . . the inherited experience and acumen of many generations of men. . . . If a distinction works well for practical purposes in ordinary life (no mean feat, for even ordinary life is full of hard cases), then there is sure to be something in it, it will not mark nothing" (Austin 1956: 11). This is practical advice about the usefulness of various distinctions we make in ordinary language. Austin then notes that "ordinary language is not the last word: in principle it can everywhere be supplemented and improved upon and super-seded" (Austin 1956: 11). The challenge here is to recognize when ordinary language is good enough and when it can be improved upon. This is a deeply normative project, not a primarily descriptivist one, and it is continuous with the kind of engineering projects described earlier in this chapter.

Something happened around 1970: much analytic philosophy of language took a sharp descriptivist turn and the various engineering projects were down-played. This turn was reflected in closer collaboration between philosophers of language and linguists. For the last forty years much of the most influential and most cited work in philosophy of language has focused exclusively on describing how various linguistic devices of English (and other natural languages) work. Paradigms include work on the semantics for anaphora, indefinite and definite descriptions, quantifiers, epistemic modals, conditionals, proper names, and predicates. The philosophers who work on pragmatics aim to describe the pragmatic mechanisms that, as a matter of fact, play a role in interpretation. None of this work has as its goal to ask how our semantics can be made better. Nor is its goal to understand how our pragmatics can be improved. The aim isn't to identify faults and then outline strategies for amelioration. These philosophers are content to be exclusively descriptivist.

I think we're now in large part blind to how bizarre this descriptivist turn in philosophy of language is. That blindness is for example reflected in Scott Soames's history of analytic philosophy (2003a, 2003b). As Soames sees it in that work, the normative (engineering) aspects played a marginal role in the origins of analytic philosophy and philosophy of language. The central aims of the analytic tradition were all descriptive (to describe various features of our linguistic practices and conceptual structures) and work towards these aims had its culmination in the work of Kripke and other externalists. In my view, this is a fundamental misunderstanding of philosophy in the twentieth century. The most crucial aspect of philosophy in that period was the normative and engineering proposals: these projects were what initiated and motivated what we now describe as 'analytic' philosophy. The descriptivist turn in the 1970s was an historical aberration (for an elaboration on this, see Cappelen 2017). What triggered the descriptivist turn? This is an interesting question, one that I don't have a full answer to. It was motivated, in part, by the perception that many of those who saw themselves engaged in various revisionary projects did not have enough understanding of what they were criticizing. In order to criticize and improve something, you first need to understand how that thing works. So the descriptivist turn was, I suspect, in part motivated by a sense that the revisionists needed more facts about language to work with.

This descriptivist turn in recent philosophy wasn't limited to those working in philosophy of language—it spread across philosophy. Epistemology is the clearest example. Since the publication of Gettier's paper in 1963, an almost unbelievable number of papers and books have been devoted to describing the exact way in which people who speak English use the word 'know', and to trying to understand why some of them don't like to apply the term 'know' in so-called Gettier cases. This purely descriptive turn is a historical aberration, as Robert Pasnau has documented (Pasnau 2013). Traditionally, what was called 'epistemology' was normative, concerned with describing epistemic ideals and strategies for improvement rather than with engaging in careful lexicology.

One aim of this book is to make these battle lines easier to see in contemporary work—making clear the contemporary battles between descriptivists and revisionists. I think that seeing the revisionist projects in various parts of philosophy as unified at a certain level of description will help strengthen those projects.

Section II

2.2 Conceptual Engineering beyond Philosophy

Philosophy isn't special. Explicit conceptual engineering takes place outside philosophy, too. Hardly any of the deficits mentioned above are restricted to speech that is distinctively philosophical. In this section of the chapter I briefly mention how something like conceptual engineering takes place in non-philosophical domains. I then turn to the view that (something like) conceptual engineering takes place whenever humans communicate using language.

2.2.1 Conceptual engineering in law and psychiatry

Two clear examples of disciplines that engage in conceptual engineering are law and psychiatry. Those creating and interpreting laws are often explicitly concerned with what certain words in laws *should* mean. The extensions of 'murder', 'fetus', 'intention', 'person', and 'tax' as they occur in various laws have massive practical importance and are the subject of extensive, explicit debate and theorizing. Similarly, psychiatrists who put together the DSM classifications for the

American Psychiatric Association and the International Classification of Diseases for the World Health Association spend a great deal of their time thinking and explicitly arguing about how terms should be defined, or about what should be in their extensions.

2.2.2 Public controversies over 'person', 'marriage', 'rape', and Biko on 'black vs. non-white'

Many of the most heated public debates can be construed as debates over what our words should mean. Peter Ludlow's book *Living Words* (Ludlow 2014) provides a very broad range of illustrations and argues that they should be understood as instances of 'meaning negotiation', or debates over what our words should mean. They are, in some important sense, metalinguistic. Here I want to focus on some of Ludlow's examples (2014: C2), rather than his theory (which I discuss in chapter 15).

Three easy examples are the debates over 'marriage', 'rape', and 'person'. In the first case, there have been heated debates over whether the members of same-sex couples should be able to stand in the marriage relation to each other. In the case of 'rape', there have been debates over, e.g., whether that term should apply to forced sex *within* marriage (this debate goes back at least 150 years). In the case of 'person', there is an ongoing debate about whether a fetus is a person or not.

Now, there are several ways to understand these debates. On one interpretation, they are irrelevant to the topic of this book: according to that interpretation, these debates are first-order debates about whether a fetus can be a person, whether a husband can rape a wife, and whether same-sex couples can be married. So construed, the debates are not about concepts. One view is right and the other is wrong—the issue isn't settled by fixing concepts. However, according to an alternative construal, these debates are about what our words *should* mean, or what concepts those words *should* express. I think this is the right interpretation of many such debates and here is an argument for that view:

Argument for these debates being, at least in part and in some cases, about what concepts our words should express.[10] It's an empirical question what is in the extension of terms such as 'marriage', 'rape', and 'person'. It's a historical accident—a fact about the history of specific words—that they ended up picking out what they pick out. Now suppose, for the sake of argument, that it turns out that the following is true about these English words:

---

[10] Here, as in many other places in Part I, I'm presenting conceptual engineering in the way others do as concerning what concepts should mean. As will become clear in chapter 12, I don't think this metalinguistic description is correct, but those objections are put aside until after my own view is presented.

- The English word 'marriage' picks out only pairs consisting of one man and one woman.
- The English word 'rape' picks out only non-consensual intercourse between people that are not married, i.e., it is impossible to rape someone one is married to.
- The English word 'person' does not pick out any fetuses.

Suppose that, as a matter of historical fact, these are the meanings that these English words have ended up with. The question is this: would these facts about the meanings of these terms settle the debate about whether, say, same-sex couples can be married? I take it that it would not. Those who advocate for same-sex marriage would be unmoved by such a fact about the meaning of the English word 'marriage'; and the best explanation for that is that they think 'marriage' *ought* to have a meaning that allows for same-sex couples to count as married (independently of what it means). Similarly, those who argue that it is possible for someone to be raped by their spouse will think the word 'rape' *should* mean something that leaves that possibility open (independently of what it happens to actually mean); and those who oppose abortion will argue that the word 'person' should mean something that includes fetuses (independently of what it actually means). I take these debates to be in part metalinguistic disputes about what the words should mean.

If you find this form of argument convincing, then the phenomenon I'm focusing on here is extremely widespread. A wide range of public exchanges can be construed as being in part exercises in conceptual engineering. Some illustrations:

- What is an immigrant?
- What is a refugee? How is the *refugee, immigrant, expat* distinction drawn?
- What is money? (e.g., is Bitcoin money?)
- What is poverty?

Here are some cases where more details can be found in Ludlow's book:

- What is a doll? (2014: 9–10)
- What is a sandwich? (2014: 10–13)
- What is a journalist? (2014: 17–19)
- What is relevant? (2014: 21–2)
- What is organic? (2014: 25–6)
- What is an athlete? (2014: 78)

For each of these case, it seems plausible that at least some of the many debates involving these terms can be construed as normative debates about what our words *should* mean (as opposed to debates over what as a matter of fact happens to be in their extension). I could fill the book up with detailed elaborations of many of these illustrations, and they are each intrinsically interesting. However, I want to try to keep the focus here on the general structure of the activity and going to great detail about any one of these would just distract from the overall goal.

That said, here is one last very vivid illustration that follows up on themes from earlier in this chapter. Stephen Biko, in "The Definition of Black Consciousness," defines 'black' and distinguishes that category from 'non-white' as follows:[11]

We have defined blacks as those who are by law or tradition politically, economically and socially discriminated against as a group in the South African society and identifying themselves as a unit in the struggle towards the realization of their aspirations.

This definition illustrates to us a number of things:

1. Being black is not a matter of pigmentation—being black is a reflection of a mental attitude.
2. Merely by describing yourself as black you have started on a road towards emancipation, you have committed yourself to fight against all forces that seek to use your blackness as a stamp that marks you out as a subservient being.

From the above observations therefore, we can see that the term black is not necessarily all-inclusive, i.e. the fact that we are all not white does not necessarily mean that we are all black. Non-whites do exist and will continue to exist for quite a long time. If one's aspiration is whiteness but his pigmentation makes attainment of this impossible, then that person is a non-white. Any man who calls a white man "baas", any man who serves in the police force or security branch is ipso facto a non-white. Black people—real black people—are those who can manage to hold their heads high in defiance rather than willingly surrender their souls to the white man.   (Biko 1971)[12]

Biko is most naturally understood as making a proposal for conceptual revision: he most likely didn't think that this is how the term 'black' was, as a matter of fact, used in his language. It is a proposal for how it should be used. Part of the goal of what follows is to find a framework for describing that kind of activity.

2.2.3 Related phenomena: semantic drift and contextual negotiations

There are two linguistic phenomena that bear more than a family resemblance to the instances of conceptual engineering given above: (i) gradual semantic drift and (ii) negotiation over how context-sensitive terms should have their semantic values fixed in particular contexts.

2.2.3.1 SEMANTIC DRIFT AND SEMANTIC PLASTICITY: A CONTINUOUS PROCESS OF CONCEPTUAL ENGINEERING?

Gradual semantic drift is the process that happens when our words change their meaning (and extension/intension) gradually over time. In a recent paper, Cian Dorr and John Hawthorne give the example of salad (Dorr and Hawthorne

---

[11] I take this to be distinct from the way race is treated in purely theoretical work on race by philosophers—Biko wasn't an academic and this proposal was primarily political, not theoretical (but these distinctions are obviously vague and fluid—and nothing hangs on it).

[12] Thanks to Brian Epstein for drawing my attention to this passage by Biko and making clear to me its relevance to the issues of this book.

2014). Here's a plausible story about that word: At some point, not too long ago, a dish had to be served cold and have a high preponderance of green leaves in order to be a salad. At that time a concoction of cold cut fruit wouldn't be a salad. That has changed. Today, fruit salads are salads. More generally, we now find it unproblematic to apply 'salad' to "various warm leaf-free concoctions" (Dorr and Hawthorne 2014: 284). If this is true about 'salad', then it is true very widely—salad isn't very distinctive in these respects. Small changes happen for very many—maybe all words—over time. More generally: the extensions and intensions of our natural language terms can change gradually over time.

For what follows, two features of 'salad' will be important:

1. 'Salad' has changed its intension over time.
2. There is nothing particularly distinctive about 'salad'—if 1. is true, then lots of ordinary language terms change their extensions over time (e.g., 'book', 'watch', 'lunch', 'healthy', etc.).

Here are Dorr and Hawthorne (2014) distinguishing two models for how semantic facts (or more broadly content facts) are determined by 'lower-level' facts such as microphysics:

Patchwork: the facts about content supervene on the microphysical facts in the same way as the facts about people's height-to-the-nearest-centimeter does. You can make little changes to people without 'the nearest centimeter' classification changing. Then, suddenly, there's a jump. As the microphysical facts change gradually, the semantic facts will respond in a jerky fashion (see Dorr and Hawthorne 2014: 316–30).

Plasticity: according to this model, the semantic facts are like the facts about people's heights: even tiny differences in the microphysical facts will induce correspondingly tiny, but still genuine, differences as regards which of them obtain (see Dorr and Hawthorne 2014: 281–300).

Plasticity seems like the right model for 'salad' and many other words in natural languages. This example is important because it generalizes very easily and very widely. The considerations in favor of gradual change in the extension of 'salad' have nothing specifically to do with salads. They concern the fact that there is nothing semantically significant about dishes with lots of green leaves—there is no sense in which this category is a reference magnetizer. There are a whole bunch of equally good candidates for the referent of 'salad' and there is no reason why we should be stuck with any one of them. This is true about a very large class of terms: *money, student, book, friendship, vacation, education*, etc.

In all these cases there are an indefinitely large number of candidate referents and no reason we should stably be fixed onto one of them for all time. Instead, there is likely to be slight instances of semantic drift over time (Dorr and Hawthorne 2014: 284–8).

Note that the example of 'salad' is importantly different from cases such as 'person', 'marriage', and 'rape'. The most obvious difference is that there has been no extensive public debate over the meaning of 'salad'—no demonstrations, no lawsuits, very little passion. Not many people seem to care very much about whether fruit-based concoctions fall into the extension of 'salad'. That said, I think that there's a lot we can learn from cases like 'salad' when thinking about cases that involve explicit efforts to engage in conceptual engineering. These cases share important features. First, cases like 'salad' illustrate the following important point: we can have change in extension *and* preservation of topic: consider people speaking and thinking about salads in the period before fruit salads were included in the extension of salads. Those people were talking and thinking about salads. There's a thing—salad—that persists throughout these changes. I later call these continuous objects topics, and they are some of the more mysterious entities I'll appeal to in this book. I elaborate this in chapter 10. Second, I'm not convinced that there's a *fundamental* difference between 'salad' and, say, 'person'. The appearance of a significant difference lies in the lack of high-profile public debates and disputes. This difference, however, might be a superficial one. In cases like 'salad', there will have been a lot of local discussion, reflections, decisions, and actions that influenced the gradual change. For example, it's likely that at some point a chef somewhere felt constrained by what she took to be unreasonable restrictions on what could go into a salad. She might have felt that these restrictions hampered her culinary creativity and her ability to construct menus for her restaurant. As a result, she started using 'salad' in a somewhat new way. She might not have thought of this act as a case of trying to change the intension of 'salad', but this and similar acts will have contributed to the gradual change. Any one such act is of course not sufficient to change the extension (initially, when she called a fruit-based concoction a 'salad', she was wrong)—but thousands of such acts combined with other factors can have that effect. But this isn't very different from the high-profile, public, and intentional efforts: any *one* article or statement or speech about what 'marriage' should have in its extension is insufficient to generate a change; what will generate a change is a very complicated combination of intentions, actions, decisions, conversations, legal maneuvers, plus a whole range of other factors we don't understand.

2.2.3.2 CONTEXTUAL NEGOTIATION AS A FORM OF CONCEPTUAL ENGINEERING?

Some expressions have their semantic values fixed in context: for example, terms like 'I', 'now', and other indexicals. According to many philosophers, the class goes far beyond these obvious cases. It is, for example, plausible that gradable adjectives and quantifiers are context sensitive: What falls into the extension of 'smart' depends on the context, the comparison class or a scale of smartness (Cappelen and Dever 2016: 16–17, 165–7). Whether it is true to say 'Everyone is here' depends on a contextually salient domain of quantification. According to some views, every expression is context sensitive along some dimensions. I'll call such views 'radical contextualist' (for more discussion of such views see Searle 1980, Sperber and Wilson 1995, Travis 1996, Cappelen and Lepore 2005, Cappelen and Dever 2016: C1).

There's a route from context sensitivity (however widespread it is) to conceptual engineering. The basic thought is this:

If a sentence S is context sensitive (an element of S has its semantic value fixed in context) then we can shape what is said by an utterance of S by shaping the relevant features of the context of utterance. We can engineer contents in context because what we say depends on the contexts we are in and we are in control of the context.

Peter Ludlow endorses a version of radical contextualism that he calls the *Dynamic Lexicon* (Ludlow 2014). This is a view that has much in common with relevance theory (Sperber and Wilson 1995, Carston and Seiji 1998, Recanati 2004, and Davidson's view in Davidson 1986). What's distinctive about Ludlow's work is that he uses these theories to advocate for the view that we have control over content in contexts and can (and do) negotiate over content in contexts. He uses his version of radical contextualism as a springboard to the view that something like conceptual engineering is ubiquitous. I discuss (and criticize) this view further in chapter 15.

Section III

2.3 The Logical Space of Conceptual Engineering: A Taxonomy

The illustrations above have the same basic structure: Some concept is considered defective along some dimension, in some cases that deficiency can be ameliorated, and various proposals are made about how to best ameliorate.

That said there's a great deal of variability among the illustrations and it would be helpful to have at least a tentative taxonomy in place. I'm not one of those philosophers who spend a lot of time building taxonomies (there just always seem to be way too many ways to do it, not enough hangs on how it is done, and it is messy), but I am making an exception in this case. Here is a proposed Taxonomy of Conceptual Engineering. This taxonomy centers on six issues: i) what the defect is, ii) the cure for that defect, iii) whether or not the revision is intentional, iv) the scope of the revision, v) whether the revision has institutional support, and vi) what norms motivate the revision.[13]

2.3.1 The varieties of conceptual deficiency

- *The semantic value is defective*: it is missing (i.e., there's nonsense) incoherence, inconsistency, vagueness (Frege and Carnap thought of this as a defect).
- *Objectionable effects of the semantic value*: it has a semantic value, but for that particular expression to have that semantic value has bad effects. So the claim isn't the concept fails semantically, but that using it can have detrimental effects. These detrimental effects can be divided into three:
  - *Morally, politically, or socially objectionable effects*: For example, if the word 'marriage' excludes same-sex couples, that might have bad effects. The claim that these are bad effects can be justified in at least two ways:
    - *Metaphysical justification*: the extensions of terms are in some cases constitutive of social reality and so insofar as it matters what our society is like it will matter what extensions our terms have (for more on this idea, see Chapter 3, sections 3.3.1 and 3.3.2).
    - *Non-metaphysical justification*: Even if you don't think meanings of words are constitutive of social reality, you can think that as a matter of empirical fact the divisions and classifications we make will have very significant social effects.
  - *Cognitive effects*: For example, if Leslie and others are right, the use of generics interferes with the cognitive processes of those using them (by, for example, making them disposed to endorse mistaken generalizations about social kinds).
  - *Effects on theorizing*: According to Clark and Chalmers (1998), the fact that we have a notion of belief that blocks the extended mind hypothesis makes it hard to develop a systematic theory of the mind (there's nothing semantically wrong with the non-externalist notion, but using it is likely to result in a non-unified theory).

---

[13] See chapter 13 for a further development of this typology.

2.3.2 The varieties of ameliorative strategies

What you do when you've identified a deficiency will depend on the deficiency it is and also on the theory of concepts that is presupposed I haven't addressed so far in this chapter, but which will be addressed in a couple of places below), but strategies can usefully be divided into three kinds:

2.3.2.1 IMPROVE THE CONCEPT AND KEEP THE LEXICAL ITEM

You have a word with a certain meaning and extension/intension. You keep the word and improve the meaning/extension/intension. In the standard case, the lexical item will be preserved, but the semantic value will be improved. This is an idea that some think is incoherent (see chapter 9), but I think there's a way to make sense of it. It's a natural way to describe many of the cases above: Railton, Haslanger, Carnap, and Clark and Chalmers want to keep the same expression, but improve its meaning. Those who pursue this strategy will have different conceptions of what it is to improve a meaning/extension/intension.

2.3.2.2 IMPROVE THE CONCEPT AND CHANGE THE LEXICAL ITEM

Another strategy is the one proposed by Chalmers in the paper "Verbal Disputes" (Chalmers 2011) and used a great deal in theoretical work: Improve the meaning/extension/intension and find a new expression—in Chalmers's case the old expression + a subscript—to attach it to.

2.3.2.3 COMPLETE ABANDONMENT

Some of those who discover deficiencies advocate total abandonment: get rid of the defective concept and the lexical item. There's nothing there to improve on. This is one way to construe some of Carnap's remarks about nonsense: he didn't think 'the absolute' should be improved. Just get rid of it.

2.3.3 Intentional vs. unintentional

Engineering projects can be divided into those that are done intentionally and those that are done unintentionally:

- *Intentional conceptual engineering:* The first section of this chapter provided many examples of philosophers who were aware of engaging in conceptual engineering.
- *Unintentional conceptual engineering:* The second section involved many examples from the social and political domain of conceptual engineering that the agents wouldn't describe as such: not all those advocating for a

change in the extension of 'marriage' are aware of being engaged in what I have called 'conceptual engineering': they might in fact deny it. What is important here is that you can be engaged in conceptual engineering even when you are not aware of it.

2.3.4 Local vs. broad conceptual engineering

Engineering projects can be usefully divided into those that have a local aim (revision for a particular purpose in a particular context) and those that have a much broader aim (revision not just for a local purpose—but a more permanent change):

- *Local and context-restricted conceptual engineering:* Engineering done on specific terms for a particular purpose in a particular context. Kevin Scharp (2013a), for example, advocates *contextually restricted abandonment*. On his view, our defective concept 'truth' works well in most ordinary contexts, but there are specific contexts in which it should be abandoned. Sometimes this strategy is described as *replacement in certain contexts*: in the contexts where the defective concept is abandoned a replacement concept is provided.
- *Global and contextually unrestricted conceptual engineering:* Engineering can be global in two senses. We can engineer a concept for the language as a whole, rather than for a particular context. The target of engineering might also be all the terms in language, rather than some restricted domain. The most general kind of conceptual engineering aims to revise *all* concepts, for all purposes.

2.3.5 Institutional vs. non-institutional

- *Explicitly regulated and institutionalized conceptual engineering (backed by institutional power):* some instances of conceptual engineering, e.g., in law and psychiatry, are highly institutionalized. They are codified (the rules for how it can be done are explicitly regulated). They are also backed by various kinds of institutional powers: the legal system by police power, for example.
- *Informal conceptual engineering:* most instances of conceptual engineering are not institutionalized, aren't governed by explicit rules, and aren't backed up by anything like police power. So, if philosophers refuse to go along with Clark and Chalmers's or Haslanger's proposals, there are no immediate and codified repercussions.

2.3.6 The kinds of norms involved

Finally, we can classify conceptual engineering projects according to the norms involved. I've talked as if the projects all involve the identification of what I've called 'a defect' and then an effort to improve. Both talk of defects and amelioration is normative. What is the relevant set of norms? Here I don't think having a classification is particularly useful and even a list might be pointless. The range of options here is as broad as that of the range of norms. So whatever your preferred classification of norms is could be inserted here.

2.3.7 Two things I haven't mentioned: holism and creating from scratch

Two important issues have been skirted around in the above outline. First, issues about holism vs molecularism vs atomism will be relevant to all instances of conceptual engineering. Put in summary form, if one engages in engineering of a particular concept, this may i) have global effects on the meaning of other terms in the language (for those who endorse radical forms of holism), ii) affect the meaning of a range of 'neighborhood' concepts, but not everything (for the molecularist), or iii) only change the meaning of that concept (for the atomist).

Second, none of the examples so far involve creating concepts from scratch. They involve improving or replacing the concepts that we already have. The instances of conceptual engineering that I have used as my illustrations all involve entrenched concepts and efforts to improve them. Those kinds of cases are the focus of this book and I won't have much to say about how best to create concepts from scratch. There are two reasons for this:

1. The philosophical tradition that I theorize about, exemplified by the illustrations above, concerns improvements of what we have. As will become clear in Part II, this tradition is my 'data point', so to speak. My central aim to present a theory of what such philosophers do—a foundation for that kind of activity. If I succeed at that, I've done okay.
2. I don't have much new to say about introducing terminology from scratch. In much of the rest of the book I rely on the externalist tradition in philosophy where the idea of baptisms and introductory definitions plays a role. I do talk about how those introductions can be defective and contested, and that's the closest I get to a discussion of the normative aspects of creating terminology from scratch.

A corollary of the focus in what follows on improvement is that the abandonment strategy, mentioned above, isn't much discussed in what follows. Abandonment might be what Leslie advocates for generics about social kinds and Scharp for the concept 'truth' (at least in some contexts). It's a widespread attitude toward pejoratives. Again, this isn't to say or imply that the abandonment strategy isn't an interesting topic. There are tricky issues about what abandonment amounts to and how it can be achieved, but they're not addressed in what follows.[14]

---

[14] It's difficult to articulate abandonment: a word can't just *disappear*. New tokens of it can occur less frequently of course and we can try to destroy or hide the old ones. Maybe in the case of, for example, pejoratives, that's what abandonment would amount to. If concepts are abstract objects, they can't disappear either—they exist eternally. If we think of concepts as psychological states of various kinds, then we can aim for the elimination of those psychological states.

3

Arguments for the Importance of Conceptual Engineering and Implications for Philosophical Methodology

In the chapters that follow, I develop a theory of conceptual engineering—the Austerity Framework. This theory describes the activity of conceptual engineering rather differently from how many of its practitioners think of it. Before turning to that critical and constructive phrase of the project, which will occupy us in Parts II and III of this book, it's worth pausing to look at very big-picture, general arguments for the significance of conceptual engineering. By 'general' I mean that these are arguments that are to some extent independent of the significance of any particular case. It's fairly easy to see the importance of the definition of 'rape', and the reasons for this importance are specific to that case. Likewise, it is not hard to see why the meaning of 'person' is important, and here too the reasons will in large part be specific. What I want to do in this chapter is to outline the most *general* arguments for the significance of conceptual engineering— arguments that apply to all cases. I think there are three such arguments: the Prudential Argument and two Ontological Arguments.

3.1 The Prudential Argument

The Prudential Argument rests on one Basic Assumption:

> *The Revisionist's Basic Assumption*: The terms or concepts which we use to talk and think about a particular subject matter can be defective and can be improved to address these defects.

I've given a range of illustrations which support this assumption in the previous chapter. That chapter also made it clear that the deficiencies that philosophers identify and their ameliorative strategies vary. For now, let's assume that the Basic Assumption is true. Now the Prudential Argument goes as follows:

The Prudential Argument: If our representational devices can be defective in ways W1...Wn, then we should be engaged in two kinds of activities: (i) investigating whether these concepts are defective and (ii) if defects are found, then ameliorating the defective concepts.

The extent to which this argument will move you depends on your attitude towards the Basic Assumption. Here are two possibilities:

- Even if you endorse the Basic Assumption, you might think that defects of the relevant kind are few and far between. You might think that the situation is a bit like this: there are presumably some defective sidewalks that have weaknesses, so that you can fall through the sidewalks into big underground holes where you will be stuck for the rest of your life. However, such defective sidewalks are *extremely* unusual. So it makes no sense to check every time you walk on one to make sure it's not one of the defective ones. It would, overall, be a waste of time. If you think linguistic defects are like that, you wouldn't exactly reject the Prudential Argument, but it wouldn't trigger immediate and urgent concern about all of our ability to talk and think. You might find it interesting to think about defects and amelioration as a theoretical issue, and for largely theoretical reasons. Conceptual defects wouldn't be an issue for the general practice of talking and thinking. Of course, even for someone with a restricted view of defects, the Prudential Argument would become urgent if much of her talking and thinking happens to be in a defective domain. If there's some reason to think that moral terms are defective, then all moral talking and thinking becomes suspect. If a subset of theoretical terms are suspect, then those who make use of those terms in that subfield must worry.
- If, however, you think the Basic Assumption is true for reasons that are not limited to a few expressions, but rather for reasons that generalize easily, then the Prudential Argument should disturb you and keep you awake at night. If large chunks of your talking and thinking are potentially defective, amelioration should be your most pressing intellectual (and indeed practical) task.

I think the second of these reactions is the right one. There are two reasons for this.

The first reason is that all the reasons that various theorists have given for thinking that some particular subset of concepts is defective *generalize easily*.

Most of the suggested deficits are such that if they apply to expression E, then they apply *much* more broadly. Recall the classification of conceptual deficits in the taxonomy in the previous chapter: most of the deficits are at least potentially ubiquitous. If Haslanger is right that gender and race terms are less than maximally helpful for pursuing the project of social justice, there is no reason whatsoever for thinking that this defect will not generalize to an extremely broad range of expressions. It's hard to see why it shouldn't also apply to 'family', 'mother', 'father', 'student', 'pet', 'money', and many, many other words. If Railton is right about the reason why we need to be revisionists about moral language, that could end up including a very large swath of terminology (everything that is, in part, normative?). If Clark and Chalmers are right about why we need to revise 'belief', then these reasons plausibly generalize beyond 'belief' to a very large set of terms used to refer to mental states. The generalization is even more obvious (and explicit) in connection with the broad revisionist project in philosophy. If vagueness and indeterminacy are deficiencies of natural language (as Frege and the logical positivists thought), then no domain of thought or speech is safe. If Carnap (and my generalization in Cappelen 2013) is right that all metasemantics (a) leave open the possibility that many ordinary language terms are without semantic foundation, and (b) this possibility is realized for many theoretical and ordinary words, then again the negative conclusion has a wide scope. Chalmers, as we have seen, thinks that philosophy is plagued by verbal disputes—i.e., that philosophers systematically talk past each other—and that what philosophers take to be substantive disagreements are pointless verbal disputes. If that is true about philosophy, it's true about all domains of speech: we should worry that all verbal interactions are plagued by pointless verbal disputes. In sum: hardly any of the reasons given by representational skeptics have a narrow scope. They might be interested in particular restricted domains, but their arguments invariably extend broadly.

The second reason for thinking that representational deficiencies are widespread is the following: *? Just a diff word ?*

The Argument from Many Alternatives: (1) If W is a word that has a meaning M, then there are many similar meanings W could have had. (2) Let M* be one of those meanings that are similar to M and could have been the meaning of W. That W ended up meaning M rather than M* is typically the result of somewhat random factors outside any particular speaker's control. (3) In general, it's unlikely that these random factors have assigned the best meaning to W—there are typically indefinitely many alternative meanings M*1...M*n that would be better meanings for W.

All of 1–3 are controversial, but 3 is particularly so. I'll start by saying a bit in defense of it. Our words ended up meaning what they do for various reasons, reasons that are not well understood. Meaning assignments will in part have been generated by past speakers' aims and purposes, needs, values, use patterns, and various other factors we don't understand well. The aims, purposes, values, etc. of those past speakers will often be very different from our current ones. Whenever that is the case, amelioration will be needed. We have no prima facie reason to think that the inscrutable metasemantic mechanisms that generated current meanings will be ideal for various contemporary theoretical, political, moral, culinary etc. aims. So, we have reason to endorse a broad and radical version of the Revisionist's Basic Assumption.

The Prudential Argument is a form of skepticism about our representational devices and our abilities to think and talk with them (in this respect it has affinities with Kripke's meaning-skeptic in the book *Wittgenstein on Rules and Private Language* (Kripke 1982)). It is, however, more pressing than that form of skepticism. This is because it is a form of skepticism that is based not on the impossibility of ruling out some recherché possibilities of mistake, error, or defect, but instead on concrete evidence that our actual representational devices are defective. As such, it's a particularly pressing form of skepticism.

3.2 Corollary of Prudential Argument: Conceptual Engineering's Effect on our Self-Understanding and the Way We Lead our Lives

So far I have focused on the cognitive significance of conceptual engineering: thinking and talking with defective concepts will make speech and talk defective in the sense that the thoughts we entertain or express will inherit the deficits of our representational devices. There is, however, a very important further implication, one that has been made particularly salient in Haslanger's work. Haslanger says the following about her proposed amelioration of gender and race terms:

… by appropriating the everyday terminology of race and gender, the analyses I've offered invite us to acknowledge the force of oppressive systems in framing our personal and political identities. Each of us has some investment in our race and gender: I am a White woman. On my accounts, this claim locates me within social systems that in some respects privilege and in some respects subordinate me. Because gender and racial inequality are not simply a matter of public policy but implicate each of us at the heart of our self-understandings, the terminological shift calls us to reconsider who we think we are.   (2000: 47)

Jennifer Saul, commenting on Haslanger's proposal, says:

There is no question, it seems to me, that Haslanger's suggestion could have the sort of effect suggested above. It is a shocking shift she suggests, and it is a shift that—if adopted—would very likely alter the way we feel about claiming identities in terms like 'woman', 'man', 'Black' or 'White'.   (2006: 138)

The points Haslanger and Saul make in the passage above generalize: they have nothing specifically to do with gender or race. Here is Burgess and Plunkett (2013a) with a more general version of this claim:

Arguably, our conceptual repertoire determines not only what beliefs we can have but also what hypotheses we can entertain, what desires we can form, what plans we can make on the basis of such mental states, and accordingly constrains what we can hope to accomplish in the world. Representation enables action, from the most sophisticated scientific research, to the most mundane household task. It influences our options within social/political institutions and even helps determine which institutions are so much as thinkable. Our social roles, in turn, help determine what kinds of people we can be, what sorts of lives we can lead. Conceptual choices and changes may be intrinsically interesting, but the clearest reason to care about them is just that their non-conceptual consequences are pervasive and profound.

(Burgess and Plunkett 2013a: 1096–7)

I think all of this is right. Conceptual engineering is not just theoretically interesting, but has important practical implications and for each of us the activity will shape who we are and what kinds of lives we lead. Again, Clark and Chalmers's proposal provides a good illustration of how this can happen in surprising ways. They suggest that if one endorses their form of active external-ism about the mind and cognition—where objects outside the 'skin and skull' boundary are part of, constitutive of, my mind—then those external things (or couplings of external objects and my biological organism) are part of me. And so interfering with those aspects of my environment is interfering with me. I will know that others are constituted by their relations to objects in their environment and so interfering with those external objects is interfering with them. It seems plausible that we don't currently think of ourselves in these ways, but should Clark and Chalmers's proposal for revision be endorsed, then this will have a wide range of significant non-linguistic implications.

3.3 Two Ontological Arguments

I turn now to what can be characterized as 'ontological reasons' for the signifi-cance of engaging in and understanding conceptual engineering.

3.3.1 The first Ontological Argument: language as constitutive of social reality

On many views of social reality, the concepts we use to describe social categories are in part constitutive of that reality. Versions of this view can be found in a wide range of authors, but in what follows I will illustrate the view and the relevance of it to conceptual engineering using Searle's theory in his book *The Construction of Social Reality* (1995).[1] First a brief sketch of Searle's view.

3.3.1.1 SEARLE ON THE CREATION OF SOCIAL REALITY

The aim in what follows is to get to the point where Searle claims that language is constitutive of social reality and then to point out that if you endorse some version of this view (whether it be Searle's or some alternative argument for the constitutive role of language) then conceptual engineering is, in part, social engineering. As we revise and ameliorate the concepts that are constitutive of some social fact, we are revising and ameliorating that social fact. That's the basic idea in the following couple of pages, and all I really do is illustrate this using Searle's account.

According to Searle, constitutive rules of the form 'X counts as Y in C' are at the core of social ontology. 'Y' denotes what Searle calls a *status function*—it assigns a status to things that satisfy the X-conditions (this is a new status that the objects don't have simply in virtue of satisfying the X-conditions). Illustration:

> Certain sorts of bits of paper are widely circulated in the United States. These pieces of paper satisfy certain conditions that constitute satisfying the X term. The pieces must have particular material ingredients, and they must match a certain set of patterns (five dollar bill, ten dollar bill, etc.). They must also be issued by the Bureau of Engraving and Printing under the authority of the U.S. Treasury. Anything that satisfies these conditions (X term) counts as money, i.e., U.S. paper currency (Y term). But to describe these bits of paper with the Y term "money" does more than provide a shorthand label for the features of the X term; it describes a new status, and that status, viz. money, has a set of functions attached to it, e.g., medium of exchange, store of value, etc. In virtue of the constitutive rule, the paper counts as "legal tender for all debts public and private." And the imposition of this status function by the Y term has to be collectively recognized and accepted or the function will not be performed.   (Searle 1995: 45–6)

Two points are important:

1. Searle thinks there has to be collective agreement or acceptance over these constitutive rules: ". . . because the physical features specified by the X term are insufficient to guarantee success in fulfilling the assigned function, there

---

[1] For an alternative framework for social construction, see Hacking 1999.

must be continued collective acceptance or recognition of the validity of the assigned function; otherwise the function cannot be successfully performed. It is not enough, for example, that we agree with the original assignment, 'This stuff is money'; we must continue to accept it as money or it will become worthless" (Searle 1995: 45).

2. And here we finally come to the point that's crucial in the current context: language is essential for the imposition of status functions. According to Searle, "language is essentially constitutive of institutional reality." This, according to Searle, is because it is "impossible to have institutional structures such as money, marriage, governments, and property without some form of language because...the words or other symbols are partly constitutive of the facts" (Searle 1995: 59).

Searle has an argument for 2, but it won't concern us here (it's not a great argument because according to Searle, language itself is a social fact, and it's a bit hard to see how language can be constitutive of itself, but I leave these concerns aside). Suffice to say that the view that language is constitutive of social reality is not entirely implausible and its plausibility doesn't depend on the details of Searle's argument here: other views might somewhat reduce the role of language in social ontology, but still assign it a central role (for a good overview of options, see Epstein 2015).

Here is the connection to conceptual engineering: According to a Searle-style view, our concept 'money' plays a constitutive role in both the creation and continued existence of money. Suppose then that these concepts evolve. Suppose we find that our current concept of money is defective; we revise and ameliorate the concept. If language is constitutive of social facts, then there is a corollary: the process of conceptual revision is also a process that involves a revision of the relevant social facts. There's a kind of dynamic evolution of the social facts that goes hand in hand with the dynamic evolution of the concepts. So conceptual engineering is engineering of the social world as much as it is of our concepts. Many think that the institution of gender is a social fact. Suppose, to make things simple, that social fact is in part constituted by the terms 'man' and 'woman'. Suppose further that a Haslanger-style ameliorative project succeeds: it changes our gender concepts in the ways she advocates. We have then changed social reality: gender has been changed.

3.3.2 The second Ontological Argument: conceptual amelioration as amelioration of the world

I just gave one argument for the view that conceptual engineering, at least in some cases, is also an engineering of the world (the social world in particular).

Later in this book (in chapter 12) I argue for a related, but more radical, view. The authors I have discussed so far describe conceptual engineering as being a process that operates on representational devices (whatever they may be). I've described it in this way because I started by describing some predecessors in philosophy who engaged in and wrote about conceptual engineering. So far I've used their terminology since that's natural to do while presenting their views. As I move on I will engage in more conceptual engineering of the very idea of conceptual engineering and the final picture will be one on which this activity has nothing to do with concepts. We're not there yet (we won't get there before my theory is presented in chapters 5 to 8), but to avoid confusion (and discrepancy between this presentational part and my positive proposal) I should at least sketch the view I'll end up with. What I have so far described as being a process that operates on representational devices is just as well—maybe better—described as an operation *on the world*. Conceptual amelioration is best described as *an amelioration of the world*. In chapter 12, this is described as the 'worldly' construal of conceptual engineering and I contrast it with views according to which we engineer the meanings of lexical items or concepts. One place where I find elements of this way of thinking is in some of Sally Haslanger's work. She has, for example, written an influential paper called 'Gender and Race: (What) Are They? (What) Do We Want Them to Be?' (Haslanger 2000). First, note that the title isn't about the words 'gender' or 'race'. Nor is it about the corresponding concepts of (say) woman, or Latino. It is about gender and race. It asks what we want those things to be, i.e., what we want gender and race to be (not what we want the words to be and not what we want the concepts to be). Applied to epistemology, the ameliorative project, so understood, is about *what knowledge ought to be*, not about what the concept 'knowledge' ought to be (see the title of Haslanger 1999).[2] On this view, an instance of successful conceptual engineering, e.g., of 'person', has the result that what a person *is* has changed. I think this 'worldly' description is the correct way to describe all instances of conceptual engineering, not just in the social domain. This sounds radical—and might raise worries about endorsing a form of linguistic idealism—but it is not. We're not creating new *stuff* using language. We are reclassifying, but on the view I develop, that reclassification can be described without going metalinguistic (i.e., without quoting words or referring to concepts).

---

[2] In other parts of the paper, Haslanger talks a lot about concepts and primarily articulates her view as one that concerns how concepts should be ameliorated. The aim here is not to engage in Haslanger exegesis, but to highlight one of the ways she describes her project.

3.4 Implications for Philosophical Methodology: Purely Descriptive Philosophy Must Be Abandoned

Many philosophers think that the aim of core parts of philosophy is either to describe our concepts or to describe the extensions of those concepts. These are often seen as competing views of the nature of philosophy. One good description of this tension is found in the first few chapters of Timothy Williamson's *The Philosophy of Philosophy* (Williamson 2007), where he contrasts the view that philosophy is largely about describing our concepts with the view that philosophy is about describing worldly phenomena. Williamson advocates the latter view (as does, for example, Kornblith 2002). Proponents of the former view include Dummett (1978) and Jackson (1998). Both the concept- and extension-focused views, however, have the following in common: they are essentially *descriptivist* views of philosophy.[3] They want to describe different things: Jackson's goal is to describe our concepts and Williamson's goal is to describe the extensions of those concepts.

If you endorse the Core Revisionist Argument, both of these strategies are mistaken. If we have reason to think that our philosophical concepts are systematically defective and that they can be improved, then our goal should be to engage in critical and constructive reflection about our concepts before we start using them. Here is my preferred way of describing the alternative, non-descriptive attitude:

The Anti-Descriptive Argument: If your aim is to think about and understand some important philosophical phenomenon—say, knowledge, causation, or freedom—you have to figure out how best to think and talk about those phenomena. The best way to talk and think about, say, freedom, isn't just to think and say true things about freedom. It is also, and just as importantly, to figure out how to represent freedom in language and thought. According to the radical version of the Core Revisionist Argument defended above, we have reason to think that our current way of representing freedom is defective, and so before we start trying to figure out truths about freedom we need to find out how best to represent it. This kind of inquiry is essentially a normative enterprise. It asks how best to represent those phenomena and what might be defective about current ways of representing them. The assessment and

Have to know what 'it' is first?

---

[3] This is not to deny that in other aspects of their work these philosophers engage in conceptual engineering. For example, Williamson's attack on the a priori–a posteriori distinction is an excellent illustration of a form of conceptual engineering (see Williamson 2013).

improvement of concepts is at the core of philosophical practice, no matter what the topic. Your goal *cannot* be purely descriptive if you accept the Prudential Argument—at the core of all philosophical activity is the continuous assessment of representational devices.

You might think this argument is not just simple, *but far too* simple. It might even be inconsistent.

> *Reply to the Anti-Descriptive Argument:* Doesn't the Anti-Descriptive Argument assume that we first engage in important *descriptive* work: figuring out whether our concepts are defective and how they can be improved? Surely that's a descriptive task, isn't it?

This reply shows a lack of understanding of the scope of the revisionary attitude which is motivated by the Prudential Argument. That argument *has no limit*: *it applies equally to the terms that occur in the 'Reply to the Anti-Descriptive Argument' above.* In other words, all the concepts involved in describing the critical/constructive project of conceptual engineering should themselves be subject to constant critical assessment and skepticism. In particular, we will need to assess the following concepts: 'concept', 'conceptual defect', 'descriptive work', etc. The very terminology in which you engage in the critical project is itself suspect. Once you endorse the Prudential Argument, there are no safe spaces. (Of course, even this articulation of the self-reflective nature of the core revisionist argument should be subject to that very same kind of criticism.)

In light of the points just made, the best way to think of the pro-attitude toward conceptual engineering that this book advocates is just that: as an intellectual attitude or as a kind of critical disposition.[4] As soon as this attitude is articulated in words as a thesis about what one should do it becomes suspect and potentially self-undermining, since it's telling you to be critical of that very articulation. (Of course, the sentence prior to this one is subject to the same criticism, and so is this one right here, but what can you do?)

Start somewhere?

---

[4] We can think of this on analogy with the critical attitudes associated with Pyrrhonian skepticism. The Pyrrhonian skeptic doesn't believe or assert that no one knows anything, but has a kind of technique for undermining any knowledge claim.

4

On the Importance of a General Theory and an Overview of the Austerity Framework

4.1 Taking Stock

Chapter 2 illustrated and categorized a kind of activity—an activity that I, for lack of a better label, am calling 'conceptual engineering'. Chapter 3 gave some general arguments for the significance of this activity. In addition to these general arguments it should be clear that the engineering of *specific* concepts takes on the excitement and significance of their domain. Consider, for example, the following questions: what should our concepts of 'truth', 'freedom', 'gender', and 'race' be? How should we develop concepts to categorize psychiatric conditions? How should our moral concepts be? (As opposed to the question, 'How *are* our moral concepts?') How should our legal concepts be? How should our central scientific concepts be? Anyone with even the slightest bit of intellectual curiosity will take an interest in such questions.

This book, however, is *not* about any specific instance of conceptual engineering. It is about the *activity* of conceptual engineering *in general*: how to understand it, how to theorize about it, and how to respond to objections to it. The topic of this book is the question of what all the examples of engineering have in common. This book is *not* primarily an exercise in conceptual engineering—except, of course, insofar as it attempts to develop a concept of conceptual engineering that can be of theoretical and practical use.

It's important to identify the most interesting and philosophically significant general questions about conceptual engineering around which we can organize a theory of conceptual engineering. Some core questions are:

- What, if anything, do the paradigmatic instances of conceptual engineering have in common?
- Why and when is conceptual engineering worth doing?

- How does a theory of conceptual engineering fit into an overall theory of language and communication?

This last question opens up a range of sub-questions. I will focus on the following:

- What is conceptual engineering about? Does it concern concepts, meanings, extensions, intensions, or something else?
- What are representational deficiencies (how can there be any?), and how can such deficiencies be ameliorated?

A certain degree of skepticism is warranted here: It's certainly possible that there isn't much interesting to say about conceptual engineering at a very abstract and general level. Maybe all the interesting work is to be done at the level of particular concepts. Maybe the kind of general reflections that I'm about to engage in is just a way to rehash old debates and nothing particularly new or exciting will come out of reflections at that very high level of abstraction. I take these kinds of worry seriously (and they made me rewrite this book many more times than I expected). Readers will be in a better position to judge whether I've succeeded or not after I've presented the full theory (and others have presented alternatives). However, even at this stage there are five things that can be said about the significance of a general theory of conceptual engineering.

4.2 Some Reasons for Thinking that a General Theory of Conceptual Engineering Is Important

First, this field will pattern with other fields, both practical or theoretical. There's a lot to be said for aeronautical engineers studying aeronautics in general and not just studying particular planes. You'll do much better both building particular planes and flying them if you do so informed by a general theory. Of course, there's an interplay between the particular and the general: we can learn from the particular to build the general theory and we can use the general theory to improve particular planes and flights. The same is true in most theoretical domains—whether in macro-economics or chemistry. It would be surprising— though of course not impossible—if conceptual engineering didn't exhibit the same pattern of fruitful interdependence between the general and the particular.

Second, there are some salient general questions that should arise for anyone engaging in conceptual engineering. A very obvious such question is this:

Important General Question: What are the things we criticize and improve? So far I've called them concepts, but if we engineer concepts we need a theory of what they are and how we go about changing them.

This is in effect a question in what has been called 'foundational semantics' or 'metasemantics'. It requires that we take a stand on what meanings (or semantic values) are, how they come to be associated with particular expressions, and how such associations can be changed. In short, the Important General Question makes it clear that our understanding of conceptual engineering will in large part be shaped by our metasemantic theory. This metasemantic theory will be general: it will be stable across particular instances of conceptual engineering. Looking ahead, the theory I propose has some salient general features (features that cut across different instances of conceptual engineering):

- It is based on an externalist metasemantics,
- It understands conceptual engineering as a form of reference change,
- It makes successful conceptual engineering extremely hard: it's a process that for the most part is out of our control, but that's not a reason for not taking it seriously (many of the things we care about are hard and in large part out of our control).

Third, there are general issues about when one's aim should be to change a concept 'C' and when the aim should be to change beliefs that people have about C. What is the difference and how do we choose between strategies? The answer to this question will in large part depend on one's view of the metasemantic issues mentioned above.

Fourth, a question that will come up in every particular instance of conceptual engineering concerns the *limits of revision*: how much revision is too much? When has revision gone too far? This cluster of issues is the topic of Part III of this book.

Finally, there are *entirely general objections* to the entire project of conceptual engineering—objections that can't be answered on a case-by-case basis, but require a general reply (a reply that applies to all particular instances of conceptual engineering). Two of these will play an important role in much of what follows:

General Objection 1:   How can conceptual engineering and externalism be compatible? If they are incompatible and externalism is true, then the entire project of conceptual engineering must be abandoned. Part II outlines this potential incompatibility and the positive theory provided by the Austerity Framework is in large part an effort to resolve it.

General Objection 2:   Strawson objects to Carnap that explication involves an unacceptable change of topic (Strawson 1963). One way to understand Strawson's objection is as a general objection to the possibility of successfully improving our representational devices: conceptual engineering will *always involve an unacceptable change of topic.* This worry comes up over and over again in the literature on conceptual engineering. Part III of this book is an effort to respond to it: the response is to develop a general theory (or in my case, a non-theory theory) of the limits of revision.

So these are five reasons for thinking it's helpful and important to make an effort to develop a general theory of conceptual engineering. I don't have satisfactory answers to all these questions and challenges. I have a framework and an account of why in many cases we should not expect a theory. I hope that, with time, there will be a plethora of general theories of conceptual engineering. Such theories will connect to foundational issues in philosophy of language and communication. It is likely that there will be as many efforts to illuminate the foundations of conceptual engineering as there are efforts to understand metasemantics. This inquiry will involve a two-way flow of ideas: on the one hand, metasemantic assumptions will shape general theories of conceptual engineering and this will shape how we understand and practice conceptual engineering. On the other hand, the activity of engaging in conceptual engineering will provide feedback to a general theory of conceptual engineering and this again will help clarify the foundations of semantics.

One more preliminary point before I start the work of developing the general theory: There's a certain kind of objection that I will not discuss here. It's a detail-focused reply, i.e., the kind of reply that goes through each of the examples of defects outlined in Part I and gives detailed and case-specific objections to the claim that they are defects. Is Railton right in what he says about the defects of current moral language? Are Clark and Chalmers right in what they say about the possible defects about our current concept of 'belief'? Is Haslanger right in her criticism of gender and race concepts? I'm not focusing on these kinds of case-specific objections in this book. I take it as a starting point that many of my colleagues and people who are not philosophers take themselves to be engaging in conceptual engineering. I simply take the fact *that they are doing it* as my starting point. None of this is meant to downplay the questions one can ask about specific proposals, e.g., about gender or race terms, or about generics. Those are questions that will become salient after a defense of the overall significance of the project of conceptual engineering. With that defense in hand, the kind of big-picture approach that this book takes can recede into the background and the focus can be on the case studies. For the purposes of developing the general theory, I don't take a stand on any of the particular cases—I don't have a favorite and my illustrations will change throughout. If the reader thinks one or a few of them are much better than the others, she is free to substitute that illustration throughout.

4.3 Overview of the Positive Theory: The Austerity Framework

Parts II–IV develop a framework for thinking about conceptual engineering. I call it the Austerity Framework. I wish there were a simply, snappy way to summarize the Austerity Framework, but I have given up on attempting to develop such a summary.[1] The Austerity Framework simply is the view I present in Parts II–IV. The view is what I say in those pages. Nonetheless, it's worth highlighting some of the view's key components.

(i) A theory of conceptual engineering should be based on a metasemantic theory. The metasemantics gives an account of how semantic values change over time. The metasemantics is distinct from the metasemantic superstructure (our beliefs about the semantics). (chapter 5)

(ii) The framework I propose is externalist. It treats all semantic change as analogous with reference change. (chapters 5 and 6)

(iii) What changes when we engage in conceptual engineering are extensions and intensions of expressions, and various external factors determine how that change happens. (chapters 6 and 7)

(iv) The kind of thing philosophers and psychologists call 'concepts' plays no role in my theory. There's no psychological or individualistic thing or event classifiable as a 'concept' that's changing or being engineered. So 'conceptual engineering' isn't a great label (see note 2 in chapter 1 for why I nevertheless chose it).

(v) Conceptual engineering understood within this externalist framework is a process we have little or no control over—and it's also not transparent to us when we engage in it. (chapter 7)

(vi) The process governing particular changes is typically incomprehensible and inscrutable. (chapter 7)

(vii) Since the theory doesn't appeal to concepts, it does not recognize incoherent or inconsistent concepts. I do, however, have a diagnosis of why so many philosophers are inclined to believe that there are such things. (chapter 8)

---

[1] I have written many books and all of them have been organized around central theses that are relatively easy to summarize and understand. These then provide a kind of focal point for the dialectic. That very tidy and useful strategy has proved impossible to implement in this case (and that made me almost abandon this book project). The topic is so broad, multifaceted, and amorphous that it doesn't lend itself to snappy slogans or tidy theoretical frameworks.

(viii) Topic continuity is compatible with changes in extension and intension—the semantic values of 'F' can change, whilst we continue to talk about F. Furthermore, the constraints on topic continuity are not fixed, but essentially contested. (chapters 9 and 10)

(ix) Topic continuity is to be sharply distinguished from the exploitation of what I call 'lexical effects': the non-cognitive, non-semantic, non-pragmatic effects of words. (chapter 11 presents a theory of lexical effects)

(x) Conceptual engineering, on the view I propose, changes the world, not just the meanings of words. (I argue for this in chapter 12)

The last part of the book, Part V, compares the Austerity Framework to alternative accounts of conceptual engineering proposed by Ludlow, Plunkett, Sundell, Haslanger, Thomassen, Chalmers, and Eklund.

Why call this framework 'the Austerity Framework'? What's so austere about it? It is austere in that it appeals to fewer theoretical entities than alternative frameworks for conceptual engineering. It's widely agreed that expressions of the kind I talk about have extensions and intensions. The kind of externalism I advocate is not universally endorsed, but the core elements of it are widely endorsed. So the core components of the theory are *few* and *relatively non-controversial*. Most of the competing theories will incorporate them. The advantage of this lack of commitments is that I need not take on board a theory of what concepts are. There are a plethora of options for thinking about concepts. I think that all of the options are problematic, so by avoiding talk about concepts I don't need to fight those battles. Many of the alternative accounts of conceptual engineering not only assume that there are concepts, but also claim that concepts perform functions. That requires an additional theory of how to identify, individuate, and change these functions. My view bypasses all that very messy terrain.

PART II

Towards a General Theory 1: Metasemantic Foundations

5

Metasemantics, Metasemantic Superstructure, and Metasemantic Base

5.1 Semantics and Metasemantics

Any theory of conceptual engineering is committed to the claim that meanings or referents can change. Such a theory will presuppose a metasemantics: a theory of that in virtue of which meanings change and what those meanings are. Here is David Kaplan's characterization of metasemantics:

There are several interesting issues concerning what belongs to semantics. The fact that a word or phrase has a certain meaning clearly belongs to semantics. On the other hand, a claim about the basis for ascribing a certain meaning to a word or phrase does not belong to semantics. "Ohsnay" means snow in Pig-Latin. That's a semantic fact about Pig-Latin. The reason why "ohsnay" means snow is not a semantic fact; it is some kind of historical or sociological fact about Pig-Latin. Perhaps, because it relates to how the language is used, it should be categorized as part of the pragmatics of Pig-Latin (though I am not really comfortable with this nomenclature), or perhaps, because it is a fact about semantics, as part of the Metasemantics of Pig-Latin (or perhaps, for those who prefer working from below to working from above, as part of the Foundations of semantics of Pig-Latin)
(Kaplan 1977/1989: 573–4).

Think of metasemantics as efforts to provide metaphysical explanations of (or foundations of or groundings for) semantic facts—the fact that an expression has a certain meaning or referent. Incorporated into such a theory will be an account of what kinds of things meanings are. There are hard questions about how exactly to distinguish metasemantics from semantics,[1] but for current purposes it will suffice to work with Kaplan's rough and ready characterization.

A theory of conceptual engineering has to incorporate a metasemantic theory because it is the facts that ground meaning that the conceptual engineer will have to

---

[1] Could semantic facts be grounded in other semantic facts all the way down? Does the account assume a form of reductionism about semantics? See the introduction to Burgess and Sherman 2014, and Kearns and Magidor 2008.

act on. To change meanings she has to change the facts that ground meaning. In order to understand conceptual engineering we need, in effect, a *Dynamic Metasemantics*: an account of how the ways in which grounding facts can change over time.

There is, however, nothing close to a consensus about what the correct metasemantic theory is. One way to proceed in light of that would be to go through various metasemantic theories and see what they have to tell us about conceptual engineering. On this way of proceeding, one would ask:

What follows about conceptual engineering if meanings are grounded in conventions (maybe along the lines of what Lewis (1969) proposed)? What follows about conceptual engineering if externalism about meaning is right? What follows if internalism is right? What follows if Davidson was right about the foundations of meaning? What follows if Lewisian reference magnetism is real? How should someone committed to the Canberra Plan think of conceptual engineering? And so on.

That's not what I'll do. Instead I will start with some assumptions about metasemantics—assumptions I think are correct—and use these assumptions as the foundation of my theory. The assumptions are drawn from the externalist tradition in metasemantics—I will take a bit from Kripke, a bit from Burge, and a bit from Williamson. None of this will add up to a set of reductive necessary and sufficient conditions for a revision in meaning, but the theory will illuminate some important aspects of conceptual engineering. The corollaries are, I suggest, far-reaching.

The aim of this book isn't to argue for those externalist assumptions. I take them to be already well established. We all have to start somewhere, and that's (one of the places) where this book starts. Of course, many will disagree with this starting point. What about those readers that don't share these externalist assumptions? Should they just stop reading now or does some of what I say generalize beyond externalism? I think quite a bit of what I say about conceptual engineering generalizes. Many of the points I want to emphasize are easier to see from within an externalist framework, but they are for the most part general lessons about conceptual engineering. To help the reader focus on some of these general issues, I'll outline what I take to be an important distinction between the metasemantic base and the metasemantic superstructure—a distinction that's important no matter what metasemantics you favor.

5.2 Metasemantic Base vs. Metasemantic Superstructure

Borrowing some terminology from Marxism, we can distinguish between the metasemantic base and the metasemantic superstructure. Think of the metasemantic base as the grounding facts for meaning and reference. Think of the metasemantic superstructure as consisting (at least in part) of our beliefs, hopes, preference, intentions, theories, and other attitudes about meanings and reference (what they are and what they ought to be). Here are two important related questions:

1. How, if at all, does the metasemantic superstructure affect the metasemantic base?
2. How much of a discrepancy can there be between the superstructure and the semantic facts (as determined by the metasemantic base)?

These are under-explored questions that have massive implication for conceptual engineering. Much of what I say in what follows will explore these questions within an externalist metasemantics. On the view I propose, what people say, think, propose, wish, and debate about meanings has very little influence on what words mean. The metasemantic superstructure has little effect on the metasemantic base and there can be a significant discrepancy between superstructure and base. This is not to say that meanings are unaffected by the superstructure. Our various mental states and beliefs have some effect on meaning, but in unpredictable ways. I make these points from within an externalist framework, but they generalize: this disconnect between superstructure and base will hold no matter which of the currently popular metasemantic views you hold. This disconnect has significant implications for the practice of conceptual engineering, which also generalize. If I am right, the way to change meanings isn't to change people's beliefs (or wishes or preferences) about meanings. It is to act directly on the metasemantic base. We don't know much about how to do that, but if certain externalist assumptions are correct, we have some rough ideas.

5.3 The Tacit Prejudice in Favor of Metasemantic Superstructure

Correct = cannot change meaning as an individ.

Much of the practice of conceptual engineering has a tacit bias against the view I just described: it's tacitly assumed that the metasemantic superstructure has *practical* significance. There's an excessive focus on what speakers think, want, intend, and agree about what words should mean. There's an underlying thought to the effect that if we could just convince people of the right views about what their words *should* mean, then their words would mean what they should. But on the view I propose, that's not even close to true. To do conceptual engineering you need to change the base, not the superstructure. Here's a diagnosis of the prejudice in favor of the metasemantic superstructure: conceptual engineers of the kind mentioned in Part I tend to occupy an intellectual in-between position:

they are in part theorists whose aim it is to describe conceptual engineering and to propose positive specific proposals for how particular concepts—race, gender, truth, freedom, belief, etc.—should be improved. At the same time they tend to see themselves as contributing to that very process—they tend to see themselves as activists, not just theorists. For those in this in-between-theorist-and-activist-position, it's tempting to think (or hope) that the two roles can be merged: that the theorizing can be a significant part of the activism. That would make life easier: the papers, books, blog posts, seminar discussions, etc. would contribute to conceptual engineering (not just to the theory of it). If I'm right, this is an illusion. Presenting an *argument* for a particular conceptual change has no more effect on conceptual change than presenting an argument for how to lower crime in Baltimore has an effect on crime in Baltimore. Both have no effect whatsoever. The activist work doesn't merge smoothly (or even at all) with the theoretical work. Doing the latter has no significant (predictable) effect on the former. As I'll make clear below, none of this is to say that our beliefs, wishes, plans, intentions, etc. are *irrelevant* to the semantic base. They might play a role, but not through 'fit'. They contribute to the base as some grains of salt might contribute to a massively complex dish or the way a tiny bit of sodium oxide plays a role in making cement.[2] So far this is programmatic. What follows is a theory that has these claims as corollaries and I think many of the alternative frameworks (with different metasemantic starting points) will have the same corollaries. I try to make clear why along the way.

(1.)greed. Uptake only happens if there is a use for it.

---

[2] Though these analogies are imperfect: we know much less about the contributions of beliefs, preferences, etc. to metasemantics than we know about the contributions of salt and sodium oxide to food and cement.

6

Externalist Conceptual Engineering

6.1 What Changes? Extensions and Intensions

So far I've talked loosely about conceptual engineering as being focused on the criticism and improvement of *concepts*. I have said nothing about what concepts are. Many of the philosophers I've used as illustrations in earlier chapters have their own views about this, but those views have so far played no significant role. In this chapter—and the rest of this book—the aim is no longer to present and systematize views of others. The aim is to present a theory of conceptual engineering. This theory takes it as a data point that philosophers and others try to engage in conceptual engineering (chapter 2 established that data point). The rest of this book is an effort to present a theory of what these people are doing—how best to understand their activity—even if that understanding differs from the explicit theories put forward by the practitioners of conceptual engineering.

The view I end up with will be surprising because conceptual engineering isn't really about what philosophers (or psychologists) have called 'concepts'. According to my view, conceptual engineering should be seen as having as its goal to change extensions and intensions of expressions, and we should think of that process within an externalist framework (where what's responsible for changes in extensions and intensions doesn't supervene only on what we think, want, believe, hope, intend, or decide).

Two notions that will play a big role in what follows are those of extensions and intensions. I use these words in entirely standard ways. Names refer to things and predicates pick out (or apply to or are true of) things. The things that a predicate picks out (or applies to, or is true of) relative to a particular circumstance of evaluation is its extension. I take the intension of a predicate to be a function from circumstances of evaluation (worlds, world/time pairs, or whatever: I'll stay neutral on this throughout[1]) to extensions, i.e., to sets—the set of

---

[1] At this point I will make no assumptions about what goes into circumstances of evaluation. I have views about this, see, e.g., Cappelen and Hawthorne 2009, but these views are not presupposed here.

things that the predicate picks out relative to each circumstance. I start with the minimal assumption that predicates have intensions and that a theory of meaning (or a semantics) will *at least* specify an intension for each predicate.

Amelioration, in my framework, always involves *the extension and intension of a predicate changing over time*. It's important not to misunderstand what I mean by that: What that means is *not* that between two times, t and t*, the extension of, say, 'person' can change because some persons die and others are born. What I have in mind are changes in extensions that are driven by changes in intensions. So relative to the same circumstance of evaluation (e.g., world/time pair) extensions can change. One way to think of this: the conditions that need to be satisfied in order to fall into the extension of 'person' (or 'woman' or 'marriage' or 'belief') have been changed by conceptual engineering, and as a result of that the intension and extension of this term have changed. Often in what follows I will for simplicity talk simply about 'a change in the extension of a concept' and what I mean is always a change in extensions resulting from a change in the intension (as just explained).

Note that all the illustrations in chapter 1 have in common that they involve changes in extension and intension.[2] To mention but three examples: the proposals from Clark and Chalmers (about an extended sense of 'belief'), Carnap (on explication), and Haslanger (on gender and race terms) all involve diachronic changes in extensions and intensions of various expression. Things that were not in the extension pre-amelioration go in, and some of what was in goes out relative to various points in time. What's picked out when we talk about counterfactual scenarios will also change. This should be fairly uncontroversial.

6.2 Externalism

Semantic externalism is a theory about what makes it the case that expressions have the semantic values that they have—it's a metasemantic theory.

---

[2] Two qualifications, one obvious and one less so: (i) The obvious qualification is that those who advocate abandonment (or replacement) don't also advocate a change in extension and intension. (ii) Some ameliorator might be advocating a change just in intension. Halsanger's view might have this consequence if the extension of 'woman' pre-amelioration matches the extension of 'woman' post-amelioration (in effect: if all actual women fall into her revised definition of 'woman' and the difference is only in how we would describe other possibilities: speaking with the current meaning of 'woman' it's possible that women repress men, but on Haslanger's revisionist proposal that would be impossible (such a world wouldn't contain anything that falls into the extension of 'woman' in Haslanger's sense)). When in the main body of the text I talk of conceptual engineering as involving something analogous to reference shifts, I mean to include such cases (where there's a change in intension but not in extension). Being more specific about this distinction will require deciding on how to characterize points of assessment, and for reasons of simplicity I want stay neutral on that throughout.

Here are a few externalist metasemantic assumptions that I take on board in what follows:

(i) *Putnam/Kripke/Burge/Williamson-style externalism is part of the metasemantic story:* the external environment that speakers are in partly determines extensions and intensions. The relevant elements of the external environment include experts in the community, the history of use going back to the introduction of a term, complex patterns of use over time, and what the world happens to be like (independently of what the speakers believe the world is like). Intensions and extensions don't supervene only *[margin: or at all?]* on the mental states of the speakers.

(ii) *The possibility of massive, fundamental mistakes and confusions about semantic values:* most or even all speakers of the language can *believe* that a predicate F applies to an object, o, but be wrong. They can all *want* o to be in the extension of F, but wanting o to be F doesn't make it so. They can all be disposed to apply F to o even though o isn't F. Humpty Dumpty was wrong: believing and wanting words to mean something doesn't make it so. (I take it to be a corollary that speakers can all think that F figures in certain explanations or in certain inferences and be wrong.) *[handwritten: What if the practice determines that it is so?]*

A corollary of this, or a slight addition, can be summarized by the following passage from Williamson, in a thesis I call 'Anti-Creed':

Anti-Creed: 'A complex web of interactions and dependences can hold a linguistic or conceptual practice together even in the absence of a common creed that all participants at all times are required to endorse.' (Williamson 2007: 125)

I should re-emphasize what I said above: These, admittedly vague, externalist assumptions are starting points for the theory. They are not argued for here. If you reject these views, you'll develop a different view of conceptual engineering: as I argued in earlier chapters, your metasemantics will in large part shape your view of conceptual engineering. This won't be a one-way influence from the theory of metasemantics to the theory of conceptual engineering. One of the conditions for being a good metasemantic theory will be that it makes sense of (or provides a realistic picture of) conceptual engineering. You might even think that this is one of the most important criteria for a successful metasemantics. If so, this book is an argument for externalism: it does a good job making sense of conceptual engineering and so it satisfies an important condition for being a good theory.

6.3 Challenges for the Combination of Externalism and Conceptual Engineering

The combination of conceptual engineering and externalism can seem problematic. Some of the prima facie problems are brought out by Burgess and Plunkett in the following passage:

> The textbook externalist thinks that our social and natural environments serve as heavy anchors, so to speak, for the interpretation of our individual thought and talk. The internalist, by contrast, grants us a greater degree of conceptual autonomy. One salient upshot of this disagreement is that effecting conceptual change looks comparatively easy from an internalist perspective. We can revise, eliminate, or replace our concepts without worrying about what the experts are up to, or what happens to be coming out of our taps. From the externalist's point of view, however, conceptual revolution takes a village, or a long trip to Twin Earth.   (Burgess and Plunkett 2013a: 1096)

Burgess and Plunkett make two points here. First, they claim that externalism anchors the contents of our expressions to features of the world that we have little or no control over—it makes it hard to see how changes of the relevant kind (i.e., changes in extensions and intensions) can happen. They are right. This and the next chapter elaborates on that point. Second, they claim that things are easier for internalists—that were internalism true, conceptual engineering would be easier. I think they are wrong about this, and I explain why in chapter 15.

6.4 How Reference Shifts

Conceptual engineering of the kind discussed in Part I typically involves a change in an expression's extension as a result of a change in its intension.[3] So a burning question for a theory of conceptual engineering is how such shifts happen. The rest of this chapter gives a partial answer to that question.

An important aim of many externalist theories is to explain how extensions can be stable across individuals and over time despite differences in beliefs, use, dispositions to use, dispositions to infer, etc. Anti-Creed above is one way to articulate an answer to this question. Securing such stability is a central motivation behind externalism. Insofar as conceptual engineering is the process of changing what our words pick out (what we are talking about), it looks like externalism blocks it or at least makes any particular instance very hard.

---

[3] See note 2 for one possible exception: maybe Haslanger's aim is to change intension but not extension.

However, since the very beginning of the externalist tradition, the *possibility* of reference change (or shifts) has been an important element of such theories. If we operate with a naive version of externalism that makes such changes impossible, very difficult, or extremely rare, it would undermine any effort to merge externalism and conceptual engineering.[4] So my version of externalism is one that incorporates the constant possibility of reference change.[5] More or less any version of externalism will give you that. Kripke's discussion in *Naming and Necessity* of Santa Claus and Evans's 'Madagascar' example are two famous examples. Kripke says:

Gareth Evans has pointed out that similar cases of reference shifts arise where the shift is not from a real entity to a fictional one, but from one real entity to another of the same kind. According to Evans, 'Madagascar' was a native name for a part of Africa; Marco Polo, erroneously thinking that he was following native usage, applied the name to an island. (Evans uses the example to support the description theory; I, of course, do not.) Today the usage of the name as a name for an island has become so widespread that it surely overrides any historical connection with the native name. David Lewis has pointed out that the same thing could have happened even if the natives had used 'Madagascar' to designate a mythical locality. So real reference can shift to another real reference, fictional reference can shift to real, and real to fictional. In all these cases, a present intention to refer to a given entity (or to refer fictionally) overrides the original intention to preserve reference in the historical chain of transmission. The matter deserves extended discussion. But the phenomenon is perhaps roughly explicable in terms of the predominantly social character of the use of proper names emphasized in the text.   (Kripke 1980: 163)

Putting aside examples from particular authors, it should be clear on general theoretical grounds that there's no incompatibility between externalism and frequent reference shifts. Externalism is the view that the grounding facts for reference consist in part of various external, non-psychological facts: that meanings ain't in the head. Some of these meaning-grounding facts might change across time. The general view is neutral on the frequency of such changes, and so it is neutral on the frequency of reference shifts. Some of the detailed workings out of the view will have implications for the frequency of reference shifts, but all versions of externalism allow for it. There are several theories about exactly how externalists should accommodate shifts in reference (see, e.g., Evans 1973, Devitt 1981) and little consensus about the details. I won't (and don't need to) take on

---

[4] There's a partly terminological and partly substantive point I won't pursue in what follows: one way to describe reference shift for externalists is the introduction of a new word or a new name. On this view, a name can't change reference, but it can be replaced by a homonymous name with a different referent. Nothing I say in what follows will depend on this issue and so it will be ignored and I formulate the issues in terms of the shift in reference of one name (Kaplan 1990, Cappelen 1999).

[5] And more generally changes in expressions' extensions and intensions.

shouldn't this be part of the metasemant)

board any particular such theory. What I do assume is that reference shifts happen. That understanding the exact underlying mechanism(s) that trigger reference shift is hard is itself an important data point for my theory. The experts on reference don't know how it happens, much less ordinary speakers. It is not that we have no clue: Evans suggested that we focus on what he calls 'dominant source of information' (Evans 1973: 199–202), Devitt has proposed a related view, and Kripke proposes, in the passage above (without elaboration), that under certain conditions the intention to refer to a particular object overrides the intention to preserve reference. Maybe one of these or some combination of them is along the right lines—but even so, it provides precious little guidance in particular cases.

Dorr and Hawthorne 2014 provides another approach to reference shift that is useful in this context because (i) it abstracts from the details of any externalist framework, and (ii) it makes shifts in semantic value not infrequent (and maybe very frequent). Recall from chapter 2, section 2.4.1, that they advocate a view according to which many expressions exhibit some degree of semantic plasticity. They base that view on the Argument from Abundance:

> [T]his argument is motivated by the thought that the number of possible meanings for that expression is enormous. In almost all cases, an expression's actual meaning is surrounded by a vast cloud of slight variants that seem just as well qualified to be possible meanings. And this abundance makes it hard to resist the conclusion that each proposition attributing any one of these meanings to the expression is modally plastic to a high degree. For if there are no differences between the possible meanings that could plausibly explain why a few of them would be much easier to latch on to than the rest, the selection of any one of them as an expression's actual meaning has to depend very sensitively on the exact values of whatever microphysical parameters are relevant to the determination of meaning. Similarly, when there are many slightly different possible contents for a speech act on some particular occasion, and no differences between these contents that could plausibly single out a few of them as being much more apt for being communicated than the rest, the fact that a certain one was singled out as the actual content of the speech act performed on that occasion must depend sensitively on the exact details of the relevant microphysical facts. Let us call arguments of this general kind arguments from abundance.   (Dorr and Hawthorne 2014: 282)

On this view, a change in the supervenience base for semantic values can trigger gradual changes. Such changes happen frequently. The resulting changes might be more or less gradual: sometimes there are a few big changes with large gaps, and other times there are very many tiny changes with very little time in between. This rough picture can be endorsed without any commitment about the exact nature of the supervenience base for semantics. The conclusion is as before: reference shifts happen, they might even happen frequently, and we have little understanding of how they happen.

In what follows it will be significant that there's unlikely to be an algorithm for figuring out how these changes can be affected. Here I find something Williamson says helpful: "Although meaning may supervene on use, there is no algorithm for calculating the former from the latter" (Williamson 1994: 206).[6] In defending epistemicism about vagueness, Williamson also says: "Every known recipe for extracting meaning from use breaks down even in cases to which vagueness is irrelevant. The inability of the epistemic view of vagueness to provide a successful recipe is an inability it shares with all its rivals. Nor is there any reason to suppose that such a recipe must exist" (Williamson 1994: 207). I think this is exactly right and it is relevant in this context: if we're looking for an algorithm for how to change meanings, we are in effect asking for a recipe for extracting meaning from use and we have no good reason to think such a recipe exists. This point is completely independent of the view of vagueness Williamson defends and is also independent of vague language in particular.

This can be illustrated by Evans's and Kripke's proposals. At the center of Evans's view is the idea that a new object is the 'dominant source of information'. What does it take to be dominant? This question has no fixed answer—there's no algorithm for deciding it. For Kripke, the core idea is that one kind of intention (to refer to a particular object) can override another (the intention to preserve reference). What's required for this override to occur? Again, I suspect no algorithm exists—it's not just that we haven't been able to articulate one, but there literally isn't one. That doesn't mean the override doesn't happen and it doesn't mean that the factors Evans and Kripke mention are not important.[7]

Here is where we are:

- The aim of conceptual engineering is to bring about a certain kind of reference change.
- Externalism of various forms allows such changes in reference.
- There's no algorithm for how such changes happen.

[6] What Williamson says about the ways meaning supervenes on use is very brief and there isn't much detail. The way I read it, his view is compatible with the various forms of externalism that I have appealed to: those are the relevant ways to spell out 'use'.

[7] It's worth emphasizing again that the theorists that I just mentioned—e.g., Evans and Kripke—talked about names and their referents. This book is primarily about predicates and their extensions and intensions. I am talking the literature on reference shifts for names and using it as a model for how to think about the analogous shifts in extension and intension for predicates. If you think predicates refer to properties (and that these again fix extensions and intensions—see, e.g., Soames 2002), this is particularly simple, but even if you don't, I assume the externalist assumptions and complications apply also for predicates.

But they both allude to social forces in changing reference.

Appeals to reference change can accommodate much of the talk of representational deficiencies I outlined in Part I of this book (but not all of it—talk of inconsistent concepts needs an additional theory, which is provided in chapter 8). Here are three illustrations:

- Consider the idea (suggested by Clark and Chalmers) that our current concept of 'belief' is defective because it doesn't pick out a natural kind and doesn't contribute to a unified theory of the mind. In the current framework that means the extension of 'belief' doesn't constitute a natural kind and that theorizing about this non-natural kind leads to a non-unified theory of the mind. A change in intension and extension will—if Clark and Chalmers are right—result in a better way to talk and think about belief. The aim will be to effect a reference shift for 'belief'.

- Consider the thought that when 'marriage' excludes same-sex couples it is defective because it has negative effects on society and that a change would be an improvement. In the current framework this amounts to the claim that 'marriage' having a certain extension has negative effects on society and that changing its extension would be a good thing: the result would be a better way to talk about marriage.

- Haslanger suggests that if the intension of 'woman' is changed so that in worlds where there are females who are not socially subordinated, they are not in the extension of women. She conjectures that if we were to talk in that way, her political goals would be advanced.

And so it goes for many of the cases discussed in chapter 2: Carnap can be understood as claiming that reducing vagueness in extensions is good for theorizing; Railton as suggesting that the extension of 'ought' should be revised; and several of the examples of efforts to change our concepts of race can be understood as attempts to change the extension of 'race'. It's important to emphasize that I'm not endorsing any of those specific claims about a need for amelioration. Each of those claims would require a great deal of work to establish. Establishing those claims isn't the aim of this book. The aim is to provide a framework for that kind of theorizing. What we have learned from the externalist tradition is that features such as introductory (baptismal) events, communicative chains, intentions to preserve reference in a chain, expert judgments and deference to experts, the speakers' environment, and complex patterns of use over time will have an effect on semantic values (extensions and intensions in particular). At the present stage of metasemantic understanding *none of this adds up to a recipe for reference change*—it doesn't enable us to understand why each of the listed changes happened, why they happened the way they did, and why other changes didn't happen. We shouldn't be in the business of trying to look for necessary and sufficient conditions for change in extension to take place. We should be satisfied with case studies and some illuminating generalizations.

6.5 Metasemantics Can Change over Time

So far I've talked about how semantic values—reference in particular—can change over time. Conceptual engineering as a project assumes that semantics isn't stable—that it's in flux. An account of the metasemantics contributes to an explanation of these changes because semantic changes result from changes in the facts that determine reference. However, there's no good reason to assume that only the semantics is in flux. We should also expect the metasemantics to be in flux. One (slightly inaccurate) way to put that: The rules for how to change the semantics can also change. A passage from Rorty can help illustrate this point. Rorty says that

philosophy is the greatest game of all precisely because it is the game of "changing the rules." This game can be won by attending to the patterns by which these rules are changed, and formulating rules in terms of which to judge changes of rules. Those who take this view hold that philosophy in the old style—philosophy as "metaphysics, epis-temology, and axiology"—needs to be replaced by metaphilosophy. Members of this school are, as it were, the metaphilosopher's metaphilosophers: since any metaphysical, epistemological, or axiological arguments can be defeated by redefinition, nothing remains but to make a virtue of necessity and to study this process of redefinition itself.
(Rorty 1961: 9)

Rorty is, at least on one reading, saying that old school philosophy should be replaced by conceptual engineering. The point I'm making in this section is that what Rorty calls 'the process of redefinition' can itself change over time; what it takes to change meanings can change. Put in my terminology: the metasemantics itself can evolve over time.

The significant element of *contestation* in many of the cases (think of 'marriage' and 'rape') contributes to changes in the metasemantics. Suppose those fighting for a change in the extension of 'marriage' were told: *Sorry, the experts have discovered that a necessary condition for a change in extension is C, and C isn't satisfied in this case, so we have to stick with the old extension.* There is no reason this should stop those advocating for a change. They would and should just say: *Okay, if it doesn't satisfy the conditions for a change of extension, let's change the conditions.* There's a significant element of contestation and open-endedness in these processes and those engaged in conceptual engineering aren't forced to follow past patterns. Of course, we're no more in control of these meta-metasemantic changes than we are in control of the changes in the semantics, but we should still think of both as being constantly in flux.

6.6 Moving on: Autonomy/Control, World Engineering, Inconsistent Concepts, and the Limits of Revision

When conceptual engineering is embedded within this kind of externalist meta-semantic framework, a number of issues become salient and the subsequent chapters address them:

- *Conceptual Autonomy/Control:* According to Plunkett and Sundell, exter-nalism undermines what they describe as our 'conceptual autonomy': it makes semantic changes very hard, harder than it would be if internalism were true. In the next chapter I argue that it is true that conceptual engineering is hard, but it is not harder than it would have been had internalism been true and it's not a surprise that it is hard (we should object to any theory that makes it easy).
- *What does the externalist framework work tell us about the subject matter of conceptual engineering?* From what I've said so far, conceptual engineering might look like a form of largely pointless fiddling with language. Is that all there is to it? In chapter 12 I argue that while it is in part about language, its effect are *worldly*: we in effect change the world and the process is not pointless.
- *How does this framework accommodate talk of inconsistent concepts?* So far it doesn't. Chapter 8 elaborates and provides an account of how to understand talk about 'inconsistent concepts'.
- *Why aren't these changes just changes in topic/subject matter? What are the limits of revision? How much change is too much?* Note that in the cases of reference change involving names—say from 'Madagascar' shifting from the mainland to the island—we have a change of topic and we can, for example, no longer disquotationally report earlier speech containing that name. There's a discontinuity. The cases I discussed in chapter 2 are not supposed to be like that: Clark and Chalmers, as I construe them, want to improve on *belief*. After amelioration, we are still talking about belief, we haven't changed the topic. I think this is an important aspect of conceptual engineering and the entirety of Part III is devoted to a discussion of these issues.

6.7 Generalization: What about Words, Sentences, and Speech that Do Not Have Extensions and Intensions?

My presentation of the Austerity Framework has presupposed that the expressions being ameliorated have extensions and intensions—roughly that their semantics enable them to pick out things in this and other worlds. That seems to make the framework unattractive or unusable for those who work in alternative semantic frameworks. Suppose, for example, that you are an expressivist about moral language. How does Austerity work then?

I am not an expressivist so that isn't the assumed background theory here, but it's worth noting that it is very easy for the framework outlined here to accommodate that view (and other alternative semantic frameworks). Here is how that would go: Suppose your favored semantics for a term like 'ought' is a very simple form of expressivism: 'A ought to Y' means 'Hurray! A Ys'. That's the semantic content. (What I say in what follows will apply equally to fancier versions of the view.) Now here is a form of amelioration you could engage in: You could argue that 'Hurray!' is, along some important dimensions, a defective attitude. Maybe our moral language would be better if the relevant attitude expressed by 'ought' was 'SuperDuper!' or 'Hurray*!'. You try to show that a language in which 'ought' expressed one of these alternative attitudes would be better, in some way. This kind of expressivist ameliorator faces challenges analogous to those mentioned above. What are the metasemantic mechanisms that connect an expression to a particular attitude and how can those metasemantic factors be changed? Do we have any kind of control over those facts? Why wouldn't such a change involve a change of topic? The change from expressing 'Hurray!' to expressing the somewhat different attitude 'SuperDuper!' is topic transforming. I suspect very much of what I have to say can be applied smoothly to such a theory, but there will also be significant differences. More generally, here is a bold conjecture (one that I won't be able to establish at this point): the structure of the view proposed here can be adjusted depending on what you think semantic values are. That is to say, it's not dependent on any specific assumptions about the nature of semantic values or what the points of evaluation are. It is, for example, neutral about whether the points of evaluation include standards or assessment contexts. In other words, the proposal could also accommodate various forms of relativist semantics (Egan 2007, MacFarlane 2014).

7

Corollaries of Externalism
Inscrutability, Lack of Control, and Anti-Luminosity

7.1 Elaborating the Austerity Framework

Here is the plan for this chapter:

- First, some elaborations of the view in the previous chapter.
- Next, a comparison with Haslanger's efforts to merge conceptual engineering and externalism.
- Finally, a reply to three objections: (i) Isn't this all just an argument for internalism? (ii) Why we should care about semantic value if my view is correct? (iii) Doesn't this all add up to a debunking project where the proper conclusion is that we should give up on conceptual engineering?

In the previous chapter, I concluded that while reference change is possible, there is no algorithm for how it is done, meaning that the conditions for successful revision might themselves be in flux. That motivates a principle I will return to throughout this book: *Inscrutable—Lack of Control—Will Keep Trying*:

Inscrutable—Lack of Control—Will Keep Trying: The processes involved in conceptual engineering are for the most part **inscrutable**, and **we lack control of them**, but nonetheless we **will and should keep trying**.

Slightly more elaborated, but still in slogan form:

(i) *An epistemic point:* In most cases the detailed mechanisms that underpin particular instances of conceptual engineering are too complex, messy, non-systematic, amorphous, and unstable for us to fully grasp or understand.

(ii) *A metaphysical point:* The process of conceptual engineering is governed by factors that are not within our *control:* no individual or group has a significant degree of control over how meaning change happens. Even if we could overcome our epistemic limitations—and know all about the relevant factors for a particular case—what we would have knowledge of would be something we had little control over.

(iii)   *A psychological point*: Despite (i) and (ii), we will keep trying to engage in conceptual engineering and, given the kinds of creatures we are, maybe we must keep trying.

This picture entails two further claims:

(iv)   *A theoretical point*: semantic and metasemantic flux is pervasive throughout our representational devices, meaning that there are no safe spaces from conceptual change.

(v)   *An epistemic point*: Conceptual engineering is not a luminous condition: you can engage in it without knowing that you are, you can think that you are doing it when you are not, and you do not know what changes to meaning you are making when you are making such changes.

7.2 Elaborations 1 and 2: 'Inscrutable' and 'Lack of Control'

According to externalists, the meaning of our words can be influenced by features of *the past*, including introductions of expressions (such as pointing and stipulations, on the understanding that these can be massively messy), and communicative chains (the 'passing along' of expressions where this is accompanied by something like reference-preserving intentions). Sources of information in the past—of the kind Evans talks about—can also be relevant to fixing reference. Other people can have an effect on our extensions: both Burge and Putnam provided good evidence that people classified as experts can play an important role. The total interaction between speakers' use and dispositions can also play an important role.[1]

This bundle of metasemantic claims entails both an epistemic point—that the metasemantics of our natural language terms are inscrutable—and a metaphysical point—that we have no control over the metasemantics.

First focus on the epistemic point: take one of the terms that are often discussed in connection with conceptual engineering, say 'person' or 'marriage'. There are two things we are ignorant of. First, to figure out the current intension

---

[1] More idiosyncratically, I think the future can influence what we talk about now—I endorse a form of temporal externalism of the kind suggested by, e.g., Wilson (1982), Jackman (1999, 2005), and Ball (forthcoming). Finally, even more idiosyncratically, thinking what happens in other possible worlds can influence what we refer to. See Cappelen and Dever (2018), chapter 5.

of a term, you would need information about the past, about introductory events, and communicative chains. It is indisputable that we don't have this information and never will. Secondly, to effectively make a change in the extension and intension of this term, you would need to understand the mechanisms of reference change. These mechanisms are also not known to any of us and might in effect be unknowable. Suppose meaning supervenes on extremely complex use patterns over long periods of time and that there's no algorithm for extracting meaning from those patterns. That makes it an illusion to think that we can be in a position to effectively predict and implement changes.

Given what I just said, it is an illusion to think that any individual or group has any significant degree of control of the reference-fixing facts. If we are not in control of the reference-fixing facts, then we're not in control of conceptual engineering because it requires us to change the reference-fixing facts. Even if we were perfectly coordinated as a group (something we are decidedly not), we would not give the group control because the actions and intentions of groups have at best a messy and unpredictable effect on our semantic values. We can of course try to influence other speakers and experts—but that will hardly ever amount to more than a drop in the ocean.

Even if we had all the information about the metasemantics of a term (about the use patterns, the histories, the sources of information, the interaction between the experts, etc.), it would appeal to factors that are in large part out of our control. For example, past facts play a role in determining the meaning of terms, but we can't change the past.

None of what I have just said assumes that externalism *excludes* intentional states from reference determination. The various externalist views appeal to intentions, beliefs, and other mental states. However, the fact such states play some role in the semantics is entirely unhelpful for those who want to oppose Inscrutable and Lack of Control. A metasemantics could put significant weight on the intentions or wishes or decisions of speakers, without the semantics being *in accordance with* those intentions, wishes, or decisions. Intentions, wishes, and decisions could play a significant role but in an unpredictable way. Maybe social change in general is like that: what we want, say, hope, etc. plays an important role in effecting large-scale changes in social structures, but not through fit.

7.3 Elaboration 2: 'Will Keep Trying'

One might think that what I've just said is a very bleak and pessimistic picture of conceptual engineering, but I don't think so. I think it's a fairly familiar predicament, and two comparisons help bring this out. First, think about trying to make a positive change to a person's life (say, that of a child you have responsibility for). For the most part, we understand very little of how such changes can be achieved and what we do know tells us that we have very little control. More often than not, what we do will either have no effect, or will have some effect other than what we intended. Nonetheless, we keep trying; there's a sense in which we can't give up.

Second, what I just said about normative theorizing about language is reflected in large swaths of normative reflections and theorizing more generally. In general, we don't make normative judgments (judgements about how thing ought to be) only when we have a worked out a strategy for how to change the world. To impose that constraint on normative reflections would exclude all but the most pedestrian of normative judgements. The various theorists canvased in chapter 1 all made suggestions for how words should change in meaning, but to criticize them for not accompanying those proposals with an instruction manual for how to implement that change would be deeply misguided and confused. It would miss the point. To take but one illustration: suppose I'm right and Haslanger has little or no control over the meaning of the English word 'woman'. That doesn't mean that her normative proposal for what 'woman' ought to mean is wrong or in some way misguided. She could be right about what it ought to mean, despite the fact that there is no algorithm for how to implement that change.

7.4 Elaboration 4: There Are No Safe Spaces Where We're in Control

When reflecting on and trying to engage in conceptual engineering there is a tempting form of hubris. It takes the form of inflated thoughts about one's own potential for impact. This tendency is natural and maybe applies much more broadly—generally in life we tend to think of ourselves as being more in control than we are and as having more impact than we have. Again, think of raising children: it's hard not to think you're in some kind of control and have significant impact, but this thought is for the most part an illusion. In the case of conceptual engineering, it often takes the form of the idea that there are safe spaces we can retreat to where we really *do* have control over the meaning of our terms. The hope would be that such safe spaces can isolate us from factors outside of our control.

As an illustration, consider writing. It's tempting to think, for example, that when I write a book, I can decide what a term, say, 'intuition', means. Suppose I just define that word in a certain way on page 2 of my book. It's then natural to think that this will determine the meaning of 'intuition' at least *as it occurs in my book* (I have, after all, told you what I want it to mean—this is sometimes called a stipulative definition). Isn't that a little bit of control? On the view proposed here, the answer is no. All you have achieved is to define a word in a certain way on page 2 of your book. Saying you want a word to mean something doesn't make it so. You have not changed the meaning of the word 'intuition'. What you say when you use that word is governed by what the word means, not by what you want it to mean. The rest of your paper is in English, not in some new language you created on page 2.[2] At best your definition will tell charitable readers how to get at the speaker's meaning, i.e., what you had in mind. However, even that isn't a move into a safe space in which we have control. The content of what's called 'speaker's meaning' is just as externalistically determined as linguistic meaning: we have no more control over that content than we have over what we say when we utter sentences in a public language.

The reaction to Lack of Control and the denial of Safe Spaces seem to many to be directly contradicted by what happens when judges, lawmakers, and others make decisions about what words as used in laws and regulations mean. In fact, that is a good test case. Let's take a particular case, say the US courts deciding that corporations are in the extension of 'person' (this is simplifying the legal situation a bit, but the simplification is irrelevant for current purposes). That looks like a case of Control: they have made a decision about what that word should mean and now that's what it does mean. So Lack of Control is false, it would seem. But this objection misdescribes what has happened in such a case. What has happened isn't that they've decided on and created a new meaning for 'person'. What has happened is that they've made/ forced certain people to misinterpret sentences containing 'person' in a par- ticular way. The US Supreme Court or any other group can no more change the meaning of 'person' than I can. They can make proposals. The difference between the legal system and me is that they have police power to back up their proposals—so even if it's an idiotic proposal, they can force people to act as if it were true. If I had a private army I could do the same to a group of people: I could get them to act as if 'pig' means 'dog', but that doesn't change the meaning of 'pig'. On that view, a better way to describe the substance of the legal decision is this: The laws treat persons and corporations in the same way along certain dimensions and in certain contexts. You then spell out those

---

[2] In chapter 15 I discuss views according to which we create word meanings and microlanguages 'on the fly'. If you find those views convincing, what I just said in response to control won't move you, but the discussion is picked up again in that later chapter.

dimensions, those contexts, and the various legal implications of treating people and corporations as the same along these dimensions in these contexts. All that can be done without saying that corporations are in the extension of 'person'. So understood, the legal cases can be turned into a defense of Lack of Control: even an institution as powerful as the US legal system (backed by police power) has failed to change the meaning of 'person'.

There's one relevant issue I've skirted so far. An important strand in the externalist tradition is the idea that there is a linguistic division of labor where non-experts defer to experts and the experts have a distinctive role in determining what we talk about. On a simple version of this view, the experts are in semantic control, in a way that others are not. I don't think anything like this simple picture of the role of experts is correct—and below I'll say why—but suppose for the sake of argument that there's some element of truth to it. That would give the experts as a group a degree of control, and it would give individual experts some control insofar as they can control the group of experts. That would be a limited exception to what I've called 'Out of Control'. However, as soon as one starts to get a bit more explicit about the exact nature of the experts' role, this exception starts to look very muddy. First, note that any good theory of the role of experts should be compatible with the fact that experts can be wrong: it is possible that experts on Fs all think that Fs are Gs, even though Fs are not Gs. So even if experts agree, say, that only Gs are in the extension of the predicate 'F', it doesn't follow that they are right. Whatever control experts have must be compatible with this.[3] A second complication with the appeal to experts is that it is unclear who should be considered experts. Who are the experts on the origin of the universe? Most people in the world think the experts are priests or religious authorities. I think the experts are physicists. Who decides who the 'real' experts are? Do we need experts on who the experts are?

I don't have good answers to all these questions and I don't have a full theory of the role of experts in reference-fixing. It is an interesting issue that deserves further exploration (and I will have a bit more to say in the discussion of Haslanger below). However, the issues raised just above show that the simple picture of the experts' semantic control is too simplistic. Whatever role the experts play, it is not one that yields an easy route to semantic control.

---

[3] Tempting thought: talk of 'experts' was just a shorthand for talk of people who are right. This would mean that we shouldn't be appealing to the sociological notion of an expert. 'Experts' in this non-sociological sense are only a genuine authority if they are right. So it's being right that matters, not being recognized as an expert.

7.5 Elaboration 5: Conceptual Engineering Not Luminous

The Austerity Framework entails that it will often be the case that you think you're engaged (or intend to engage) in conceptual engineering, but you are not. It will also often be the case that you think you're engaged in an effort to change someone's beliefs (say about what marriage is or what constitutes a person), but what you do will contribute to conceptual engineering. Engaging in conceptual engineering is not what Williamson (2000) calls 'a luminous condition': We can do it without being aware of doing it and we can think we're doing it when we're not doing it. When we are doing it, we are also not in a position to know what meaning changes we are contributing to. This point is an extension of and a strengthening of 'Lack of Control': not only do we lack significant control over the mechanisms that lead to conceptual amelioration and revision, but we're not even in control of when our actions contribute to that project. Again I see a parallel with efforts to effect social change. We might contribute to such changes even when we're not intending to, or make changes different to those that we intended. So it should be unsurprising that this lack of luminosity also holds for conceptual engineering, which is after all a kind of social change in the realm of meaning.

7.6 A Sharp Contrast: Haslanger on Externalism and Amelioration

In many of Haslanger's writings, revisionist or ameliorative projects are com- bined with an externalist view of the semantics for social kinds.[4] My way of incorporating externalism into conceptual engineering contrasts sharply with Haslanger's. This section outlines some of those contrasts.

Some of the important differences between our ways of combining externalism and amelioration can be extracted from the following two passages:

Social constructionists can rely on externalist accounts of meaning to argue that their disclosure of an operative or a target concept is not changing the subject, but better reveals what we mean. By reflecting broadly on how we use the term 'parent,' we find that the cases, either as they stand or adjusted through ameliorative analysis, project onto an objective social, not natural, type. So although we tend to assume we are expressing the concept of immediate progenitor by the term 'parent' in fact we are expressing the concept of primary caregiver (or some such); the constructionist shows us that our

---

[4] See note 6 in chapter 1 for remarks on the relation between Haslanger (2000) and Haslanger (2006).

assumptions about what we mean are false, given our practice. This is not to propose a new meaning, but to reveal an existing one.   (Haslanger 2006: 110)

For most conversations the incomplete hold we have on meanings doesn't matter, for we are good at figuring out enough to communicate and get by. But the indeterminacy of our grasp of meanings also allows for confusion and mystification; one goal of social theory, as I see it, is to clarify meanings with social justice in mind. Although Putnam, Kripke, et al. were keen on the holistic nature of our inquiry, they also tended to be biased in favor of the natural sciences in seeking the a posteriori conditions for membership in a kind. But an externalist bias towards the natural sciences is not warranted, for social kinds are no less real for being social. I argue that in the social domain we should rely on social theorists, including feminist and antiracist theorists, to help explicate the meanings of our terms. Much can be gained, I believe, by including both social science and moral theory— broadly construed—in the web of belief that has a bearing on our inquiry.

(Haslanger 2012: 15)

I'll focus on three aspects of Haslanger's view:

> *Haslanger sees amelioration as revelation:*   "Social constructionists can rely on externalist accounts of meaning to argue that their disclosure of an operative or a target concept is not changing the subject, but better reveals what we mean."
>
> *Haslanger sees social scientists as reference-fixing experts:*   "we should rely on social theorists, including feminist and antiracist theorists, to help explicate the meanings of our terms."
>
> *Haslanger advocates the view that reference-fixing is in part normative:*   "one goal of social theory, as I see it, is to clarify meanings with social justice in mind." One (somewhat stretched) way to read this is as suggesting that references of social kind terms are whatever satisfy certain normative conditions, e.g., the extension of 'family' is determined, in part, by whatever promotes a just social order.

There are aspects of this picture that are congenial to the Austerity Framework. Most importantly, we agree on the importance of finding a way to incorporate externalism into the project of conceptual engineering. In large part, this book is an effort to think through the ways that this can be done. There is, however, a *fundamental* point of disagreement with Haslanger about how externalism and conceptual engineering combine. Getting clear on that point of disagreement will, I suspect, help make my view easier to understand.

7.6.1 Some points of agreement between Haslanger and the Austerity Framework

Before turning to the Big Point of Disagreement, some points of convergence. According to Haslanger, reference-fixing is in part guided by norms: the norms of social justice figure in some way in the reference-fixing mechanism. A version of that view is a corollary of what I call 'the contestation theory of topic continuity' (which I suggested in 6.5, and will develop further in chapter 10). According to this view, contestation over topic continuity is often a battle of norms. This isn't true just about terms for social kinds, but also for natural kind terms, terminology for sports activities, food, art, and any other domain. However—and here I think I disagree with Haslanger—I don't think the right norms (or the norms I endorse) are the reference fixing ones. Whoever wins wins—if the wrong norms win in the long run, they also win the reference fixing game.

I also agree with the idea that social scientists (and also philosophers) are experts and can play a role analogous to that of experts in the natural sciences. I think experts play some role, but as argued in the previous section, the nature of that role is unclear and confusing. However, there is also an important disanalogy between experts in the natural and social sciences: normative choice points are often more pressing for research into the nature of, say, gender, race, democracy, or family than they are for research into the molecular causes of cancer. The salience and centrality of the normative in these domains makes it unlikely that there will ever be the same level of consensus and convergence, as there is in, e.g., cancer research. The lack of consensus and convergence will make the very notion of an expert—who counts as an expert—an endlessly contested subject in these fields. Who counts as an expert will be at least as contested as the first-order questions. This makes it less likely that an appeal to experts will resolve much, if any, of the central points of dispute in these areas.

7.6.2 A big point of disagreement between Haslanger and the Austerity Framework

Now to the Big Point of Disagreement over how externalism and ameliorative projects combine. As I see it, amelioration as revelation undermines the basic idea behind ameliorative projects: Haslanger, in effect, treats externalism as *the end of amelioration*. What we thought was amelioration (i.e., improvement of our representational devices) turns out to be revelation of something that was there all along. This means that Haslanger effectively gives up on the ameliorative project. After incorporating externalism, what she ends up advocating is essentially *a purely descriptive project*: the aim is to figure out what the extensions really are, and what externalism tells us is that a) this can be really hard to figure out, b) that it can be very different from what we think it is, and c) that normative considerations play a content-determining role.

My view is *more radical* because it is *more revisionary*. The Austerity Framework incorporates externalism and in so doing recognizes that the actual extensions of our terms can be very different from what we think they are. It then goes further, and says that given what we think the extensions of our terms are, we might want to improve them (where improvement involves changing actual extensions and intensions). A couple of illustrations can bring out the contrast between my view and Haslanger's. Suppose as a matter of historical fact that given the way 'marriage' was introduced, it ended up with an extension and intension *that excludes* same-sex couples.[5] It's unclear whether this is true or false, but for the sake of argument assume it's true. I then think amelioration/ conceptual engineering kicks in: you would want to change the extension and intension of 'marriage' in a way that preserves topic. You still want to be talking about marriage, but you want it also to include same-sex couples. That process of amelioration is hard for reasons that I have gone into above, but it is the core part of the ameliorative project. Compare this with the view of conceptual engineering as revelation. Haslanger tells us that "[s]ocial constructionists can rely on exter- nalist accounts of meaning to argue that their disclosure of an operative or a target concept is not changing the subject, but better reveals what we mean" (Haslanger 2006: 110). But in the case I just imagined, the revelation of what our term meant revealed something we object to—it reveals that the word doesn't denote what it ought to denote. That, as I see it, is the point where conceptual engineering kicks in. The first stage, the revelation of what we refer to, is a descriptive project, and is not distinctively ameliorative.

Has a point here, but CE can also change.

7.7 Objections to the Austerity Framework

7.7.1 Objection 1: Isn't this just an argument for internalism?

In this chapter I have articulated Lack of Control and Inscrutable as theses that go hand in hand with externalism and the Austerity Framework. Can internalism give us more scrutability, and more control? Recall Burgess and Plunkett's claim:

The textbook externalist thinks that our social and natural environments serve as heavy anchors, so to speak, for the interpretation of our individual thought and talk. The internalist, by contrast, grants us a greater degree of conceptual autonomy. One salient upshot of this disagreement is that effecting conceptual change looks comparatively easy from an internalist perspective. We can revise, eliminate, or replace our concepts without worrying about what the experts are up to, or what happens to be coming out of our taps.
(Burgess and Plunkett 2013a: 1096)

[5] And that is compatible with the reference-fixing mechanism being in part normative—it might just turn out that norms I don't agree with play that role.

An internalist could say: 'One condition on a good metasemantic account is that it makes sense of various conceptual engineering projects. You've just shown that externalism makes the process inscrutable and practically impossible. That's an argument against externalism and in favor of a more conceptual engineering friendly account of the nature of meaning.' To assess this line of thought, let's first consider whether internalism, as such, puts us in any more control of the facts that determine meaning. Internalism is a supervenience claim: it claims that the extensions and intensions of expressions supervene on features of individuals (and then lots of bells and whistles to elaborate on this in various ways, but the bells and whistles don't matter right now). Suppose the meaning of my words supervenes in that way on *me*. Note first that this is compatible with the meanings and extension supervening on features of me that I have no control over. It's also compatible with it being unsettled and unstable what combination of internal features ground reference. So there's just no step from Internalism to our having control over the extensions and intensions of our expressions.

Moreover, even if you're an internalist who thinks meanings and extensions supervene on something we have 'introspective access to', this view won't lead to Control: I can have introspective access to my headaches, but I have little control over them. We also have minimal understanding of what causes them. Moreover, even if meaning supervenes on something internal that I have control over (I don't think there are any such internal states, but put that aside for now), Control doesn't follow: it could supervene on something we could control, but the determination relation from the supervenience base to meanings/extension could still be out of our control. For example, even if there's supervenience on what we want or intend or decide, the supervenience relation doesn't have to make it the case that semantic values are what we intend for them to be, what we want them to be, or what we agree on them to be (for all we know, it could be a total mess or get us to the opposite of what we want, intend, or decide).

So, there's no shortcut here from Internalism to Control. Internalism makes it just as hard to get control. Or, put in terms of a challenge: an argument is needed a) that there are inner states that are scrutable and under our control, and b) that meaning or concepts supervene on those inner states. However, even that isn't enough. Even if you think (a) and (b) are true, you don't have a position that guarantees scrutability or control. You still need (c) the determination relation from the supervenience base to be scrutable and within our control. As far as I know, no internalist has ever even tried to argue for the conjunction of a–c.

7.7.2 Objection 2: Why care about semantic values if they are inscrutable?

One might object that if extensions (and intensions) are inscrutable, incomprehensible, out of our control etc., why think they play important roles in our cognitive lives? Surely, such 'hidden' meanings are irrelevant to anything we should care about. They are some kind of exotic creatures that have no genuine significance for us.

The reply is that despite Inscrutability, we have easy access to and knowledge of the extension of our terms, it's just a form of access that's not very useful for the conceptual engineer. We all know, for example, that the extension of 'belief' consists of all and only beliefs and that the extension of 'person' consist of all and only persons. That kind of disquotational knowledge is true, informative, and accessible to us despite Inscrutability. So Inscrutability doesn't imply that we can't know what we're talking about. Accordingly, contrary to the objection, we are *not* ignorant of what, e.g., 'person' denotes. We know *exactly* what's in its extension. And that matters to someone who wants to understand what persons are. If you are interested in what persons are, then you are interested in what is in the extension of 'persons'. One condition on a good answer is that it includes all and only persons. However, saying just that is very uninformative and is unhelpful for most theoretical purposes, meaning that someone asking that question will typically want more. But what she does not want is an answer that's not about persons—that simply wouldn't answer her question.

7.7.3 Objection 3: Isn't this just a debunking project? Comparison with ideal theory in political philosophy

Some readers of early drafts of this manuscript found it weird that I present it as a defense of the importance of conceptual engineering, but at the same time defend theses like 'Lack of Control—Inscrutable—Will Keep Trying'. They asked whether this book is in effect a debunking project, disguised misleadingly as a defense and whether this book it in effect an extended argument that conceptual engineering is impossible.[6] I understand this reaction, but it's a mistake for reasons I've already mentioned. As I emphasized above, that the processes underlying change are inscrutable and uncontrollable is a familiar point from other normative domains. Theorists are comfortable reflecting on and proposing theories of justice, for example, without having a recipe for how they can be implemented. More generally, we can make judgments about what ought to be the case without knowing how

---

[6] Alex Byrne read an earlier draft and articulated this concern in a particularly helpful way: "By his (HC's) lights (it seems to me), his conclusion should be that there is no such thing (as conceptual engineering), and that its proponents deserve the guillotine. And that kind of reign-of-terror conclusion is much more Cappelenesque anyway." There's a part of this I agree with: If you come to the field of conceptual engineering with certain expectations, then this book debunks those expectations and perhaps with them your conception of the field.

to make the world that way (or even having a plausible strategy in mind). Those are just different projects: figuring out what ought to be the case and making the world that way. Moreover, normative theories (and all other theories) inevitably abstract from the messy details of reality in order to make systematic theorizing possible. Those thinking about defects of concepts and ameliorative strategies should be allowed the same leeway.

8

The Illusion of Incoherent/ Inconsistent Concepts

8.1 Explaining the Appearance of Incoherent or Inconsistent Concepts

So far, the Austerity Framework doesn't have the resources to explain *all* the various kinds of deficiency used as illustrations in Part I. In particular, it's not yet clear how I can explain the talk of *inconsistent, incoherent, and indeterminate* concepts that I presented in chapter 2 (Part I). Richard, van Inwagen, Scharp, and many other conceptual engineers start with the idea that concepts can have those properties. Such characterizations seem to presuppose very rich notions of concepts. For example, it's relatively easy to see how you can endorse the idea that concepts can be inconsistent if you think of concepts as entities governed by rules: inconsistency in a concept can then be understood as an inconsistency in the rules (e.g., Spicer 2008, Scharp 2013a: C2). The Austerity Framework doesn't appeal to constitutive rules of concepts. The externalist component of the Austerity framework (including *Anti-Creed*) is opposed to it.[1] The Austerity Framework doesn't appeal to concepts at all. It is, in effect, conceptual engineering without concepts.

In light of that, I could just say that the philosophers who talk about inconsistent or incoherent concepts are misguided: trapped in a false theory that leads them to mischaracterize the phenomena under discussion. But that's an unsatisfying and simplistic way to proceed. I think appealing to incoherent concepts is a natural thing to do, and that the Austerity Framework can explain why this is. What I can provide is in effect an error theory of such appeals.

---

[1] This is not the place to argue for that claim: see the exchange between Williamson and Boghossian in Boghossian 2011 and Williamson 2011. Main point: it's an effort to avoid that kind of view—to see how far you can come without it.

The view I propose has two central components:

a) According to the Austerity Framework, there are no incoherent or inconsistent concepts, but we can explain why some philosophers are inclined to
   think there are;
b) The Austerity Framework locates the appearance of incoherence or inconsistency in three places: (i) inconsistent beliefs, evidence, and conceptions,
   (ii) inconsistent introductions, (iii) metasemantic messiness.

8.2 Inconsistent Beliefs, Evidence, and Conceptions and Inconsistent Introductions

According to the kind of externalism that I endorse, there's no cluster of beliefs
(or dispositions to endorse) that are analytically true or are required for being a
competent user of a predicate. Speakers can be deeply committed to *all kinds* of
false beliefs about Fs and still be competent users of 'F' and use 'F' to say false
things about Fs. You could for example be completely devoted to the idea that
pencils are alien creatures and that doesn't in any way prevent you from using
'pencil' to talk about pencils (and say false things about them, e.g., that pencils are
aliens). By extension, you can be deeply convinced that there's evidence that all Fs
are both G and not-G. You can be deeply convinced that a particular object that
has the property F is both G and not G. None of that means that you're not a
competent user of 'F'. It also doesn't mean that your concept of F is inconsistent.
It just means that you're inclined both to believe that all Fs are G and that they are
not-G (or that this particular F is both G and not G). That's *your* problem—not
the concept F's problem. Nor is it a problem for things that are F.

As an illustration, consider again van Inwagen's claim:

There are seemingly unanswerable arguments that...demonstrate that free will is incompatible with determinism—and there are seemingly unanswerable arguments that...dem-
onstrate that free will is incompatible with indeterminism. But if free will is incompatible
both with determinism and indeterminism, the concept 'free will' is incoherent, and the
thing free will does not exist.   (van Inwagen 2008: 327–8)

One thing that happens to people (even people who think carefully) is that their
beliefs about some topic end up internally inconsistent. They might encounter
evidence that points in conflicting directions—where it's hard to see how to
resolve the inconsistency. This kind of thing can easily happen when thinking
about very complicated phenomena such as freedom (or justice, or gender, or
knowledge). Talk about 'incoherence' or 'inconsistency' in concepts can then
(misleadingly) be used to characterize having incoherence or inconsistency in
your beliefs or evidence. This talk doesn't characterize something called 'the
concept of freedom' and certainly not freedom.

Here's the same point put in a different terminology: Distinguish between concepts and conceptions, e.g., the concept of freedom and conceptions of freedom. Some of those who appeal to this distinction think that people who share a concept can have different conceptions of that concept—they share a concept of freedom, but they have different conceptions of freedom. A challenge for such views is to tell us what the concept of F is, how it is distinguished from conceptions of F, and how conceptions again are distinguished from beliefs about Fs. Without going into details, one way to articulate the proposal above is that someone's conception of F—say freedom—can be inconsistent, even though the concept isn't.

None of this justifies a claim of the form: *the concept of F is inconsistent*. That's almost always the wrong way to go because the right response is almost always a version of Modesty/Humility:

> *Modesty/Humility:*   We just can't figure this out. It's too hard. We don't know how to collect more evidence and the evidence we have doesn't resolve the issue of whether Fs are G or not G. Given our limited cognitive capacities, this happens a lot. Consider an example: There's strong evidence that the butler did it. There's also strong evidence that the butler didn't do it. But we have no way to figure out whether he did it or not. The evidence could in principle be inaccessible to us. Nothing follows about the concept of a butler or murderer (nor should we be inclined to say that butlers or murderers don't exist).

Modesty/Humility is a recognition of our epistemic limitations and tells us to not project those limitations onto something called 'the concept'.

8.2.1 Inconsistent or incoherent baptisms or reference-fixing descriptions

In a Kripkean framework there are introductory events (some expressions are introduced through pointings (baptisms) and other terms through reference-fixing descriptions) and then expressions are passed along in causal communicative networks. Focus on the introductory events. Here are some inconsistency-like features that can, at least in principle, occur at that stage: a term can be introduced through reference-fixing descriptions that impose incoherent or inconsistent conditions on the referent. This need not be blatantly so. Introductory events are not likely, in real life, to be brief isolated events. If we imagine there is an introductory event for a term like 'freedom', it will most likely have involved many people acting over a period of time (more on this in the next section). For now what I want to point out is that in such a reference-fixing process, incoherent or inconsistent conditions can be imposed. The speakers involved in this introduction could decide that 'Freedom' should denote both something that satisfies conditions G (e.g., not being caused) and other conditions F (e.g., being within the agent's control), without realizing that the idea of something being both G and F is incoherent. If so, we can get a structure that's much like that of what is called an inconsistent concept.

8.3 General Source of the Illusion of Inconsistency: Metasemantic Chaos

Those of us who endorse various forms of externalism should expect a great deal of metasemantic messiness. This messiness can have results that will lead some philosophers to describe a concept as incoherent or inconsistent.

To see this, consider one of the more influential passages of twentieth-century philosophy:

Someone, let's say, a baby, is born; his parents call him by a certain name. They talk about him to their friends. Other people meet him. Through various sorts of talk the name is spread from link to link as if by a chain. A speaker who is on the far end of this chain, who has heard about, say Richard Feynman, in the market place or elsewhere, may be referring to Richard Feynman even though he can't remember from whom he first heard of Feynman or from whom he ever heard of Feynman. He knows that Feynman is a famous physicist. A certain passage of communication reaching ultimately to the man himself does reach the speaker. He then is referring to Feynman even though he can't identify him uniquely. He doesn't know what a Feynman diagram is, he doesn't know what the Feynman theory of pair production and annihilation is. Not only that: he'd have trouble distinguishing between Gell-Mann and Feynman. So he doesn't have to know these things, but, instead, a chain of communication going back to Feynman himself has been established, by virtue of his membership in a community which passed the name on from link to link...   (Kripke 1980: 91)

The picture Kripke outlines here is obviously a massively sanitized version of any real linguistic history. Kripke's description abstracts away from a great deal of real-world complications, and he is very much aware of this. For example, just a couple of pages later he says:

[M]y characterization has been far less specific than a real set of necessary and sufficient conditions for reference would be. Obviously the name is passed on from link to link. But of course not every sort of causal chain reaching from me to a certain man will do for me to make a reference. There may be a causal chain from our use of the term 'Santa Claus' to a certain historical saint, but still the children, when they use this, by this time probably do not refer to that saint. So other conditions must be satisfied in order to make this into a really rigorous theory of reference. I don't know that I'm going to do this because, first, I'm sort of too lazy at the moment; secondly, rather than giving a set of necessary and sufficient conditions which will work for a term like reference, I want to present just a *better picture* than the picture presented by the received views.   (Kripke 1980: 93)

What exactly are the details of an externalist metasemantics that appeals to chains of communication? I don't have a full story, Kripke doesn't offer one, and Kripke is right that this isn't what we should be looking for. What is clear is that however the details are worked out, the externalist metasemantics *can go wrong* and be *messy*. This kind of messiness can be mistaken for conceptual inconsistency. To see how that could work, consider some concrete illustrations of metasemantic messiness.

8.3.1 Evans on reference change

First reflect on reference change and in particular what can happen during the messy period of reference change. Gareth Evans's description of this process is helpful (though none of the details in Evans matter much). Evans describes a situation in which reference change happens, but in a transition period there's no reference at all and sentences containing the expressions fail to have a truth value:

Suppose one of a group of villagers dubbed a little girl on holiday in the vicinity 'Goldilocks' and the name caught on. However suppose that there were two identical twins the villagers totally fail to distinguish. I should deny that 'Goldilocks' is the name of either—even if by some miracle each villager used the name consistently but in no sense did they fall into two coherent sub-communities. 'NN' is originally used to denote x but we're in a transition period and y is *now the dominant source of information*: At this point, I think we can say that the name 'NN', as used in this practice, no longer has a referent. The persistent identification of y as NN has undermined the connection which tied the name uniquely to x. It is certainly no longer possible to report what has happened by referring to y and saying 'This is not NN.' Indeed, such a remark will not have any definite truth-value.   (Evans 1973: 203)

Evans-style reference failure isn't inconsistency, but is easily mistaken for it. We're in a situation where 'Goldilocks' is satisfying some conditions for referring to *a* and some of the conditions for referring to *b*. If *a* is F and *b* isn't F, then we'll be inclined towards assenting to both 1 and 2:

1. Goldilocks is F.
2. Goldilocks is not F.

The general point has nothing specifically to do with Evans's theory. Any semantic theory should leave open the following two possibilities:

- A condition for being semantic value can be partially satisfied
- At time t, an expression E has two equally good candidate extensions: *a* and *b*.

In this kind of situation, something about E will be *defective*. In some cases this kind of defectiveness is mistaken for a concept being incoherent or inconsistent (when we have two or more equally good candidate referents). The pattern generalizes from names to other kinds of expressions.

8.3.2 Other kinds of metasemantic messiness

Suppose you like the picture given in Kripke's *Naming and Necessity*, as I do. I think a good story about reference includes the following factors. (i) Introductions of expressions. These come in at least two kinds: pointings and stipulations using descriptions. (ii) Communicative chains: expressions are passed along in communicative chains. The 'glue' of these communicative chains includes at least reference-preserving intentions. I also think deference to experts plays an important role in reference-fixing: for some speakers, what they refer to using 'F' will depend on what the F-experts denote using 'F'. All of these factors will in real life be immensely messy. By 'messy' I don't just mean that it will be unclear when the conditions are satisfied, though there will be that too. I mean also that what counts as satisfying the conditions will be up for debate, controversial, and not determined by any rules.

As an illustration, consider the two main categories of reference-determining factors. First, the introductory events, ostensions, or descriptions that fix reference. Here we encounter issues such as:

- What counts as an adequate introduction;
- What is pointed to;
- Who gets to point, i.e., whose pointings matter;
- Whose stipulations matter for introducing the term;
- What counts as an adequate reference-preserving intention;
- Who counts as an expert.

Who counts as an expert is not an issue settled by the language faculty or by a set of rules that we have to obey. It is something we get to decide on along the way: we negotiate and deliberate over it as we do with most other social matters. The same is true of the other items on the list.

With that in mind, the following is a constant possibility (and I think a constant reality): according to one way to resolve the metasemantic conflicts, o is in the extension of F, while on another way of doing so, o is *not* in the extension of F. Insofar as a speaker is sensitive to these metasemantic tensions (and the extent to which we are is an open empirical question), she will be 'pushed towards' endorsing 'Fo' and also pushed towards accepting 'Not Fo'. Moreover, *there can seem to be no empirical facts that will settle the matter for her.*

I think that's a situation we frequently are in with respect to philosophical terms and it is one that leads people to the mistaken impression that there are inconsistent concepts. Think about applying something like Kripke's model to the following expressions of English:

- Freedom
- Woman
- Justice
- Belief
- Truth
- Child

The real history of these terms—e.g., the introductory events, the millions of links in the communicative chains, the expert opinions, and so on—is unimaginably complex. Messiness of the kind described above is bound to arise. I grant that proving that this is the source of the sense of incoherence that some philosophers claim to feel will be hard, but it is, I propose, one fairly plausible diagnosis.

One version of this kind of metasemantic deficiency is worth singling out: In some cases descriptions are used to fix reference. In real life cases the correct descriptions can end up being incoherent. Nothing in the Kripkean picture rules that out. It's unclear what happens in those cases. If a theoretical term, say 'true', is introduced through descriptive conditions that are internally inconsistent, it's again not unlikely that the result could be a sense of incoherence and inconsistency.

In sum, what I'm proposing is again an *error theory/diagnostic*: those who talk of inconsistent concepts have in some cases confused these kinds of metasemantic messes for inconsistency or incoherence in something they call 'concepts'. This isn't to say that there's no deficiency there. There's a metasemantic deficiency that leads to a term's having defective semantic content and to defective thoughts. So there is work here to do, but it is not work that involves fixing an inconsistent concept. It is, instead, work that involves improving the conditions for meaningfulness, i.e., the metasemantic foundations.

8.4 The Liar Paradox, Inconsistency Theories, and the Austerity Framework: A Comparison

Some of those who write about inconsistent concepts do so in connection with efforts to solve paradoxes such as the liar. Eklund takes seriously the possibility that our intuitions in such cases really are inconsistent and that this is because the principles that are constitutive of the concept of truth are inconsistent (Eklund 2002). Similarly, Scharp's view has as a central aim to find a solution to the Liar Paradox (Scharp 2013a).

The kind of view proposed by, for example, Scharp differs from the view in this book both in substance and motivation. The section above outlined various ways in which the substance of our views differs, but the motivational differences are as important. They reflect a fundamental difference in our approaches to conceptual engineering:

- *My motivation:* I'm interested in conceptual engineering because I think our linguistic and cognitive devices can be defective along many varied dimensions and that it's important to explore a variety of ameliorative strategies. This is reflected in the wide range of illustrations found in Part I of this book. A theory of conceptual engineering should explore all these potential deficiencies, say something about their interconnections, and compare ameliorative strategies.
- *Inconsistency theorists' motivation:* Scharp is interested in conceptual engineering because he wants to solve the paradoxes. For him, the project of understanding conceptual engineering is successful just in case it contributes to a solution to the paradoxes. The appeal to inconsistent concepts serves that purpose and so does the development of replacement concepts.

So my motivation is broader than that of, e.g., Scharp. It's not much of an exaggeration to say that Scharp's motivation is *very* idiosyncratic. First, it's motivated by an effort to solve paradoxes. Most philosophers are not so motivated. However, most of those who are interested in, e.g., the Liar Paradox, don't turn to conceptual engineering. It's only if you think *none* of the standard solutions to the paradoxes work that you will be attracted to the kind of inconsistency view that Scharp advocates. That view (the view that 'truth' is an inconsistent concept) is endorsed by only a very small minority of those who work on the paradoxes. So the Scharp path into conceptual engineering is very narrow indeed. My view of conceptual engineering, by contrast, is entirely open-ended: I don't start with assumptions about what the deficiencies are. I don't start with assumptions about what the available ameliorative strategies are. Finally, I don't have to endorse a particular view of concepts to be interested in conceptual engineering. That's all up for grabs. This has the advantage that it makes the research project attractive to anyone interested in representational deficiencies, not just to those who are interested in the paradoxes, happen to find all the standard solutions unacceptable, and believe concepts can have inconsistent constitutive rules.

As a corollary, our views differ in that my framework doesn't aspire to make an original contribution to the literature on the paradoxes. Most of the standard solutions to the paradoxes are of course available to someone who thinks about conceptual engineering in the way I do.[2] Paradoxically, one solution that's not available is the inconsistency view—the very view that has made philosophers like Eklund and Scharp interested in conceptual engineering. That said, I suspect quite a bit of the material appealed to by inconsistency theorists can be accommodated by the Austerity Framework. The general strategy for such accommodation is to model what they describe as *inconsistencies in the constitutive principles of a concept* (or as: *inconsistencies in what is required for semantic competence*) as *inconsistencies in the metasemantic principles or mechanisms that underpin (or govern) that domain of discourse*. The extent to which this can capture the details of various inconsistency views, I will leave for later work (or as an exercise for inconsistency theorists looking for an alternative).[3]

[2] For an overview of the options, see sections 4.1 to 4.4 in Beall, Glanzberg, and Ripley 2016.

[3] A central idea in Eklund (2002) is that paradoxes exert a pull on us. The way Eklund defines 'pull' is highly theoretical and connects pull with constitutive principles of concept possession. Since I reject the appeal to such constitutive principles I reject the phenomenon of pull as defined by Eklund. There is, however, a more informal sense of 'pull' in which paradoxes exert a pull on us. In that informal sense it means that some people (especially some professional philosophers) find the premises pre-theoretically acceptable, the inference pre-theoretically good, and the conclusion pre-theoretically unacceptable. If that's what the phenomenon of pull amounts to, then I suspect the features I appeal to in this chapter can at least partially explain the phenomenon that Eklund calls 'pull'. However, we shouldn't expect or demand a theory of pull (if understood in this informal way). There will be all kinds of reasons why some people find something pre-theoretically acceptable—it's not the sort of thing that lends itself to systematic theorizing.

PART III

Towards a General Theory 2:
Topic Continuity as the Limits
of Revision

9

The Limits of Revision
Topic (Dis)Continuity and Miscommunication

9.1 Revision and Continuity

In chapter 6 I described conceptual engineering as the effort to change the extensions and intensions of expressions. I modeled that process on how names can change their referents and I appealed to familiar examples from that literature, such as Evans's 'Madagascar' case in which the referent of 'Madagascar' changed from a part of the mainland to an island. Here is an important feature of Evans's example: there's an obvious *change of subject matter*. The result of the change is that we are *no longer talking about the same thing*. Pre-change users of 'Madagascar' talked about a part of the mainland; post-change, they talk about an island. This is very important. It has the result, for example, that those who spoke sentences containing 'Madagascar' before the reference change *can no longer be reported in indirect reports using that word*. If pre-reference change Sally said, "There's treasure in Madagascar," we can't now report her as follows: "Sally said that there's treasure in Madagascar."[1] If we want to recall or pass along the information she expressed, we will have to use a different word.

This part, Part III is concerned with the following question: does conceptual engineering always involve topic revising in this way or can conceptual engineering in some cases preserve topic? This is a central question for anyone interested in conceptual engineering and its foundations. The answer affects all particular instances of conceptual engineering because all particular efforts must be sensitive to the limits of conceptual engineering. We need to know: how much engineering is too much?

---

[1] What we could say instead is: "Sally uttered the sentence 'There's treasure in Madagascar.'" Given the change in referent of 'Madagascar' it doesn't follow that she said that there's treasure in Madagascar.

9.2 The Strawsonian Challenges

According to Carnap, philosophers should engage in explication (see chapter 2, section 2.1.10). A successful explication changes the extension of vague and indeterminate terms, and makes them precise. In response to the idea that Carnapian explication is central to philosophy, Strawson says:

[T]o offer formal explanations of key terms of scientific theories to one who seeks philosophical illumination of essential concepts of non-scientific discourse, is to do something utterly irrelevant—is a sheer misunderstanding, like offering a textbook on physiology to someone who says (with a sigh) that he wished he understood the workings of the human heart. . . . typical philosophical problems about the concepts used in non-scientific discourse cannot be solved by laying down the rules of exact and fruitful concepts in science. To do this last is not to solve the typical philosophical problem, *but to change the subject.*   (Strawson 1963: 505)

This Strawsonian concern has been at the center of Haslanger's work (even though she doesn't make the connection to Strawson explicit). It's a concern she addresses again and again in her various papers on the topic. Here is Haslanger articulating Strawson's challenge:

In asking what race is, or what gender is, our initial questions are expressed in everyday vocabularies of race and gender, so how can we meaningfully answer these questions without owing obedience to the everyday concepts? *Revisionary projects are in danger of providing answers to questions that weren't being asked.*
    Given the difficulty of determining what "our" concept is, it isn't entirely clear when a project crosses over from being explicative to revisionary, or when it is no longer even revisionary *but simply changes the subject.*   (Haslanger 2000: 34)

Mark Richard (forthcoming) says:

For that matter, doesn't the A-project [the ameliorative project] as Haslanger executes it cross the line between conceptual therapy and stipulative rebranding? Isn't the fact that people perceive it in just this way a reason to think that in *this* case we are better off pursuing a B-project instead of an A-project? These sound like rhetorical questions, I know. But I don't intend them that way. After all, there are examples of conceptual revision that are versions of the A-project that involve revisions that look similar to those Haslanger proposes, but don't seem to involve anything like changing the subject—ones that in fact seem like natural, though hardly inevitable, examples of conceptual evolution. This might be said of the conceptual transformation inherent in the appropriation of racial or sexual epithets by their targets; of proposals to rework the notion of gender so that it is a (choppy) continuum, not a binary division (Fausto Sterling (2000)); of the campaign by 19th and 20th century feminists to get the legal and social world to reconceptualize rape; and of the ongoing attempt to drag the social world towards a concept of marriage on which it is a bond between persons of any sex.

In retrospect, none of these seem odd or perverse conceptual turns—indeed, they seem to many of us in some sense the way the relevant concepts ought to have evolved. Noticing this, one might wonder whether resistance to Haslanger's version of the A-project isn't just unwarranted theoretical conservatism, something that stands to philosophy of language as a horror of government mandated health insurance stands to practical politics.   (Richard forthcoming)

Peter Ludlow (2005) comes close to saying that an epistemologist who advocates a revisionist account of 'knows' (i.e., one that's not faithful to its current semantics) it is *missing the point*:

[F]irst, and most obviously, any investigation into the nature of knowledge which did not conform to some significant degree with the semantics of the term 'knows' would simply be missing the point. . . . [E]pistemological theories might be rejected if they are in serious conflict with the lexical semantics of 'knows'.   (Ludlow 2005: 13)[2]

Railton says about the revisionist project:

Revisionism may reach a point where it becomes more perspicacious to say that a concept has been abandoned, rather than revised. No sharp line separates tolerable revisionism and outright abandonment, but if our naturalist wishes to make his case compelling, he must show that his account of a person's good is a rather clear case of tolerable revision, at worst.   (Railton 1989: 159)

This part of the book is about this cluster of concerns.[3] My goal in articulating these concerns is not to capture exactly what all these authors had in mind. The goal, instead, is to explore three important and complicated issues in this vicinity that I take to be central issues in the foundations of conceptual engineering:

(i) Conceptual engineering and change of topic, continuity of inquiry, verbal disputes, and saying what others said.
(ii) Conceptual engineering and truth relativism.
(iii) The alleged incoherence of conceptual engineering.

---

[2] I take this quote from Pasnau, who notes: "This seems just as doubtful as saying that ontology—the study of what things there are in the world—must conform with the semantics of the term 'things'" (Pasnau 2013: 988 n. 1).

[3] In addition to these articulations of the worry, there's an entire literature on how to respond to Strawson's challenge to Carnap (Maher 2007, Justus 2012, Olsson 2015, Schupbach 2015, Brun 2016). A brief side note: for reasons I don't quite understand, whenever I present this material (and it's in a lot of places all over the world), one consistent reaction is that I make too much of the Strawsonian objection. For reasons I make clear below, I think that the Strawsonian concern is very important, and that responding to it is a central task for any theory of conceptual engineering. The passages quoted above as well as the entire literature on Strawson's reply to Carnap show that this attitude isn't idiosyncratic.

Each of these circles around similar themes, and perhaps, on some ways of individuating the objections, they are instances of the same objection. Nonetheless, I will discuss them in turn. I'll also, for each objection, give a preview of the reply I'm about to give.

9.3 Change of Topic, Continuity of Inquiry, Verbal Disputes, and Saying What Others Said

By generalizing Strawson's objection to Carnap we get an objection to the project of conceptual engineering along the following lines:

- Change of extension and intension[4] (and so also change of sense, if you believe in those) is a change of topic, so revisionary projects of the kind described in chapter 2 are bound to fail. Even if the revisions succeed, they do not provide us with a better way to talk about what we were talking about; they simply change the topic.

Here's an example. Suppose at t the extension of 'belief' is E and that E excludes the kinds of cases that Clark and Chalmers want to include. Clark and Chalmers then engage in conceptual cngineering and as a result 'belief' changes its extension and intension: it now includes a wide range of cases that were excluded from E, in particular it now includes cases where the believer is assisted by various external devices. The objection now says: that's not an improvement on 'belief', it's a change of topic. Sure, there's *some* overlap in extension; there is also overlap in extension between 'English' and 'Londoner', but the former can't be an improvement on the latter. If you replaced the current extension and intension of 'Londoner' with that of 'English', you would just be changing the topic. The same point can be raised against Haslanger's proposal for a new extension and intension for 'woman': what she is doing is changing the topic, not improving on 'woman'.

One way to think about this is ask yourself if you can improve on the concept of the number 1 (whatever that might be). Here is a clearly absurd thought:

Absurd thought: 1 isn't quite big enough, it should be a bit bigger. Maybe it should be more like 1.00001.

---

[4] Recall from chapter 6, section 6.1 that when I talk about change in extension as the result of conceptual engineering, I mean a change that is accompanied by a change in intension (so relative to the same circumstance (e.g., world/time pair) extensions can differ). One way to think of this is: the conditions that need to be satisfied in order to fall into the extension of, e.g., 'woman', or 'marriage', or 'belief' have changed by conceptual engineering, and as a result of that the intension and extension have changed.

Surely, that's *not* the kind of process that those advocating conceptual engineering would include as an instance of conceptual amelioration. 1.00001 is just a different number from 1. There is no conceivable way in which 1.00001 is an *improvement* on 1. 1.00001 might be the answer to a question that 1 isn't an answer to, but it *can't be a better concept of 1 than 1*. That idea doesn't even make sense. But, you might reasonably wonder, isn't all conceptual engineering like that?[5] If the answer is 'no', why not?

> *Preview of my reply:* I think that all the objections I discuss in this chapter can be responded to. The responses are developed over the next two chapters. Nonetheless, it will be helpful to give super brief indications of where this is going (it will also help us to see continuity in the objections). So, here, in super brief form, is my reply to the change of topic objection: topics are more coarse-grained than extensions and intensions, and so expressions that differ with respect to extensions and intensions can be about the same topic.

I just articulated the objection by appeal to the notion of 'topic' and 'continuity of topic'. There are some different, but closely related, ways to articulate this kind of objection and in what follows I go through three of those:

a. *Lack of continuity of inquiry:* Suppose a group of people are trying to answer a set of questions where the topic is denoted by some expression E. So they are interested in questions like: 'What are Es?' or 'Why are Es F?' Two illustrations:

- Consider the ordinary term 'woman'. We are interested in questions like 'What is it to be a woman?' or 'Why are women paid less than men?'
- Consider the ordinary term 'belief'. We are interested in questions like 'What is a belief?' or 'Are there norms of belief?'

Suppose someone tries to improve on the meaning of 'belief' or 'woman' and, as a result, changes the extension of the word. Now suppose we try to answer the questions that we formulated using those words pre-amelioration using the words with *new* extensions, i.e., we respond with sentences like 'women are...' and 'belief is...'. The objection is that the answers employing terms with the new extensions fail to answer the original questions. These answers concern something new—not what we were originally talking about when we used the

---

[5] Another case it's useful to think about (if you think the mathematical case is unrepresentative): Could *dark red* be an amelioration of *red*? No, says this objection, you haven't improved on *red*, you have just started talking about something else.

expressions 'woman' and 'belief'. We have the illusion of an answer, but it's a purely verbal illusion. There's a lack of continuity of inquiry: the old questions are not being answered.[6] We're answering new questions. We found that concern in the Haslanger quote above and it's also articulated by Annti Kauppinen:

Moral responsibility, for example, is not a technical notion, though some terms that philosophers use in explicating it may be. Indeed, why should anybody care about what philosophers do if they just argued about their own inventions? People want to know if they have moral responsibility or knowledge of other minds in the very sense in which they ordinarily talk about responsibility or knowledge, and to get at that sense one must work with the folk's own concepts. By and large, philosophers oblige; revisionism is a last resort, to be used only when one is convinced that the folk concept is hopelessly confused or too imprecise for one's purposes.   (Kauppinen 2007: 98)

b. *Verbal disputes:* Why keep the same linguistic expression when you are changing the meaning? Why should Haslanger continue use the word 'woman' with a new meaning, rather than employing a new expression, say 'Woman*', to mark the distinction with her new, ameliorated meaning? After all, those using 'woman' with Haslanger's proposed meaning plausibly express different thoughts from those who were using it with the pre-amelioration meaning. This is bound to create massive confusion when the ameliorators try to talk to the non-ameliorators or try to say what people said pre-amelioration. Wouldn't every-thing be much easier if we marked the distinction in meaning by a distinction in lexical item? (This concern is a version of the Change of Topic challenge above.)

c. *Saying what others said:* Suppose Clark and Chalmers succeed in their revi-sion of 'belief', i.e., they succeed in changing our concept of 'belief'. As a result, the word 'belief' now has a new extension and intension. Things that were not in the extension of 'belief' before now are. Okay, so how, then, do we report on past speech that contains the word 'belief'? If we use the word 'belief' with its new meaning, then it looks like we're misquoting past speakers. So the right thing to do would be to just quote them—to say that they used the word 'belief', but not to use that word to say what they said. This is the flipside of the verbal dispute point in the previous paragraph: if the ameliorators don't switch to a new linguistic expression during the amelioration, then they will have to change expression when reporting on what others said, otherwise they will end up misreporting past speakers.

All the objections articulated in this section concern what I think of as *the continuity of thought, talk, communication, and inquiry.* In later chapters I will

---

[6] Recall Haslanger's version of the Strawsonian worry according to which revisionary projects are in danger of answering questions that were not being asked.

refer back to this as *the continuity data* (and I will argue that many other theories fail to account for it). Conceptual ameliorators will often want to engage in all kinds of ways with the thoughts and speech of pre-amelioration speakers. Quoting them won't do because that is just to say what words they used, not to say what they said in uttering those words. There's a very strong pressure towards disquotational/homophonic reporting—we are more or less hardwired to do it. We also do it intra-personally: when Clark and Chalmers think about what they thought about beliefs before their ameliorative effort, they will do so *using* 'belief' (with its new meaning) to describe what they thought or said when they used 'belief' in the past. As a matter of fact, this is what we do. Amelioration seems to make a total mess out of this practice.

And new meaning is different [handwritten margin note]

> *Preview of my reply:* As soon as you recognize that *what we talk about* and *what we say* is more coarse-grained than extensions and intensions, then *we can say the same* and *talk about the same things (the same topics)*—more generally have continuity of talk and thought—even when our representational devices differ with respect to their extensions and intensions. Here's another way that I will put this: We can talk about *the same topic*, e.g., knowledge, belief, freedom, or marriage, even though the extension and intension of 'knowledge', 'belief', 'freedom', and 'marriage' change. As those terms undergo semantic changes we can still use them to talk about the same topic. Not only can there be continuity of topic through changes in extension and intension, but these changes can be *improvements*—*better ways to talk about the same topic.* On this way of thinking, a revisionist about moral language is still talking about what we ought to do, but she does so in a better way (if the revision is successful). The next chapter spells out this reply in more detail.

9.4 Assessing What Others Have Said: Truth Relativism?

How does an ameliorator assess pre-ameliorated speech and thought? It looks like amelioration makes the following situation possible. Let S be a sentence containing a term that's a candidate for amelioration ('marriage', 'belief', 'ought', etc.):

Pre-amelioration: What is said by an utterance of 'S' is true.
Post-amelioration: What is said by an utterance of 'S' is not true.

So far, so good. The problem occurs when a speaker post-amelioration reports what was said by a speaker pre-amelioration. Suppose a speaker post-amelioration reports on Nora's pre-amelioration utterance of 'S' by saying: 'Nora said that S', i.e., by using 'S' when saying what the pre-amelioration speaker (i.e., Nora) said. If this is acceptable (and I think it is), it looks like we end up committed to the following: what Nora said is true prior to amelioration, but false post-amelioration. So don't we end up committed to a form of relativism about truth?

Preview of my reply: The argument above misdescribes the situation or relies on a mistaken reading of 'what Nora said is true prior to amelioration'. Here is the correct description: pre-amelioration, Nora used 'S' to express a proposition p that is true. Post-amelioration, it is true to describe Nora as having expressed a different proposition, p*, that is false. What's important is that the truth values of p and p* are insensitive to assessment contexts. What varies is what it is that Nora has said. This is a form of what Cappelen (2008a and 2008b) calls content relativism (as opposed to truth relativism).

9.5 The Alleged Incoherence of Conceptual Engineering

This is the version of this objection Mark Richard discusses: *You can't improve on a concept by changing its intension and extension because that very idea is incoherent.* Concepts have their intensions and extensions *essentially*. So a change in intension or extension always involves abandoning a concept, and can never be an improvement of the old concept. Insofar as conceptual engineering rests on the idea of changing a particular concept's intension and so extension, the entire project is incoherent.

Preview of my reply: Conceptual engineering and amelioration are mislabeled: it's not about improving concepts—in fact, it's not about concepts at all. The process involves better ways to talk about topics, e.g., belief, marriage, and what we ought to do. As a corollary, I don't think a theory of conceptual engineering is hostage to a theory of what concepts are. And that's good because the nature of concepts is one of the most disputed topics in philosophy and psychology: there's a plethora of theories, no agreement on theoretical role, and significant pressure towards eliminativism (Machery 2009). This lack of consensus or even convergence would be a problem for a theory of conceptual engineering. My version of conceptual engineering bypasses this cluster of problems because it doesn't require an appeal to *concepts* at all.

9.6 Brief Note to Those Not Moved by (and Impatient with) the Strawsonian Objections

Some readers of earlier drafts of this material thought that I take the various versions of Strawson's objection too seriously and that spending two chapters replying to it are excessive.[7] Here is a motivation for their dismissive attitude towards this cluster of issues:

Dismissal: The idea that even a slight change in extension—e.g., a slight sharpening of a vague term (as in a Carnapian explication)—should have all the negative implications outlined above is too implausible to take seriously. It is obvious that, for example, a *slight sharpening* of an extension will not lead to a change in topic, undermine samesaying, lead to discontinuity in inquiry, or lead to relativism. It obviously doesn't have these consequences. Focusing on that issue distracts us from the really important issues. The 'really important' issues are then articulated in various ways:

(i) *Really important issue version 1:* When does an amelioration have the result that we have lost *what we care about in the pre-ameliorated concept?* On this construal the central issue is figuring out 'what we care about' and how to preserve it.

(ii) *Really important issue version 2:* Many of those who theorize about conceptual engineering think that concepts do *jobs* for us—they perform *functions.* For those who think like that, the really important issue is how to preserve a valuable function/job while getting rid of conceptual deficiencies. So the key challenge is not to understand topic continuity, but to identify and preserve functions—to find something that can do the important job of the concept while leaving its deficiencies behind.

Readers devoted to some version of Dismissal could skip the next two chapters and move straight to chapter 12. However, for two reasons I don't recommend reading this book in that way:

- First, I think the Strawsonian challenge is very much worth taking seriously and that none of the questions asked can be easily dismissed. It's a mistake not to be captivated by that cluster of challenges. Moreover, understanding why changes (both big and small) in extensions and intensions can preserve topic will illuminate some of the central aspects of conceptual engineering.
- One reason the cluster of issues tied up with the Strawsonian challenge are so important is that they make us focus on the limits of revision: anyone who has thought seriously about conceptual engineering worries (or should

---

[7] Tristram McPherson pushed this point forcefully and made me see the dialectic more clearly here.

worry) about the limits of it. How much revision is too much? What does 'too much revision' mean? Strawson worried about it, Carnap worried about it, Railton and Haslanger worry about it. Clark and Chalmers (and all other engineers of specific concepts) should be worrying about it. Starting with Strawson's challenge helps to put a focus on that crucial issue.

Finally, I don't think it's helpful to approach conceptual engineering (and questions about the limits of revision) through the idea that concepts have functions or jobs (and so we shouldn't ask: how do we preserve a function or job?). I reject this way of thinking in chapter 16, where I argue that there's no good way to account for the relevant notions of 'job' or function.[8]

[8] I should note that Carnap had a reply to Strawson's objection. He says:

A natural language is like a crude, primitive pocketknife, very useful for a hundred different purposes. But for certain specific purposes, special tools are more efficient, e.g., chisels, cutting-machines, and finally the microtome. If we find that the pocket knife is too crude for a given purpose and creates defective products, we shall try to discover the cause of the failure, and then either use the knife more skillfully, or replace it for this special purpose by a more suitable tool, or even invent a new one. [Strawson's] thesis is like saying that by using a special tool we evade the problem of the correct use of the cruder tool. But would anyone criticize the bacteriologist for using a microtome, and assert that he is evading the problem of correctly using a pocketknife? (Carnap 1963: 938–9)

This reply has a kind of rhetorical charm to it, but I don't find in it a careful response to the clusters of concerns articulated in this chapter. It seems as if Carnap just didn't want to acknowledge the depth of Strawson's objection.

10

Reply to Strawson 1

Continuity of Topic, Samesaying, and the Contestation Theory

The previous chapter raised objections to the very idea of conceptual engineering. This chapter and the next begin the task of responding to those objections.

10.1 Overview of the Two Strategies for Responding to Strawson's Challenge

In what follows I offer two kinds of responses to the Strawsonian objections. You can't easily make use of both at the same time, but either strategy can be pursued against either objection. First, let me offer a brief sketch of the two strategies. I then spend the rest of this chapter on the first strategy, and the next on the second strategy.

First Strategy. *Appeal to the Coarseness of 'Samesaying' and 'Topic'*: This strategy for responding to Strawson's challenge appeals to data about when we correctly describe people as *having said the same thing*. I use the expression 'samesaying' to describe that phenomenon. If there's some p such that both A and B have said that p, then I'll say that A and B are 'samesayers'. The argument I appeal to has two steps:

- The first step in this argument points out that A and B can samesay each other using a sentence 'Fa', even though the extension of 'F' in A's speech differs from the extension of 'F' in B's speech. I'll illustrate this point in two ways: (i) by data about uses of context-sensitive expressions (and what I call inter-contextual samesaying[1]) and (ii) by thinking about diachronic samesaying.[2]

---

[1] This argument draws on material from Cappelen and Lepore 1997, Lepore and Cappelen 2005, and Cappelen and Dever 2016.

[2] Here I draw on points made by Dorr and Hawthorne 2014.

- The second step in the argument says that if samesaying is possible despite differences in extension, then so is 'talking about the same topic'. Sameness of topic goes hand in hand with samesaying.

The core of this reply to Strawson is to say that we can talk about the same topic even when we change extension and intension. Sameness of topic doesn't track sameness of extensions and intensions. Sameness of topic is more coarse-grained than that.

An underlying thought is this: 'extension', 'intension', and 'content' are *theoretical* terms, and are not things on which we have a pre-theoretic grasp. By contrast, expressions like 'what she said', 'what she was talking about', and 'talking about the same topic' are important *pre-theoretic* notions.[3] These pre-theoretic notions are more coarse-grained than the theoretical notions that philosophers have used in the last one hundred years. 'What was said by utterance u' is much more coarse-grained than 'the semantic content of u' (relative to context). As a corollary, two sentences with different semantic contents (where semantic content is understood as, at least, having the same extension and intension) can be used to say the same thing, or to talk or be about the same topic.

Second Strategy.   *Appeal to Lexical Effects:* According to the second strategy someone engaged in conceptual engineering should respond to Strawson's challenge by saying: *I don't care about whether I'm changing the topic or failing to answer the old questions. I care about the effects of my speech. The effect is in part a function of which lexical items I use. I've picked these lexical items (say 'woman') because doing so has good effects, despite changing the topic.*

I call the effects which this strategy appeals to 'lexical effects', and they are not part of semantic or even pragmatics as typically conceived. An illustration: imagine a proponent of same-sex marriage is convinced that the word 'marriage' at some point had in its extension only couples of different genders. She might react in one of two ways. (i) She insists that after the change in extension she is still talking about the same thing. There is preservation of topic, i.e., the topic is still marriage. However, she might also say the following: (ii) *Even if I am changing the topic or subject matter, I want to keep the lexical item. I want to use that same lexical item because using that term has important effects. And we want to preserve those effects.* The next chapter explores this strategy further.

---

[3] There is also a theoretical notion of topicality in linguistics. That literature addresses different issues from those in this book and so is not helpful here.

10.2 Coarseness of Samesaying and Sameness of Topic

In the remainder of this chapter, I will develop the first strategy for responding to Strawson's challenge. I start by what for many readers will be a reminder of why the following thesis is true:

Coarseness: Sameness of topic doesn't track sameness of extension.

The arguments I'll give appeal to data about how expressions like 'same topic' and 'saying the same' are used. Most of the basic data points are very familiar, and so I will only sketch the data briefly here and direct the reader to further literature. If for a few paragraphs this seems to be too remote from the significant versions of Strawson's challenge, then I urge patience—the relevance will become clear below.

10.2.1 Data from samesaying using context-sensitive expressions

Gradable adjectives (such 'cold', 'happy', and 'expensive') are context-sensitive. Their extensions change between contexts. Just what element of context determines the extension is a complicated matter. Maybe it's a comparison class, maybe a cutoff point on a scale, maybe some combination of the two, or maybe something else altogether. No matter what it is that determines extension, the mechanisms involved are very fine-grained. There are infinitely many potential extensions for an adjective like 'smart' or 'interesting', since there are infinitely many possible comparison classes and cutoffs on different scales. As a result, two utterances of a sentence like 'S is interesting' in different contexts will almost always vary at least a bit in their extensions (and, thus, since extension is functionally determined by intension, the utterances will vary at least a bit in their *intension*, too. In what follows, I'll sometimes leave this further qualification implicit, to avoid being overly wordy). Despite this difference, we can often describe two people who utter the sentence 'A is an interesting theory' in different contexts as having *said the same thing*. They both said that A is an interesting theory. It is a fact about our reporting practice that we don't, in such cases, require the comparison class of interesting theories or the cutoff point on a scale of interestingness to be identical. If that were required for the truth of samesaying reports, it would be a minor miracle if we ever managed to say the same thing.[4]

---

[4] This kind of argument may be familiar to some readers from defenses of semantic minimalism (e.g., Lepore and Cappelen 2005), but it's important to note that *nothing* in what follows will depend on endorsing all of semantic minimalism. The way in which the argument is used here relies on much weaker premises. I'm just observing that we very often can engage in such disquotational speech reports when there's good reason to think that the exact extensions differ. For more on the data see also Cappelen and Lepore 1997, Cappelen and Hawthorne 2009, and Cappelen and Dever 2016.

These kinds of examples are familiar, and I will give just one more here: consider two separate conversations in which people talk about Serena Williams and her tennis-playing. A utters 'Serena is really smart' and B utters the same sentence. A, B, and their contexts are different in many ways. The conversational context is somewhat different, their background assumptions about Serena are somewhat different, their assumptions about smartness differ, and so on. Despite all this, there are contexts in which it is true to say:

A and B both said that Serena is really smart
A and B agree that Serena is really smart
A and B both described Serena as being really smart
A and B said the same thing about Serena.

These descriptions of them as samesayers are true even if it turns out that A's and B's respective contexts fix somewhat different extensions and intensions for 'smart'. This establishes the following important point: *we don't require identity of extension for 'smart' in order to treat A and B as samesayers.*

This point generalizes. Our language is filled with context-sensitive expressions, i.e., with expressions whose extension is sensitive to minute and obscure aspects of the context in which they are uttered. In most of these cases, the contextual parameters that determine an extension relative to a context are unknown to us (not even theorists who spend their whole lives thinking about these parameters agree on what they are for even a single context-sensitive expression!), but we can still use disquotational reports with confidence. Cappelen and Hawthorne describe this phenomenon as the 'easiness of disquotational speech reports' (Cappelen and Hawthorne 2009: 105 n. 8). Disquotational speech reports are those that use the very sentence reported on in the complement clause of an indirect speech report. So if S is the sentence uttered by A, then 'A said that S' is the disquotational speech report. A *collective disquotational speech report* takes the form of 'A and B said that S' when both A and B uttered S. The point above can be put as follows: if A utters a sentence containing a context-sensitive expression e in context C, I can frequently disquotationally report her in another context C*, even though the semantic values associated with e in C* (i.e., e's intension and extension) are somewhat different from what they were in C.

These points have been much discussed[5] and it's worth noting that *in the entire literature hardly anyone has advocated the view that identity of semantic value is required for samesaying.* There has been disagreement about the *extent* of the variability, but hardly anyone has tried to defend the view that in order for A and

---

[5] See Preyer and Peter 2005.

B to say the same, they have to utter sentences with identical semantic values. So looking at this debate over the last forty years, the flexibility view has won.[6] As we will see below in section 10.3, this claim has important implications for the Strawsonian objections.   *Not sure this part carries over.*

10.2.2 More on coarseness: Dorr and Hawthorne on plasticity and disquotational reports

In a recent paper[7] Cian Dorr and John Hawthorne have made a point similar to the one I made about contextual variability. Their data is helpful and put in slightly different terminology, so I will go through it here. I conclude that their data provides more direct support for *Coarseness*.

As I mentioned in chapter 2, section 2.4.1, Dorr and Hawthorne distinguish two models for thinking about ways in which semantic facts supervene on non-semantic facts (for simplicity, treat these as all the microphysical facts). Here's a quick recap of *Patchwork* and *Plasticity*.

Patchwork: the relevant semantic facts supervene on the microphysical facts in the same way as the facts about people's height-to-the-nearest-centimeter. The continuous space of possible microphysical configurations of the world is divided into a discrete collection of cells, within each of which the exact same facts (from the given subcategory) obtain. As we vary the microphysical facts smoothly, the semantic facts will respond in a jerky fashion.

Plasticity: the relevant semantic facts are like the facts about people's heights: even tiny differences in the microphysical facts will, almost always, induce correspondingly tiny, but still genuine, differences as regards which of them obtain.

Dorr and Hawthorne think that when a term tracks a so-called 'joint in nature', *Patchwork* is the right model. However, in many cases there are no relevant joints in nature, which means that *Plasticity* is the right model. They say:

In almost all cases, an expression's actual meaning is surrounded by a vast cloud of slight variants that seem just as well qualified to be possible meanings. And this abundance makes it hard to resist the conclusion that each proposition attributing any one of these meanings to the expression is . . . plastic to a high degree. . . . When there are many slightly different possible contents for a speech act on some particular occasion, and no differences between these contents that could plausibly single out a few of them as being much

---

[6] This is to say, one central thesis of Cappelen and Lepore 1997 is now more or less common ground among those who participate in this debate.

[7] Dorr and Hawthorne 2014.

more apt for being communicated than the rest, the fact that a certain one was singled out as the actual content of the speech act performed on that occasion must depend sensitively on the exact details of the relevant microphysical facts.   (Dorr and Hawthorne 2014: 282)

Note the analogy to the above point about context-sensitivity: the point above was that context-sensitive expressions are sensitive to tiny changes in context. The point now is that more generally, meanings of words are sensitive to small changes in the microphysical facts, and so since microphysical facts change continuously, meanings will change continuously. Here is a great illustration from their paper concerning temporal plasticity:

Suppose—not implausibly—that the use of 'salad' has evolved gradually over the last few centuries, from a situation in which people only applied the word to cold dishes with a high preponderance of green leaves of some sort, to the current state where we comfortably apply the word to various warm, leaf-free concoctions. The meaning of 'salad' is evidently not the same at the beginning and at the end of this history. It follows that there has been at least one second-long interval such that the meaning of 'salad' was not constant throughout that interval. But given the gradual character of the underlying changes, there is no principled microphysical basis for singling out just a few of the second-long intervals as intervals during which the meaning of 'salad' changed. This makes it tempting to conclude that semantic changes occurred during all of the intervals, or at least during some substantial proportion of them.

(Dorr and Hawthorne 2014: 284–5)

The meaning of 'salad' supervenes on the microphysical facts. The microphysical facts change constantly and, according to *Plasticity*, there is constantly some slight change in the meaning (and so in the extension) of 'salad'.

The crucial point is that they then go on to note that despite this change in meaning, we remain comfortable with disquotational reports across time. They say:

In many circumstances, we confidently use homophonic methods in reporting speeches made in the not-too-distant past. For example, we hear Sally saying 'Salad is delicious', and five minutes later we utter:

(1) Sally asserted that salad is delicious.   (Dorr and Hawthorne 2014: 286)

Note that this is in effect the same point as the one I made above about cross-contextual disquotational reports: the time parameter of the context has changed and so, assuming plasticity, has the semantic value. We treat ourselves as samesaying an utterance of S in a different context, despite the fact that the difference between our contexts is likely to mean that there is at least a slight difference in extension (a tiny bit of semantic drift). Dorr and Hawthorne point out that if we make certain assumptions about attitude reports more generally, the point applies to pretty much any cross-temporal attitude report (and thus any inter-contextual attitude report) (Dorr and Hawthorne 2014: 285–7).

REPLY TO STRAWSON 1: CONTINUITY OF TOPICS   113

Dorr and Hawthorne also ask us to consider counterfactual speech reports involving speech and attitude reports (2014: 286), e.g.:

(2) If we had taken Sally to Giorgio's, she would have asserted that salad is delicious.

(3) If I had the courage, I would tell them to stop making fun of my baldness.

(4) No matter which graduate school I had gone to, I would probably still have been insisting that monetary policy can prevent recessions.

The supervenience base of these reports is likely to be somewhat different (the microphysical facts aren't typically going to be identical when we make such reports), but, as Dorr and Hawthorne point out, it would be a disaster if we had to give up on such counterfactual reports (2014: 313).

10.3 The Relevance of Coarseness to the Strawsonian Objections

In the previous chapter I sketched various versions of what I labeled 'the Strawsonian objection'. Here is the relevance of the above to each of these versions:

(i) *Conceptual engineering and change of topic, continuity of inquiry, verbal disputes, and saying what others said:* If samesaying is more coarse-grained than extensions, then sameness of topic is as well. Here is why: *if A and B said the same, then they are talking about the same thing and their topic is the same.* If A and B both said *that women are F*, then both of them spoke about women and so they talked about the same thing, i.e., women. *If samesaying doesn't require identity of extension, then same-topicality doesn't either.* This is a direct reply to the 'change of topic' version of Strawson's objection. According to the objection, conceptual engineering involves a change of topic because it involves a change of intension and extension. We now know that's wrong.

I articulated three additional, closely related, versions of the 'change of topic' objection, and we are now in a position to respond to each of them:

a. *Lack of continuity of inquiry:* As a corollary, we have a reply to the objection that the result of conceptual engineering is a failure to answer questions asked in pre-engineered language. If the question (articulated in pre-engineered language) was: *Are women F?* then we can answer: 'Women are not F' using the post-engineered language and still have answered the question despite a change in the extension of 'woman'. We can do that because the question was *about women*, and so was the answer.

b. *Verbal disputes*: Topic continuity enables us to avoid verbal disputes. Extensions and intensions might have changed, but as long as we're still talking about the same thing, the danger of verbal dispute is avoided.

c. *Saying what others said*: The evidence from inter-contextual reports and semantic drift shows that disquotational reporting can be sustained through amelioration, i.e., through a change in extension and intension. I can say what you said, using the very same words you used, even if those words have different semantic contents from the ones they have when you say them.

(ii) *Assessing what others have said: content—not truth—relativism:* Conceptual engineering has weird and surprising effects on our assessment and report of others' speech. The weirdness can be brought out by thinking about how we assess indirect reports. Here is a sketch of the weirdness:

- At t A uses F with semantic value V. She utters 'b is F'. Let's suppose this is true.
- Then later, at t*, F has undergone amelioration, so it now has a new semantic value, V*. Now consider 'b is F' uttered at t*. It is, suppose, false.
- Next imagine a disquotational indirect report of A's utterance (which was made at t) made at t*: 'A said that b is F'.
- I claim this report can be true (since indirect reports don't require that the semantic value of the complement clause is identical to the semantic value of the reported utterance).
- However, we're now in the following situation: call the proposition that your indirect report attributes to A, p*. p* is false. Call the proposition that A expressed in uttering 'a is F', p. p was true.

I embrace this view. I see it as a feature, not a bug. You can disagree with this, but that would take us into a full-blown discussion of the semantics for indirect reports and while that's a topic close to my heart, it's not for this book (for my views on this see Cappelen and Lepore 1997 and 2005 and Cappelen and Hawthorne 2009). What I want to point out there is that there's no relativism about truth involved. The indirect report is monadically true. The proposition A expressed was monadically true. The complement clause of your indirect report is monadically true. There's no implication that truth assessment is relativized to context of assessment (as proposed by, for example, Kölbel 2002, 2009, and MacFarlane 2014). What this does imply is a version of what I have called *Content Relativism*. (For more on content relativism, see Cappelen 2008a, 2008b. That view is also incorporated into Cappelen and Lepore 1997, 2005.)

There's a great deal more to be said about how revision, amelioration, and conceptual engineering more generally affects our reporting practices. Jennifer Saul (2006) raises some of those issues. In a response to Haslanger, she says:

Imagine that Amanda takes a feminist philosophy class and is convinced by Haslanger's views. She decides to use the terms 'woman' and 'man' in the way that Haslanger suggests in order to explain to her friend Beau what she has learned. Amanda utters (1):

(1) All women are subordinated by men.

Beau does not use 'woman' and 'man' in the way that Amanda uses these terms. He uses them, let's say, as sex terms. A first question is what Amanda has said. Since the speaker and audience have different meanings in mind for the contextually-shifting terms, it is genuinely unclear what the right answer is. Possibly, the right answer is that Amanda has failed to say anything. This seems strange. Perhaps more plausibly, Amanda has said one thing and Beau has understood her as saying another. But if that's the case, Beau will have trouble even reporting what Amanda has said. It should be, it seems to me, that Beau's utterance of (2) is true.

(2) Amanda said that all women are subordinated by men.

But we're assuming that the content of 'women' in Beau's mouth is different from its content in Amanda's. What Amanda has said is not something that Beau can report (at least not without a lot of work). There are other options, but all face difficulties. These difficulties—regarding what is said in a mixed context, and what we say when we report the speech of those who use the terminology in a different way—point to the seriousness of the confusion that is possible with a contextualist version of Haslanger's view. In so doing, they offer some reason for resisting it.   (Saul 2006: 141–2)

I disagree with Saul's claim that Beau can't use (2) to report on Amanda's speech (that's the central thesis above: if there's topic continuity, then the report is acceptable, though weird for the reasons just given). However, I do agree with Saul that there's a great deal of messiness and potential for confusion and misunderstanding stemming from conceptual engineering. That in itself is an interesting data point: conceptual engineering has disruptive effects on communicative exchanges. An important research topic is to explore those disruptive effects further. For example, Sterken (forthcoming) argues that it is important for ameliorators to engage in speech that involves 'transformative communicative disruptions', where these are understood as speech acts that in a sense are both misleading and dishonest, but still serve an invaluable purpose.

(iii) *Conceptual engineering and incoherence:* The 'Richard' version of Strawson's objection says that the very idea of improving a concept through changing its extension and intension is incoherent: these are essential features of concepts and cannot be changed. Our reporting practices reveal that the pre-theoretic notions of 'saying the same' and 'talking about the same topic' are more coarse-grained than the semantic notions of *extension*. Richard (forthcoming)

Again seems to rely on ambiguity between direct + indirect speech reports considers (in order to reject) the idea that the semantics of a concept determines its identity—where semantic changes implies change in concept. Here is the response: 'concept' is a theoretical notion we should get rid of, at least for the purposes of thinking about conceptual engineering (which, of course, makes salient how unfortunate that label is). Maybe in a certain tradition it is used in the way Richard claims. That, however, shouldn't worry us as long as a change in concept doesn't lead to a change in topic—that is, as long as it doesn't lead to a failure to answer questions asked in the pre-engineered language.

10.4 Objection: What Kinds of Changes (Relative to a Context) Are Compatible with Preservation of Topic?

So far I have only said that we can have changes in extension while preserving topic. But nothing so far answers the questions: *What kinds of changes are compatible with topic preservation? What are the limits of revision? When have ameliorators gone too far?* My response has two important components:

a. I won't give you a set of necessary and sufficient conditions for acceptable revisions. Searching for necessary and sufficient conditions here is a waste of time (as it is in most areas of philosophy). Instead, I suggest studying genealogy and conceptual histories. That, however, won't add up to a set of necessary and sufficient conditions.

Agreed

b. Insofar as I have a theory, it's best described as the *Contestation Theory of the Limits of Revision*: just as there are no fixed rules for how conceptual change can be implemented, there are no fixed rules for how far revision can go. The limits of revision are themselves up for revision, contestation, and negotiation. If there are any rules here at all, it's that we make up the rules along the way.

It's helpful to start with a comparison. Many think that one goal of semantics is to specify the contribution that various parts of sentences make to the semantic value (or content or meaning or truth conditions) of the whole sentence. Semantics starts with an assignment of semantic values to the expressions of a language and then tries to show how they compose. Indexicals and other context-sensitive expressions don't have stable semantic values and so semanticists try to characterize the ways in which contexts determine semantic values. In doing so, they typically assume that there are rules for how expressions get their semantic values in context. David Kaplan called such rules 'characters' (Kaplan 1977/1989).

Classic Semantics for compositionality

The process I'm now trying to describe doesn't fit into either of those categories. The process is one where the semantic value of a non-context-sensitive expression is changed (or the character of a context-sensitive expression is changed). The question we are asking is at the most general level: What are admissible ways of changing a language? More specifically, I'm asking: What are the conditions under which such changes still count, relative to a context, as leading to continuity of topic?

The process of changing the rules that govern the language isn't itself governed by the rules that are being changed. So semantics won't help us here. Nor will an understanding of characters or, more generally, the ways in which context-sensitive terms get their semantic values fixed in contexts. There is also little help to get from the inquiries that are often labeled 'pragmatics'. This is, for the most part, the study of how content that goes beyond semantic content can be communicated or presupposed. That's not what we are looking for. So what to do? I suggest we need, first, a better understanding of genealogy and conceptual histories.

10.5 The Significance of Genealogy and Conceptual Histories

In response to the Strawsonian objections, I have argued that we can preserve topic while changing extension and intension. I then asked what kinds of changes are compatible with topic preservation. To answer this we can study the ways conceptual evolution has happened in the past and then try to induce on the basis of these cases to get a general theory of what kinds of revisions are admissible. We look at a case like 'salad' and observe how it has changed over the last fifty years from a leaf-based concoction to something that doesn't require leaves. How did that happen? Why did speakers of English go along with that change? We then consider many other cases and look for common patterns.

There's a long tradition of studying conceptual histories or genealogies. Philosophers, historians, and others have contributed to that literature. Philosophical terms have histories that in some cases are very well documented. Oxford University Press has a series of books covering the history of concepts such as *Eternity* (Melamed 2016), *Memory* (Nikulin 2015), *Evil* (Chignell forthcoming), and *Space* (Janiak forthcoming). There is an important and extensive body of work in developmental psychology on how children's conceptual repertoire changes over time (Carey 2009). In jurisprudence, there is extensive work on the various ways in which legal concepts evolve in the context of particular legal systems. So here's a thought: why not try to synthesize the work from all these fields with the aim of coming up with a unifying theory? That is, to synthesize a theory that is the sort of thing that could answer the question: *What kinds of conceptual revisions are topic-preserving?*

While I think this is a strategy that is important and very much worth pursuing, I have three crucial reservations:

- First, this is an entirely empirical project. It requires understanding and interpreting connections between details of historical events that in many cases are extremely hard to uncover. We have, for example, no good reason to think that the crucial events in conceptual change were recorded in writing—it seems plausible that in many cases there's no 'crucial event' that triggers a change, but just tiny little effects of many verbal and nonverbal interactions between people. So the recommendation that one engage in genealogy is compatible with the view that we are far away from fully understanding even a single case. We can't even explain rather simple cases like changes in the meaning of 'salad'. To answer the question 'how exactly did that change happen and what made it possible?' would require knowing minutiae about salad-related linguistic practices that no one—as far as I know—has access to. Who was the first person to start changing the extension? Why? Did he or she meet initial resistance? And so on.

- Second, what has so far been categorized as 'conceptual histories' (e.g., the works referred to above) fails fundamentally to distinguish between changes in people's beliefs about Fs (say, persons or space or torture) and changes in the extensions and intensions of 'F'. On the view proposed in this book, these two kinds of change are fundamentally different. Often the extension and intension of F remains stable as people's beliefs about F change radically. On the flip side, often the extension and intension of a predicate, 'F', will change without salient or very significant changes in beliefs about Fs. What in current literature is labeled 'genealogy' makes no effort whatsoever in distinguishing between these kinds of changes. For genealogy to be useful for those trying to understand topic preservation through changes in extensions and intensions, more refined notions of genealogy are needed.

- Third, suppose we had exquisitely refined tools for doing conceptual genealogy of the kind I am advocating and we used those for hundreds of years of gathering such data, so that we have a large set of complete case studies in hand. This still won't add up to a recipe for how to go about it in new cases. This is because those interested in conceptual engineering will also want to be revisionary about what counts as admissible engineering. This point is developed further in Section 10.6.

10.6 The Limits of Revision: The Contestation Theory

So far I've been talking as though we are looking for a descriptive account of when conceptual revision has gone well—i.e., of what *as a matter of fact* counts as successful revision. But that question is too restrictive, particularly in this context. We should also be interested in how it *should* be done—i.e., what *should* be considered successful. Past instances of revision, as revealed by genealogy and the other kinds of empirical work outlined above, might tell us what *has* happened, but the conceptual engineer might not want to be restricted by facts about past revisions. She might want revision to happen in ways in which it has hitherto not happened.

We can think of many of the proposals that philosophers have put forth about constraints on conceptual engineering as falling into this latter category. I particularly have in mind proposals from those in the Carnapian tradition (including Carnap himself) and from philosophers such as Sally Haslanger. I used to think of these proposals as efforts to provide descriptively adequate conditions for concept revision (and earlier drafts of this book were focused on showing that as such they failed). I now think the right way to think of them are as *recommendations* for how conceptual engineering *should* be done. Here is the thought. Suppose someone responds to a particular revisionist proposal with one of the following: *Sorry, that's not going to work because that's not how it has been done in the past.* Or: *Sorry, that's not how children as a matter of fact do it.* Or: *Sorry, can't do that in a legal context because it's not how it has been done in the past.* Here is a legitimate response:

Okay, maybe what you're saying about what has happened in the past is all true, but I think we *should* make this revision anyway. What's at issue is not how we have done it in the past or how it is natural for children to do it, but it's how I think it should be done.

This response treats the constraints on conceptual engineering as *themselves* up for engineering—they can be molded and shaped. This is a continuation of the fundamental spirit of conceptual engineering: *don't take what's given to you for granted—question everything and in particular the concepts handed to you.* That kind of critical and questioning spirit is naturally applied to the constraints on 'sameness of topic'.[8]

---

[8] There are connections here to some of the literature on so-called 'essentially contested concepts' (Gallie 1955, MacIntyre 1973, Kekes 1977, Swanton 1985). That literature is focused on specific subsets of expressions often assumed to be characteristically contested. On the view suggested here, however, there's nothing in principle distinctive about 'rape' compared to, say, 'salad': these processes are all contested. In this respect I agree with the central criticism of the literature on essentially contested concepts found in Pekka Väyrynen (2014).

10.7 Comparison: Railton on Topic Preservation

None of this is to say that there's *nothing* to say about topic preservation. We can learn from the past history of conceptual evolutions even though we are free to make and negotiate adjustments. So one thing worth trying to do is come up with a kind of checklist for topic preservation (when extensions and intensions have changed). It would be a kind of empirically gathered set of guidelines that in broad outlines fits many cases (but, given what I said in the previous section, could be renegotiated).

There is something to be learned here from some remarks by Peter Railton. As pointed out in chapter 2, section 2.1.4, Railton's naturalistic program in moral philosophy is revisionist, but not topic-changing. Railton doesn't think sameness of topic isn't determined by sameness of extension and intension. It is, instead, determined by something he calls 'job descriptions' (Railton 1993: 46). Two speakers converge on a common topic, according to Railton, if they converge on a job description (and they can converge on a job description while disagreeing on what extension and intension satisfy the job description). Here is how, for our purposes, we can construe Railton-style job descriptions:[9]

> The job description of a concept, say 'Freedom', has three components:
> (i)   Truistic claims about Freedom (e.g., it has something to do with agency, responsibility, volition, etc.)
> (ii) Paradigm instances of Freedom (e.g., *those* are instances of free acts)
> (iii) Inferential relations that Freedom figures in (e.g., *if some act reduces freedom, then it is—ceteris paribus—bad*).

Railton doesn't endorse the so-called Canberra plan (Jackson 1998). His job descriptions don't provide the basis for an account of analyticity (e.g., the truisms are not analytically true and it is not analytically true that the paradigms are instances of freedom). Endorsement of the claims that figure in a job description is not a condition on concept possession: one can reject all of it and still use 'freedom' to talk about freedom. For example, if A and B use a (not context-sensitive) term 'F' in their common language, they will both be talking about F, even if they disagree on all elements of the job description (i.e., they disagree on what the relevant truisms are, on paradigms, and also on inferential roles). Finally, job descriptions are not reference fixers. In short, they play none of the traditional roles that senses do for Fregeans and neo-Fregeans.

---

[9] I'm grateful here to Peter Railton, who in conversations made clear to me the relevance and status of job descriptions.

So what do they do? If A and B are engaged in conceptual engineering and advocate different extensions and intensions, what then secures sameness of topic *is convergence on job descriptions*. This could allow for debate, negotiation, and dispute over how to weigh the various parts of the job description (so that could incorporate some of the features in the previous paragraph).

I like the idea of this as a kind of checklist for topic preservation. What I find problematic about Railton's proposal is that the proposal is made without detailed empirical backing. Railton's proposal seems to be the result of primarily armchair reflection by Railton himself. I don't think we should trust our armchair assumptions about topic preservation. In order to propose a theory an enormous amount of careful empirical work is needed. Whether the topic has been preserved is not even in the neighborhood of an a priori question. A proposal like this should be backed up by many, many detailed case studies. We would need to keep an eye on whether in these cases there could be topic continuity without continuity in job description or whether there could be continuity in job description without continuity in topic. That's data we simply don't have. Even in a seemingly simple case like 'salad', we have no clue what went on. Are there, for example, cases like the following? A and B disagree about the job description of salad. A has standard salad views. B is a devotee of a salad conspiracy theory according to which salads are devices for aliens to enter our bodies etc. Work this out so they really do disagree fundamentally on the job description for 'salad'. Would that kind of situation suffice to undermine topic continuity? My own conjecture is: not necessarily. The notion of sameness of topic is massively malleable and, given the right context, there could still be topic continuity, e.g., because A and B are part of a relevantly similar causal history (this reflects the fact that there's something deeply ahistorical and somewhat internalist about the way Railton describes his job descriptions).

— 'Job descriptors' like 'topics' then?

11

Reply to Strawson 2
Lexical Effects

11.1 Beyond Topic Continuity

I ended the last chapter by trying to describe the limits of revision. I described those limits as the point where there's a discontinuity of inquiry, where disquotational reporting breaks down, and where verbal dispute begins. From the previous chapter, you might have gotten the impression that I think that these limits should never be crossed; that going beyond the limits of revision would be bad. That, however, would be wrong. I didn't say or presuppose that. This chapter explores the possibility that going beyond the limits—where there's no continuity of topic, where disquotational reports break down, and where verbal disputes proliferate—might be a good thing. At the end of the chapter I argue against going beyond the limits, although I am aware that this argument is based on value judgments that are probably not widely shared.

11.2 Lexical Effects and Conceptual Engineering: An Overview

Let's consider someone engaged in a process that she thinks of as improving a concept, C. If she were successful then the extension and intension of C would change. The Strawsonian objection says: you aren't proposing to improve on C, you're just trying to develop a device for talking about something else, C*. Here is the response on the part of the conceptual engineer that will be considered in the remainder of this chapter:

I started out with a lexical item, L, that has C as its extension. What I propose is to change the extension of L without preservation of topic. I openly admit to proposing a change in topic. What I care about is that this lexical item should be used in relation to this new extension. I don't care about topic preservation, I don't care about whether I'm using the same concept, or whether I'm answering the same questions.

This response takes its inspiration from some remarks by Haslanger, who in response to her version of Strawson's objection says:

[I]f our goal is to identify a concept that serves our broader purposes, then *the question of terminology is primarily a pragmatic and sometimes a political one*: should we employ the terms of ordinary discourse to refer to our theoretical categories, or instead make up new terms?   (Haslanger 2000: 34–5 italics added)

I think that someone with this attitude might reason as follows: for pragmatic, political, and *any number of other reasons*, I want to keep the old terminology, *even when it involves a change in topic*. So what might those reasons be? This is where I think the idea of a *lexical effect* is helpful.

11.3 Lexical Effects: Some Illustrations

Expressions have effects beyond what philosophers and linguists classify as their semantic and pragmatic effects.[1] An expression can have cognitive and emotive effects over and beyond (and in some sense independently of) any of its semantic and pragmatic properties. I'll give a bunch of examples of this below, but first, consider the relevance of this phenomenon to the Strawsonian objection. Suppose lexical item L has lexical effects E. Someone might develop the following plan: I like these effects, i.e., I like E, so I am going to keep L. I'll do that even though doing so will change the topic and might lead to various verbal disputes, because the benefits outweigh the disadvantages.

I'll start with some illustrations of lexical effects and then give some brief general remarks about what they are and how they are generated.

11.3.1 Names

Suppose that today a child is named 'Hitler'. Suppose its parents didn't know about the evil bearer of that name. It was a typographical coincidence: the ignorant parents happened to like those letters organized in that way. There is no semantic, pragmatic, or other connection between the child and the evil bearer of the same name.[2] Now imagine people being asked to use that word to refer to the child. Those asked to do so can know what I just said, i.e., there's no connection whatsoever to the evil person. Still, the name will doubtlessly have emotional and cognitive effects on those who are aware of its former bearer. It will affect how people who talk about the child think about and relate to the child. It is not part of the meaning or sense of the name (if you believe in such things),

---

[1] Where I take 'pragmatic' to denote the kinds of linguistic and speech act properties discussed in standard overviews of pragmatics. See Korta and Perry 2015.

[2] If you like to use the word 'name' in such a way that it's a different name it makes no difference (see, e.g., Kaplan 1990, Cappelen 1999)—the point is that it is the same lexical item—i.e., the same letters in the same order.

and it is not related to the referent. It is simply an effect of the name itself. That lexical item triggers certain negative emotional and cognitive effects.

11.3.2 Pejoratives

Maybe the easiest way to see the lexical effects of pejoratives is to note that some of the world's leading newspapers, e.g., the *New York Times*, don't even allow quotations of pejoratives. Timothy Williamson thinks this is because people don't understand the use-mention distinction (Williamson 2009). He is right, but even so, it is an indisputable fact that the very presence of the lexical items associated with pejoratives has an effect on us and it is this effect that these newspapers guard against. These effects are exhibited by the many public debates over uses of the words 'niggardly'. The very appearance of a pejorative expression inside another expression that does not itself have any connection to that pejorative has repeatedly been the source of social sanction. Again, any explanation of this will have to talk about lexical effects (where these are not semantic or pragmatic).

11.3.3 Brand names

The point made in connection with 'Hitler' can be brought out in connection with brand names. There is a reason why companies spend enormous amount of resources protecting their brand names. It is often claimed that close to 80 percent of the value of the Coca Cola company lies in its ownership of the name 'Coca Cola'. What does that mean? It is of course complicated, but one thing it means is that if the company had to change the name of its core product, then the value of the company as a whole would decline dramatically. What's important for our purposes is this: in a scenario in which the brand name of the drink was changed, even among a population that knows about the change in name (and knows that nothing about the drink had changed), people's propensity to buy the drink would decline. The change in lexical item would change their behavior. More generally, one lesson from reflecting on brand names and the theory of brand names (something philosophers of language and linguists should do much more) is that lexical effects are immense. The lexical items themselves have broad cognitive and emotive effects which are not captured simply by talking about Gricean implicatures, presuppositions, or other standard pragmatic phenomena—in part because they are not entirely, or even for the most part, cognitive effects (they don't add another level of content).

11.3.4 Davidson on the effects of metaphor

Another way to get a feel for lexical effects is to think about (my interpretation of) Davidson on metaphor (Davidson 1978) and then apply some of these lessons to what George Lakoff says about lexical effects. A warning: what happens in the next couple of paragraphs is a bit of a roundabout way into the topic of lexical effects, and it's important not to get too hung up in Davidson exegesis or even the theory of metaphor. As will become clear, this is just to give you a way to think about lexical effects.

Here is a super-brief summary of my reading of Davidson's view of metaphor:

According to Davidson, "What distinguishes metaphor is not meaning but use. And the special use to which we put language in metaphor is not—cannot be—to 'say something' special, no matter how indirectly" (1978). At the core of Davidson's view of metaphor is the thesis that *no metaphorical content is conveyed*. Metaphors, according to Davidson, have only their literal meaning, and what they express is typically false ('Juliet is the sun' has only one meaning: that Juliet is the sun—and that is false). The goal of the use of a metaphor is not to convey some special message. Since what the metaphor prompts or inspires in most cases is not entirely, or even at all, recognition of some truth or fact, the attempt to give literal expression to the content of the metaphor is simply misguided. So what is the goal? He compares metaphor to a picture or a bump on the head and says that "There is no limit to what a metaphor calls to our attention, and much of what we are caused to notice is not propositional in character." Metaphors 'inspire' 'visions, thoughts and feelings'.

Here is what I want to take away from Davidson: words have all kinds of non-cognitive effects and cognitive effects that go far beyond their literal meaning (and their implicatures and presuppositions). Maybe you think that's not enough for a good theory of metaphor. I don't care about that. What I care about is that he's right: words have the kinds of effects that he describes.

Okay, suppose you're on board so far. Now, ask: what is *characteristic* of metaphor? What makes it *distinctive*? What makes it different from regular non-metaphorical speech? After all, metaphors have their literal meaning (which is typically false). In that respect they're not distinctive (there are lots of literal falsehoods around). So the idea must be that they are distinctive because they have these non-cognitive effects. That, however, would be surprising. If Davidson is right about the effects of metaphorical speech—they can inspire visions, thoughts, and feelings—then what's the argument that what we would classify as literal speech can't also have those effects? It would be extremely surprising if those kinds of effects are restricted to what we naturally classify as metaphor. Suppose I tell you: "Tomorrow, Nora will get dressed, have breakfast, make a shoe, play the cello, and then go to a yoga class." This is literal speech, but it can inspire thoughts and feelings. Nothing Davidson says about the effects of metaphor isn't also true about literal speech. Now, I don't care about this point as an objection to Davidson. What I care about is this: if you follow this line of thought—as I think you should—then this is a way to get to my notion of a lexical effect—i.e., an effect that words have that go very far beyond anything they say, implicate, or presuppose. That is, words have effects that go far beyond their semantic and pragmatic properties (unless you like to use the word 'pragmatic' to denote non-semantic effects, which is not how I use it in this book).

11.3.4.1 BRIEF DIGRESSION: CAN AN UNDERSTANDING OF LEXICAL EFFECTS PROVIDE A UNIFIED THEORY OF PEJORATIVE AND METAPHOR?

I'm appealing to features of pejoratives and metaphor to give some illustrations of what I have in mind when I talk about lexical effects. It's worth noting, as a brief digression, that there are some implications here for how to think about metaphor and pejoratives: such speech has lexical effects, and it has these in common with 'regular' speech. The difference is a matter of degree and maybe especially conversational salience. Sometimes the lexical effects of speech are important (more important than the literal content). This is a unifying feature of what is often classified as 'metaphor' and 'pejoratives'. If this is so, then the study of metaphor and pejoratives should at least in part be the study of various kinds of lexical effects and how they can be raised to salience. I'm attracted to the view that this is all you need in order to develop a theory of pejoratives and metaphor, i.e., that what you need for a unified theory of metaphor and pejoratives that merges neatly with a theory of conceptual engineering is a theory of lexical effects, their kinds, and ways to make them more salient than literal meaning. To establish this point here would require engaging with the extensive literature on those topics and that would take us too far afield. All I need for present purposes is to be able to use these illustrations of cases in which lexical effects are salient.

11.3.5 Lakoff on metaphors, frames, and political branding

Some of what George Lakoff says is best understood as appealing to what I call lexical effects. Much of his work is about the non-literal effects of combinations of expressions. He has applied those theories to what can be described as political branding: calling inheritance tax 'death tax' (in order to make it less attractive), using the expression 'pro-life' (to make laws restricting abortion more attractive), using 'tax relief' rather than 'tax cuts', etc. Here is Lakoff's description in the first pages of his book *Don't Think of an Elephant!*:

When the word *tax* is added to *relief*, the result is a metaphor: Taxation is an affliction. And the person who takes it away is a hero, and anyone who tries to stop him is a bad guy. This is a frame. It is made up of ideas, like *affliction* and *hero*. The language that evokes the frame comes out of the White House, and it goes into press releases, goes to every radio station, every TV station, every newspaper. And soon the *New York Times* is using *tax relief*. And it is not only on Fox; it is on CNN, it is on NBC, it is on every station because it is 'the president's tax relief plan.' And soon the Democrats are using *tax relief*—and shooting themselves in the foot. It is remarkable. I was asked by the Democratic senators to visit their caucus just before the president's tax plan was to come up in the Senate. They had their version of the tax plan, and it was their version of tax relief. They were accepting the conservative frame. The conservatives had set a trap: The words draw you into *their* worldview. That is what framing is about. Framing is about getting language that fits your worldview. It is not just language.   (Lakoff 2004: 4)

Lakoff's account of these kinds of cases is massively cognitive. Expressions trigger (or express or are associated with) what he calls 'frames'. He says that "[f]rames are mental structures that shape the way we see the world. As a result, they shape the goals we seek, the plans we make, the way we act, and what counts as a good or bad outcome of our actions" (Lakoff 2004: xv). I don't think that there are such things, i.e., I don't think there are mental structures that shape the way we see the world. Since I don't think there are such things, I also don't think they are triggered by (or associated with) expressions.[3] That's too big a point to argue here and so it won't play an important role in what follows. What will play an important role is that there's something less grandiose we can say that does at least some of the explanatory work that Lakoff's frames are doing. Suppose you like the idea that metaphors are a bit like a bump on the head. They can make you see things differently; words can trigger thoughts, feelings, and visions that are unrelated to their semantic and pragmatic properties. Suppose you're also on board with the idea that if this is true about metaphor, it's also true—albeit maybe to a somewhat lesser degree—about non-metaphorical speech. Lakoff, like Davidson, points out the rather obvious fact that words have a range of powerful cognitive and emotive effects that go infinitely far beyond their literal meaning and their pragmatically conveyed content. As Lakoff, among many others, points out, this fact is exploited in the kind of political branding that I mentioned earlier. And as soon as one sees that, it is obvious that these effects are everywhere—in ordinary speech and conversation, in theory-building, and in theoretical writings

---

[3] Lakoff says: "In politics our frames shape our social policies and the institutions we form to carry out policies. To change our frames is to change all of this. Reframing is social change. You can't see or hear frames. They are part of what cognitive scientists call the 'cognitive unconscious'—structures in our brains that we cannot consciously access, but know by their consequences: the way we reason and what counts as common sense. We also know frames through language. All words are defined relative to conceptual frames. When you hear a word, its frame (or collection of frames) is activated in your brain" (Lakoff 2004: xv). Here is the trivial reading of that: we have a brain and thoughts supervene on what goes on in the brain. What's not trivial is that clusters of contents are systematically 'activated' by words or that they define words. None of that is argued for in Lakoff's work—it's simply asserted. He also seems not to care much about the difference between 'activation' and 'definition' or the relation between them.

of all kinds. That's a view you can endorse even if you don't think that words are 'defined' by 'mental structures that shape the way we see the world'.

11.4 Lexical Effects and Conceptual Engineering

With these illustrations as a background, let's consider a range of cases closer to the topic of conceptual engineering. One place to start is with terms that have been subject of extensive public debate and negotiation, such as 'marriage' and 'rape' (and 'organic', 'hacker', 'refugee', 'immigrant', 'combatant').[4] The central assumption I make in this section is that such words have significant lexical effects. For 'rape' they are on the negative side of a spectrum and for 'marriage' on the positive side. So you can imagine people wanting to exploit these effects (negative or positive). In particular, someone proposing a change in extension for 'rape' or 'marriage' might explore the following justificatory strategy:

> *Lexical Effects Defense of Conceptual Engineering:*   I agree that the proposed amelioration doesn't preserve topic in this case (or I just don't care about that issue). What I care about is preservation of the lexical effects that come from calling these new topics 'rape' and 'marriage', respectively. I want to use the negative effects of the expression 'rape' and I want the positive effects of the expression 'marriage'. I want to exploit these effects for, as Haslanger calls it, 'pragmatic and political' reasons. (As emphasized above, these should not be thought of as 'pragmatic' effects in the way that linguists and philosophers of language use the term.)

It would be an absurd prejudice to assume that those engaged in 'serious' theorizing are immune to lexical effects. They are obviously not. How we label our views and the choice of central theoretical terms can have all kinds of non-cognitive effects that scholars often exploit (for the most part without being aware of doing it). The use of a particular term can be a way to indicate allegiances, trigger associations, make appeal to authority (some famous person used this word), and sometimes just to show off. Turning to philosophy (though the point here has nothing specifically to do with philosophy), I suspect that the choice of whether to use terms such as 'reductionist', 'feminist', 'experimental philosophy', 'intuitive', 'anti-realist', 'relativist', 'analytic', etc. is often in large part guided by the non-semantic and non-pragmatic lexical effects the use of these terms will have. Roughly, the idea is: *show me which words you use, and I'll tell*

---

[4] See Ludlow 2014 for a wide range of good illustrations that in some cases might involve the exploitation of lexical effects (though this isn't how Ludlow would construe the cases).

you who your friends are (or who you want your friends to be). We can imagine a
(I would say) defective intellectual discipline or practice where the primary goal
was to choose grammatical combinations of lexical items *with the right lexical
effects*—i.e., the primary goal of writing was to exploit lexical effects (as opposed
to saying something true or justified). This is may be one way to understand
François Recanati's description of Lacan's followers. In the paper 'Can We
Believe What We Do Not Understand?' (1997), Recanati characterizes some of
the sentences used by followers of Lacan in the following way:[5]

- They defer to Lacan, i.e., central concepts are used by the followers to mean
  whatever Lacan meant by them.
- Lacan didn't mean anything by those terms—he failed to introduce terms
  with meaning.

Why did Lacan fail? There might be no point in speculating about the details.
It could be some kind of cognitive failure on his part or it could be intentional
deception—we simply don't know. What matters is that, according to Recanati,
we have a fundamentally defective introduction of terms. The terms are passed
along among those who speak and write about Lacan, and, put simplistically, they
defer to the meaning they assume Lacan has given those words. Recanati concludes that in these cases there is no content:

In Lacanian cases the accepted sentence possesses a deferential character but the attempted
deference fails: No user x has the cognitive resources for determining the content of the
term to which the deferential operator applies, hence no content is expressed, in that
context.   (Recanati 1997: 92)

Here is a way to think about this situation (assuming for the sake of argument
that Recanati is correct): the followers of Lacan were using meaningless lexical
items in order to exploit the lexical effects of those terms. The use of these terms
could, for example, indicate allegiance to Lacan, membership in a group aligned
with Lacan in various ways. This is fairly extreme case: there is no meaning and
so all there is to exploit is the lexical effects (for more on the meaninglessness of
these terms, see Cappelen 2013).

It might be overly optimistic to assume that *we* (by which I mean roughly:
contemporary analytic philosophers) are entirely different from the Lacanians in
this respect. It might turn out that even for us, a significant amount of our work
consists in trying to trigger the right kinds of lexical effects. Given some of my

[5] Recanati speaks with some authority on this issue: before his interest turned to analytic
philosophy he was one of Lacan's most prominent students.

own views (not argued for or presupposed in this book), I find it very natural to think that many sentences written by many contemporary analytic philosophers are produced primarily in order to exploit lexical effects. I think, for example, that terms such as 'intuitive' and 'de se' are, literally, meaningless (Cappelen 2013, Cappelen and Dever 2013). So those who use those terms in sentences are not doing it because it results in a sentence expressing a thought (since there are no thoughts expressed by sentences containing those expressions). So why do they produce them? They might think those sentences will express thoughts and that is certainly part of the explanation. But I think an equally plausible conjecture is that they do so in order to signal certain kinds of social and intellectual allegiances (and connections). By using 'de se' you indicate that you belong (or want to belong) to a certain group of philosophers and that you have read certain papers and that you are aligned with certain other philosophers. Of course, this is not the full story. My conjecture here is just that this is (a not insignificant) part of the story.

11.5 A General Theory of Lexical Effects?

I've given you some illustrations of lexical effects, but not a general theory. I don't have one. I think they are a hugely varied category. They can inspire, trigger associations of various kinds, make you happy, cheerful, motivated, sad, angry, etc. They can certainly affect your dispositions to behave. This is a point made particularly vivid by brand names, but if a name like 'Coca Cola' can make you more likely to spend money on bottle of liquid, then most likely a name can also make you more disposed to accept, say, a philosophical theory (it is, after all, cheaper to accept a philosophical theory than to buy a bottle of Coke, so we should expect the barriers to be lower).

In sum: I think the study of lexical effects is potentially enormously significant. It is also deeply empirical. Fields such as sociolinguistics might provide insight. Priming studies in psychology can provide insight. Business schools have entire departments of marketing and one thing they study are the effects of brand names. They train people to do what I think of as creating and changing lexical effects. I suspect there's a lot that philosophers interested in lexical effects can learn from these varied fields. Some conjectures:

- Lexical effects will be of many kinds, both cognitive and non-cognitive.
- There will not be stable lexical effects across large populations.
- These effects are also temporally unstable: they change easily over time.
- These effects are non-compositional: even if you can characterize the lexical effects of two expression E1 and E2 in isolation, you can't predict or calculate

the lexical effect of their combination, i.e., the lexical effects of 'E1E2'. The effects of combinations are entirely unsystematic and unpredictable. One reason for thinking that is that it's not possible to write an algorithm that predicts the effect of metaphor.

- Even if you know the lexical effect of an expression on an individual, that effect will interact with other features of the individual in ways that are largely unpredictable and will vary wildly across individuals.

11.6 Why Are Lexical Effects Largely Ignored in Philosophy of Language?

Lexical effects have not been at the center of philosophical reflections about language in the twentieth century. Why not? Since the origins of analytic philosophy, our focus has been on understanding phenomena such as analyticity, the sense-reference distinction, reference-fixing, informativeness, substitutivity in opaque contexts, compositionality, and the nature of representation. This cluster of issues more or less ignores the nature of lexical items themselves and their non-semantic and non-pragmatic effects. One can, of course, see traces of an interest in this topic here and there. Frege, for example, made a few cryptic remarks about what he called 'coloring', but he didn't do much with it.[6] (Maybe there are ways to spell out Frege on coloring in ways that make it about lexical effects—I'm not sure, and as always in my work I stay as far away from anything in the neighborhood of Frege interpretation as I possibly can.)

In short: lexical effects have not been seen as providing answers to any of the core questions in philosophy of language and mind. That's one important reason why it has been largely ignored. Another reason is this: there's a sense in which philosophers of language, at least, have been focused on describing the thoughts expressed by uses of sentences—their content (specified, for example, as truth conditions). This has also, in a sense, been the focus of pragmatics, which has been the study of other thoughts expressed in a more indirect way (e.g., through implicatures or presuppositions). All of this is focused on contents and thoughts. Lexical effects bring in another dimension: how the symbols make you feel and affect you. As a result, this topic is very alien to most theorizing about language in the twentieth century.[7]

---

[6] According to Frege, coloring has no effect on the logical properties of words, and so he more or less ignored it. See Dummett 1973: 84–5, and also Neale 2001.

[7] This could be a significant mistake even for those of us who have focused on the traditional questions in philosophy of language: if lexical effects affect our judgments about truth and falsity (and it's an empirical question whether they do), then these effects might directly influence fundamental data points for semantics.

11.7 Playing with Fire: Deception and Communicative Breakdowns

Exploiting lexical effects to push changes in meaning in a way that does not preserve topic is *risky*. The central risk concerns the possibility of verbal disputes (and fake agreements) and more generally breakdowns and discontinuity in communication. In other words, the worries are all ones I described as Strawsonian in chapter 9. Here is an illustration of the worry:

> *Risks:* Suppose a speaker S has implemented the strategy I have just outlined: she is using an old expression, E, with a new extension and does not care about whether this process preserves sameness of topic. And in fact, the revision *does not* preserve sameness of topic.[8] Those who don't know about what S has done will interpret her utterances of E as having the *pre*-revision meaning (and there is no way to exclude such audiences, such that one only speaks to those 'in the know'). Anyone *not in the know* will be inclined to report S using a sentence like: "S said that E is F" and will in so doing *mis*report her, because 'E' in the ignorant reporter's mouth does not denote what E denotes in S's mouth. The problem goes the other way too: if S isn't careful, she will easily engage in disquotationally reporting others' use of E and so misrepresent what others said. We're pretty hardwired to go for disquotational reports of people who speak our language (except when they use obviously context-sensitive expressions, like 'I', 'here', 'now', etc.). To make samesaying reports across a revision of meaning that is not topic preserving could be communicatively disastrous.

Here is an illustration: suppose, for the sake of argument, that the FBI's definition of 'rape' is correct:

Penetration, no matter how slight, of the vagina or anus with any body part or object, or oral penetration by a sex organ of another person, without the consent of the victim.[9]

Suppose you want to advocate for a broader definition—e.g., one that *does not require penetration*. You can do that in two ways: you can pursue the first strategy in this chapter and say that this is a better way to talk about rape (and so what you are talking about is still rape). Alternatively, you're not interested in defending

---

[8] Note that given Lack of Control and the lack of luminosity of conceptual change, an engineer's attitude toward the topic preservation of her proposed change will not necessarily match with whether she actually preserves topic. Someone who wants to change the topic might end up preserving it, and vice versa.

[9] That's the definition currently given on the FBI's website: https://ucr.fbi.gov/crime-in-the-u.s/2014/crime-in-the-u.s.-2014/offenses-known-to-law-enforcement/rape. Before 2011, their definition was: 'carnal knowledge of a female forcibly and against her will'.

topic continuity; instead, your aim is to exploit the effects of using the word 'rape' to talk about these new cases. The claim then is that these effects outweigh the disadvantage of potential verbal disputes (more on such weighing below).

Anyone choosing the second strategy runs the risks outlined above. Suppose S's utterance of 'A is a rapist' is interpreted by someone, H, who is not in the know—i.e., H is not aware of the ameliorated use. Suppose also that H trusts S. Then, if A is in the post-amelioration extension of 'rapist' but not in the pre-amelioration extension, H will end up with a false belief about A. When H then tells others what S said, H will use her word 'rapist' to report and so this false claim will spread widely through testimonial chains. There are ways to try to guard against such effects, but there's no way to guarantee that they won't happen. In transition periods, i.e., when the ameliorated use has not yet been established, these kinds of effects are likely to happen no matter how much one tries to guard against it.

How to balance the value of lexical effects against the dangers of miscommunication is a complicated empirical question. One could argue that these kinds of communicative disruption are strategically useful, so that you could exploit not only the lexical effects but also the effects of the miscommunication. According to this view, the miscommunication itself is part of the larger communicative strategy (see Sterken forthcoming in Burgess, Cappelen, and Plunkett forthcoming for an exploration of this option).[10]

11.8 Why Exploitation of Lexical Effects Should Be Avoided

If I were in charge, the kind of lexical exploitation that I have just outlined would be banned. Here is why:

> *Exploiters:*   Call conceptual engineers who exploit lexical effects without an effort to make the case that the revision is topic preserving (i.e., without trying to make the case that it's a better way to talk/refer) *Exploiters.* Exploiters undermine rational discourse by encouraging verbal disputes and in so doing undermine continuity of inquiry. They treat speech as a medium of manipulation, not as a medium for communication (i.e., as a medium for the exchange of thoughts and

---

[10] One might think that there is one lexical effect that always supports keeping a word: familiarity. It seems like an important feature of 'woman' that I know that every English speaker will be familiar with it. I can't rely on their familiarity with a proposed replacement. On the other hand, that familiarity is a double-edged sword: it leads people towards disquotational interpretations and, as we have seen, that can lead to communicative breakdowns in the context of conceptual engineering (thanks to Matt McKeever for pushing the point about familiarity).

ideas). There are of course Exploiters with good intentions, but the overall effect of their exploitation is to contribute to and encourage a use of language that undermines what we should treasure the most about it: the continuous exchange of ideas. Exploiters are in effect *anti-intellectualist opportunists that contribute to a destruction of genuine communication.*

If you have a value system in which the preservation of language as a medium of communication isn't placed very high, then you'll no doubt be more sympathetic to Exploiters and also inclined towards Exploitation yourself. Not much of what follows will hang on my assessment of Exploitation, though I'll mention it here and there. That said, those with Exploitative sympathies should be able to be on board with most of what follows. What is important for the overall dialectic of the book is the recognition of Exploiters as an interesting category of conceptual engineers; my assessment of their work is less important.[11,12]

---

[11] What about metaphorical use of language? Didn't I say that it was characterized at least in part and maybe entirely by the exploitation of lexical effects? I did, and that illustrates the point above: metaphorical use of language in literature doesn't present itself as an effort to be literal communication. On the contrary, it marks itself as not being that. *What's Exploitative is to present oneself as engaging in literal communication and then intentionally be an Exploiter.*

[12] Am I being too hard on Exploiters? The condemnation of Exploiters in the main body of the text is couched in generic terms and as such it is compatible with a wide range of exceptions. Moreover there will be many cases where other norms overrule those appealed to in the text. That said, I think the general attitude of condemnation is justified in much the same way as one can be generally against stealing or lying (acts that are sometimes acceptable because the relevant norms are outweighed by other norms).

PART IV

Towards a General Theory 3: Worldliness and the Varieties of Conceptual Engineering

The three brief chapters in this part complete the presentation of the Austerity Framework. Chapter 12 emphasizes that conceptual engineering, as described in earlier chapters, can be described on the object level, without devices for denoting words or concepts. Conceptual engineering can be described as being about freedom, causation, gender, or salad. Chapter 13 puts some of the pieces together from earlier chapters and describes the varieties of conceptual engineering. Chapter 14 responds to some objections.

12

The Worldliness of Conceptual Engineering

12.1 What Is Conceptual Engineering About?

When we talk about conceptual engineering *what* is it that is being engineered? As a heuristic, we can divide answers into three categories:

- *Option 1: Something Conceptual:* On this kind of view, conceptual engineering is about concepts (whatever they may be), the constitutive principles for concepts (whatever they may be), or the constitutive principles for concept possession (whatever they may be). Haslanger's project is about the concept of woman and Clark and Chalmers are interested in the concept of belief (or the constitutive principles for that concept or the possession conditions).[1]
- *Option 2: Words and Their Meanings (or Extensions):* On this view, conceptual engineering is about words of a specific language and their meanings. So construed, conceptual engineers are interested in, e.g., the English words (lexical items) 'woman', 'torture', 'freedom', etc. Their goal is to change these meanings.
- *Option 3: The World—Object Level:* On this view, conceptual engineering is about the world. It is about, for example, marriage, persons, torture, or freedom. So construed, the result of conceptual engineering can be described as an object-level change: we're changing what gender, freedom, salad, marriage, etc. *are.*

---

[1] Since no one agrees on what concepts are, they often try to refer to them by talking a natural language word and writing it in italics or caps—and then the assumption is that they have succeeded in referring to a concept and that the readers know what is referred to. In the main text I sometimes write in that way when presenting the views I disagree with, but ultimately I don't think any of those devices for referring to concepts make sense. They are defective linguistic devices and defenders of concepts need to do some conceptual engineering on their concept-referring devices. (See footnote 2.)

The aim of this chapter is to make a case for Option 3, the worldly description of conceptual engineering. In sum, I argue for the following:

- Option 1 is unhelpful: concepts—construed as the theoretical entities that some philosophers and psychologists appeal to—play no significant role in understanding conceptual engineering.
- Option 2 has an element of obvious truth in it: as I have described conceptual engineering it involves changing the extensions and intensions of expressions. Moreover, those who exploits lexical effects are focused on the effects of certain lexical items (and the combinations of lexical items). However, and this is the key point in what follows, this isn't the only correct description of the effects and aims of conceptual engineering.
- Surprisingly, there is a construal of Option 3 that is true, and that is worth emphasizing over both of the first two options. I defend Option 3 in a *metaphysically lightweight* way—it's a not a form of idealism or social constructionism about everything. Option 3 ends up being true because of interesting interactions between semantic content and speech act content: The discrepancy between the two allows us to say something true when we say that, for example, marriage, persons, torture, or freedom has changed. In none of these cases will the semantic content be true, but what we say is true.

12.2 In Favor of the Worldly Characterization of Conceptual Engineering

To see how the view proposed here gives room for worldly descriptions, it'll be helpful to have a concrete example to work with. I'll use 'family'.[2]

Suppose that between two points in time, t and t*, the semantic value of 'family' changes, i.e., its extension and intension change as the result of conceptual engineering. So there's some set of people that relative to a point of evaluation, say a world/time pair, is in the extension of 'family' at t*, but not at t. To make this vivid, let's suppose it's the set of two women and a child that's not the offspring of either (at a certain time in a certain world). Using 'family' with the meaning it had at t, this set of people is not in the extension of 'family' (at that time and that world). Using 'family' with the meaning it has at t*, they are in the extension (at that time and that world).

Now here is a sense in which what a family is *hasn't* changed: Suppose we use 'family' with the semantic value it had at any *one* of these times, then what counts

---

[2] It might seem significant whether I'm choosing the name for a social kind or not, but it isn't and I'll explain why below.

as being a family hasn't changed relative to *any* point of assessment—informally: the conditions imposed on being in the extension are stable relative to all points of assessment. What we can pre-theoretically think of as 'what it takes to be a family' hasn't changed, as long as we use just one of the meanings (the one 'family' had at t or at t*). So it looks like we're stuck: no matter which meaning we use—the one at t or the one at t*—it looks like we're not able to express a true proposition by uttering something like 'what a family is has changed between t and t*' or 'families have changed between t and t*'.

However, this is too simplistic. Not everything we say is fixed by the semantic value of our expressions. What we say goes far beyond the proposition semantically expressed. What we say (or one of the propositions we say[3]) when we utter a sentence can be true even though the proposition semantically expressed is false. In particular, a salient proposition in certain settings will be one where the intension of 'family' is variable—where, so to speak, what it takes to be a family at t is different from what it takes to be a family at t* (and where these differences correspond to the different meanings 'family' had at t and t*). This proposition—this part of what is said—will in some settings take some effort to focus in on, in other settings less so. What it makes possible is the truth of utterances of sentences such as:

What families are has changed.
Families have changed.

These will express one true proposition (in addition to the false proposition semantically expressed). In speaking like that we are talking about families—the topic that is more coarse-grained than the semantic values of expressions. In general, as soon as we allow saying to include contents beyond the semantic values (those that have changed), we can recognize additional contents that reflect the semantic changes—and there can be a plurality also of such contents. None of these need to quote words and talk about their semantic values.[4]

This connects to a central theme above: the coarse-grainedness of topics relative to semantic values. The semantic values of the expression 'family' has changed, but the change has been topic-preserving and so what we talk (and think) about is family. That's also why it makes sense to talk (and think) about what families ought to be—when what it ought to be is different from what it is.[5]

---

[3] On my view, each utterance expresses a very large number of propositions—only one of them the proposition semantically expressed (Lepore and Cappelen 2005).

[4] Though what we say can include such contents as well—the aim here isn't to exclude such contents, but show how we can also describe the change at the object level.

[5] Again it's crucial not to misinterpret this way of talking: the thought I am trying to characterize is the thought that *what it takes* to be a family ought to be different from what it is.

In all these cases one can coherently think that *it*—that very thing—ought to be different from what it is.

When describing conceptual engineering as operating on the object level, it can give the impression of having very heavy metaphysical implications. The above remarks should make clear why I think that worry is misplaced: the underlying mechanisms involve expressions changing their extensions and intensions and a recognition that these changes are topic-preserving. The result is that we can say truly that, e.g., families have changed (and we can see that change as a result of conceptual engineering). What has changed is not the English words or some kind of abstract object called the concept of 'family'. Families are worldly phenomena and they have changed. However, none of this is a commitment to new and spooky ways of creating families. The families that end up existing at some time/world pair is the result of familiar facts about people creating bonds in various complicated, but non-spooky ways. There are true object-level ways that can be used to describe the results of conceptual engineering, but none of that means we have discovered new and linguistically driven ways to procreate or become a parent.

12.2.1 Brief digression: more on topics and our talk about them

I've talked about topics a great deal—their coarse-grainedness (compared to semantic values) has been crucial at various junctures above. What are topics? I don't have a metaphysics of topics and their identity conditions over time. Instead, I have an account (or a description) of the contestation over when it's legitimate to say, "They're still talking about (or discussing, describing, or...) marriage (or freedom or...)." The model gives the conditions under which we describe two people as samesayers: they can be samesayers even when the semantic values of their words diverge (see chapter 10), but what makes that true isn't a new semantic value that is identical between the two of them. There's no new level of content that they converge on. That would both lead us into a regress and be non-explanatory. And the situation is similar with respect to topics: there's no point postulating a new entity—topics, to account for the continuity in topic—that will do no explanatory work.

Again there's a useful analogy here with intercontextual variability. Suppose 'knows' is context sensitive. Suppose two speakers utter 'A knows that p' in two different contexts that determine somewhat different semantic values for 'knows'. We can still describe these two utterances from a third context *using* 'knows', not mentioning it. For example, we can say:

1. They both talked about what A knows.

We can also say:

2.   They both said that A knows that p.

[handwritten margin note: B/c you are exploiting the fact that 'it' has a common meaning]

Note that I don't need to quote 'knows' in order to say this and nothing is gained, when theorizing about these phenomena, by adding a new meta-proposition— one that they both expressed. The reports in 1 and 2 above are true because the speakers stand in the samesaying relation to each other. Analogously, nothing is gained by adding a new level of content corresponding to topics.

12.3 Against Conceptual Engineering Being about Concepts

Many of those who write about conceptual engineering are unclear on the exact nature of the entities being engineered. Others are clear, but have very different views from those outlined above. Some of these alternatives are extensively discussed later in the book. Option 2 is discussed further in chapter 16. Option 1 sees conceptual engineering as focused, not on the object level, but on some kind of intermediary, typically described as a concept. The first item on the agenda for such views should be to specify what concepts are, and then present an account of how concepts so construed can be engineered. There's of course already a smorgasbord of options for how to think about concepts:

Smorgasbord (selection of options):   prototypes, Platonic objects or Fregean senses (whatever they might be); there's the theory-theory, and a range of other options. You can be a nativist or not. You can be an atomist or not.

However, and this is the strange part, those who talk of conceptual engineering as operating on concepts *don't* start by making choices on this smorgasbord. They often just talk about 'concepts', their engineering, and then leave it at that. That's unfortunate because it makes the view hard to assess—you don't really have an account of conceptual engineering unless you make an explicit choice here (assuming you're someone who thinks of conceptual engineering as operating on concepts).

Those who are theoretically committed fall into three categories:

(i)   Concepts are entities that fulfill functions.
(ii) Concepts are entities with constitutive principles.
(iii) Concepts are entities that persist over time.

Option (i) is discussed in chapter 16. The next two sections are focused on (ii) and (iii).

12.4 Conceptual Engineering as Being about Constitutive Principles (of Concepts or Concept Possession)

Among those interested in conceptual engineering, advocates of option (ii) include Matti Eklund, Kevin Scharp, and quite a few of those I described as inconsistency theorists above: they think there can be inconsistent concepts and that those inconsistencies are to be understood in terms of inconsistent constitutive principles. There's a sense in which this book is a direct challenge to such views and a sense in which it isn't. I don't think concepts are constituted by (or have) constitutive principles. I also don't think concept possession requires adherence to, commitment to, or entitlement to (anything like) constitutive principles. My arguments for these views are largely those of Timothy Williamson's (2007) and are reflected in the thesis I call Anti-Creed above. Rehashing this entire debate in this book would take us too far afield. It would in effect be a book of its own and distract from the central narrative of this book. The view in this book shows how you can construe conceptual engineering without any such complicated commitments. The direct challenge to people like Eklund and Scharp is: why not construe the activity along the lines suggested here? I appeal to non-controversial ingredients that you already have at your disposal, I leave out all the controversial machinery, and I can explain the same phenomena.[6] Simplicity recommends the Austerity Framework over these more baroque, and controversial, alternatives.

The appeal to simplicity is powerful and it can be elaborated by thinking through all the added challenges taken on by an appeal to constitutive principles. Here are some of them:

- First you need to argue that there are constitutive principles of the relevant kind. That involves responding to a battery of objections from, e.g., Williamson (Williamson 2007). Scharp attempts to frame a notion of constitutive principles that avoids these objections. Discussing whether he succeeds—I don't think he does—is something that would take us too far afield (and would involve an assessment of Scharp's appeals to entitlement—a notion that I find even more obscure and problematic than the original appeal to

---

[6] Including an explanation of why there *appear* to be inconsistent concepts; see chapter 8.

constitutive principles). For current purposes, it suffices to note that given the strength of Williamson's arguments this is a substantial commitment. It would be an advantage to not have to take it on.

- Then, having responded to those challenges, you need to show that all relevant concepts (the ones that are candidates for conceptual engineering) have such principles. For example, Paul Boghossian, in his reply to Williamson, ends up with the view that just a few logical constants (maybe *just* 'and') have constitutive principles. On these extremely restricted views, there wouldn't be much conceptual engineering to do (if conceptual engineering is restricted to the fixing of inconsistent principles) and the activity would be more or less irrelevant to philosophical practice. So the most prominent reply to Williamson, i.e. Boghossian's, isn't available to someone who (a) thinks that appeal to constitutive principles plays an essential role in conceptual engineering, and (b) thinks a broad range of concepts can and should be engineered.

- Suppose you have a reply to Williamson that broadens the range of concepts that have constitutive principles. Suppose you also think—as Scharp does—that the aim of conceptual engineering is to hunt down inconsistent constitutive principles. You then need an effective procedure for distinguishing inconsistency in constitutive principles from:
  - Inconsistency in people's beliefs
  - Metasemantic chaos that provides the illusion of inconsistency (see chapter 8).[7]

Take freedom as an example. One option when encountering claims about incoherence or inconsistency is that these characterize some non-constitutive beliefs that people have about freedom. Another option is that the metasemantics is messy. The proponent of constitutive principles takes on the task of distinguishing inconsistency in constitutive principles from these superficially similar phenomena. No easy task.

- Those who place constitutive principles at the heart of conceptual engineering typically focus almost exclusively on *inconsistency* as the defect that engineering aims to ameliorate. That approach leaves out very much of what I described as conceptual engineering in Part I. At the end of chapter 3 I gave

---

[7] I'm assuming here that even if you are a devotee of constitutive principles, you must also recognize the possibility of metasemantic chaos: there's some metasemantic mechanism that makes it the case (grounds) that a concept has the constitutive principles it does have. That metasemantic mechanism can be messy along the lines described in chapter 8.

a taxonomy of defects which includes much more than inconsistency. So yet another challenge is this: give an account of all those other forms of defects. Constitutive principles (if there are any) are well suited to capture inconsistencies, but they are not well suited to, for example, account for the kinds of deficiencies people who work on gender and race concepts draw our attention to. A natural reply here is to say that these are just very different concerns and it was a mistake to lump them together: Haslanger-style amelioration isn't the same kind of activity as the kind of replacement required when we encounter an inconsistent concept. Note that this reply leaves open a reconciliation strategy: the lovers of constitutive principles could appeal to their inconsistent principles when hunting inconsistent concepts, and could then use my theory for all the other kinds of defects.

None of this aspires to a proof that you shouldn't approach conceptual engineering through an account of concepts (i.e., by starting with an account of concepts and then developing the theory of conceptual engineering around it). Had this book been much longer it would have included a chapter that showed how conceptual engineering looks from the point of view of all the main theories of concepts. That's an important research project, but it is best left to proponents of these various theories of concepts.

12.5 Conceptual Engineering as Being about Entities That Persist over Time (Richard's View)

Richard (forthcoming) suggests that we think of concepts as entities that persist over time and can change their extension and intension. One way to compare our views is to see this as a reification of what I call topics. I could have said: topics are things that persist over time and they change their extensions and intensions. To see why I think this is unhelpful, first some background and context for Richard's view.

Richard describes the incoherence version of Strawson's objection to conceptual engineering (chapter 9) and says that those who endorse that view tend to think of a concept as a thing with a semantic essence: its intension. He thinks that's a mistake. Concepts, according to Richard, are things with histories and across those histories intensions can change. The way Richard develops his view draws on a number of distinctions, for example between articulations, practicums, official notions, core notions, conceptions, and the interactions between all of these. I will have a bit more to say about these notions in the later chapters; however, my central point in this connection can be made without going into those details. Here, roughly, is the structure of what Richard wants:

Consensus within the L-community — necc/absolute

1. *Stretched-concepts*: He proposes that we recognize a temporarily stretched out object: this is the species model of concepts. This stretched out concept can change over time—in particular, its intension can change.

2. *Time-slices of stretched-concepts*: A stretched-concept consists of time-slices.

The question I have been concerned with in previous chapters is when a change in extension and intension results in a change of topic. Richard's model, no matter how the details are developed, will not in itself address that question. The question when put in terms of stretched-concepts is: *In virtue of what are different time-slices part of the same stretched-concept?* The model itself gives no answer to that question. It provides a way of *asking* the question (i.e., the italicized part two sentences ago), not an answer to the question. I think Richard agrees with this. He says an advantage of his view is that it allows us to articulate questions such as this: "[H]ow do we select or project, from the various accounts we might give of what makes different synchronic conceptions 'fit together' to make up a single 'concept stage', to an account of what relations various concept stages must have, in order to be 'stages of the same concept'?" This is in effect the question of how to account for conceptual continuity over time.

The core question—'Under what conditions is a time-slice part of the same stretched-concept?'—isn't answered by this structure itself. So what he sees as the central advantage of his view is that it enables us to articulate the question in a particularly *useful* way. However, I'm not convinced it's doing even that. There's a simple way to articulate this issue and it's the one I have been using throughout this book:

At some point speakers of L use F with extension E. At some point later, F's extension has changed. If speakers of L are still talking about the same topic when they use F, then there's a relevant kind of continuity.

I have suggested that we model that continuity on what we say about diachronic samesaying and inter-contextual samesaying. For example, we wonder how two speakers uttering 'N is smart' can say the same thing (both say *that N is smart*) even though in their respective contexts 'smart' picks out somewhat different extensions. Suppose someone suggested the following:

What we need is a new entity: the inter-contextually-stretched-concept. This is the concept of 'tall' that is built out of contextual slices. We can then usefully ask the unity question as follows: how do contextual slices of 'tall' make the big inter- contextually-stretched-concept of tallness?

My reaction to this is: Sure, I guess you could ask the question this way, but it isn't particularly helpful. It's not that you can't make sense of this question, but we know much simpler ways of talking about these issues. The same can be said about the diachronic case: it's not exactly wrong to postulate a new object, but it also isn't particularly useful. What we need to understand better are a) the metasemantic mechanisms that generate reference change, and b) the conditions under which such changes are properly described as cases of samesaying or topic preservation. Richard mentions a variety of phenomena (theoretical role, similarity in extension, similarity in what he calls 'articulation'). Those things will in some way contribute to shifts, but as I said above, I'm not in the business of trying to specify necessary and sufficient conditions for when extensions change or for continuity of topic when extensions change. We can look at case studies, some generalizations will be useful, but this is not an area that lends itself to the specification of strict conditions.[8]

12.6 Worldliness and Recent Metaphilosophy

Conceptual engineering, as it is understood in this book, is congenial to the strand of contemporary metaphilosophy that's vehemently opposed to the view of philosophers as people who sit around fiddling with concepts. The kind of view I have in mind is articulated in the first few chapters of Williamson's *The Philosophy of Philosophy* (Williamson 2007). Philosophy, on this view, isn't about analyzing concepts; it's not about trying to specify necessary and sufficient conditions that somehow constitute concepts or concept possession. It is, instead, about various features of the world: knowledge, freedom, morality, perception, language, etc. Epistemology, for example, isn't about the concept of knowledge, it's about knowledge. Someone attracted to this picture of philosophy would and should be prejudiced against the very idea of conceptual engineering. On the face of it—in the very name!—it seems to be advocating concept-fiddling, which is just what should be avoided. My version of conceptual engineering, however, isn't like this at all: it is directly about the world, there are no concepts to fiddle with, and there isn't any fiddling. There are words, but we're not fiddling with the words (they remain the same). What I have described is a process that operates directly on extensions and intensions (i.e., things in the world). In that sense, the

---

[8] An analogy might help see why stretched-concepts won't be much help: it's—somewhat—agreed in the 4d vs. 3d debate about objects that both theories seem to be able to capture the same data (at least as concerns change). It would be surprising if in debates about concepts going 4d about them would suddenly make a decisive difference.

process I describe as conceptual engineering is about knowledge, freedom, what is right, women, marriage, and salad. It's not about the words (except in the few cases where the lexical effects are exploited) and it's not about concepts (I don't appeal to any). As I said at the end of chapter 3, the terminology Haslanger often uses to describe ameliorative projects is appropriate: *when doing conceptual engineering, we are deciding how these things should be* (Haslanger 1999, 2000).

This has always been the point of linguistic philosophy — people like Williamson just choose to misinterpret it.

13

Varieties of Conceptual Engineering

13.1 Three Varieties of Conceptual Engineering

The paradigmatic instances of conceptual engineering have one important common feature:

> *Core-Commonality:*   The paradigmatic instances of conceptual engineering are efforts to assess and improve our representational devices.

This is an important commonality and it bolsters the claim that there's unity to the various illustrations given in chapter 2 of this book. That said, there are many different ways to go about doing this. Chapter 2 gave an overview of varieties of conceptual engineering found in the literature I surveyed. I'm now in a position to add to that classification, using the terminology and distinctions in the Austerity Framework. As a heuristic, I divide conceptual engineers into three categories. I'll have more to say about each of these below, but here is the initial characterization:

Topic-improving engineers

The first kind of conceptual engineering starts with an expression that has a certain extension (and intension) and then they try to change the extension either by extending it (in the case of Clark and Chalmers) or narrowing it (as in the case of Carnap). If successful, they end up with an improved intension—where an improved intension for F is understood as *a better way to talk about Fs*. But, crucially, they don't thereby change the topic. Topic preservation is what Carnap aimed for, it's what Clark and Chalmers aim for, it's the goal of Railton's naturalistic project in moral philosophy and some of Haslanger's work on race and gender concepts. It's also likely to be a fair description of what happened with 'salad': for various reasons (best known to people who think carefully about salad-related issues and their histories) it is better to talk about salad in the broader way where dishes of chopped fresh fruit are salads. This is the kind of conceptual engineer that, if she takes her task seriously, will worry a great deal about the Strawsonian objection and the limits of revision.

Semantic engineers

This is the kind of conceptual engineer whose focus is on the kind of semantic defects discussed in chapter 8: there I outline how the metasemantics can fail to generate a semantic value in the way it is supposed to do (see, e.g., 8.2.1 and 8.3). In chapter 8 I explained why it is not right to describe this as resulting in an 'inconsistent concept'. That is not to say there is no deficiency generated in such cases. We can describe it as a 'semantic defect' insofar as the metasemantics failed to do its job of generating a proper semantic value for the expression.

Lexical effect-exploiting engineers (aka exploiters)

These are the 'bad boys' of conceptual engineering: their primary focus is not on the content of speech, but on the lexical effects of the expressions they use—a change in topic (and discontinuity of inquiry) isn't, for such engineers, a fatal flaw. They're happy as long as the lexical effects kick in as expected. At the end of chapter 11 I argued that if you put a high value on communication as a device for exchange of ideas, then you should shun this strategy.

From a practical, non-theoretical point of view, there isn't always a sharp distinction between these three kinds of engineers. These aren't distinctions that those who engage in the activity have articulated to themselves—they're unlikely to come up with one of these positions if asked what they were doing. These positions are my theoretical reconstructions of what is going on. Some philosophers may employ different strategies for different cases, and some instances of conceptual revision will mix the three strategies.

When is conceptual engineering worth doing? The answer will depend in part on whether the focus is on topic, semantic, or lexical engineering.

1. For topic-preserving engineers conceptual engineering is worth doing when there is some kind of deficiency in the original intension of an expression. The supposed deficiencies are varied: for Carnap it is vagueness and indeterminacy, for Haslanger it is the political effects of current gender and race classifications, for revisionists about truth it is the generation of paradoxes. According to Clark and Chalmers, the original concept of belief is shallow, fragmented, and not sufficiently useful in explanation. According to Railton, in our ordinary language moral concepts fail to integrate smoothly with his favored form of naturalism. For those who advocate a change in 'marriage', the problem is that the old, traditional extension had unfair

political and personal effects on a group of people. And so it goes. Most of these cases have something in common—*they are efforts to find a better way to talk about Fs.*

2. For semantic engineers, conceptual engineering is worth doing when encountering an expression that is <u>*semantically* defective</u> (where this is understood as in chapter 8). 'Semantically' in the previous sentence is italicized because that marks the difference between the semantic engineers and the topic-improving engineers. The latter don't start out with an extension they think is semantically defective. They start out with an extension that's not a good way to talk about a topic. Semantic engineers think that a particular semantic defect (or set of defects) is undesirable for some reason and then they try to fix it. Typically, the fix is for some particular conversational purpose or for the purpose of some particular inquiry. If, for example, you agree with van Inwagen that 'freedom' is defective, then one aim you can have as a philosopher is to ameliorate it—you've noticed that many or all of those using the expression 'freedom' have gone wrong because of this defect and you develop a strategy for amelioration. If, like Carnap and Cappelen (2013), you think that many important terms are meaningless (they have no semantic foundation—they're empty and give rise to empty thoughts), then you might want to find strategies for making those expressions meaningful.

3. For lexical effect-exploiting engineers, conceptual engineering is worth doing because exploiting the lexical effect(s) associated with a particular word can help you achieve some desirable effect, and the value of that effect outweighs the risks. At the end of chapter 11 I argued that, in general, non-topic-preserving engineering is a bad idea and that if you value communication, you should shun this kind of lexical engineering. I also mentioned that not everyone shares my values—some value communication less and so that argument wouldn't move them. Indeed, as a matter of fact, I think the exploitation of lexical effects plays an important role in many conceptual engineering projects. (I also think most of those who exploit lexical effects don't do so knowingly—see the point about Anti-Luminosity in chapter 7, section 7.5.)

13.2 The Interconnections between the Three Varieties of Conceptual Engineering

The distinctions above are theoretical reconstructions using my theoretical vocabulary, and no particular instance of actual conceptual engineering will neatly fit into only one of the categories. There will typically be elements of each kind going on simultaneously. That said, here are some salient questions triggered by that rough division:

1. Can those engaging in semantic engineering also be doing topic engineering?
2. Can those who engage in lexical exploitation also be doing topic and semantic engineering (assuming we have a clear idea of the connection between the latter two)?
3. What are the criteria for doing either of these well? What counts as success?

I have a reasonably good grip on 2, but much less of a clear sense of what to say in response to 1 and 3. First, some possible answers to 1:

1a.   When there's a semantic defect, there is no topic there and so no room for topic engineering.
1b.   Semantically defective expressions still have topics, so the two kinds of engineering will go hand in hand.
1c.   Some semantic deficiencies exclude there being a topic, but other semantic deficiencies don't. So in some cases the two kinds of engineering will go hand in hand, but not in others.
1d.   Semantic deficiencies come in degrees and whether there is a topic there or not also comes in degrees. So whether one can engage in the two kinds of engineering simultaneously is a matter of degree: the two can coexist more or less.

The Austerity Framework leaves all of 1a–1d as live options. The reader will have noticed that I haven't given a very detailed account of any specific defects here: the framework is compatible with many ways of understanding specific semantic deficiencies (I don't, for example, have an account of whether and how 'freedom' or 'truth' are defective). My default assumption is that either 1c or 1d is correct, but nothing in what follows depends on that assumption.

In response to question 2, the answer is a clear 'yes'. Lexical exploiters can and often are also topic engineers and semantic defect engineers. To a certain extent we might be exploiting lexical effects whenever we use language. The positive answer to 2 above is just a corollary of that.

A range of answers to question 3 are compatible with the Austerity Framework. Here are some of the complexities: What counts as *semantic* success or improvement will depend a great deal on the details of the metasemantics. It, in a way, is the effort to tell us what counts as having a semantic value. On my view, metasemantics is inscrutable and so we're unlikely to have a good grasp of what counts as success in improvement. Even if you're convinced you know what the current metasemantics is, it can change in the future (since, as I argued in chapter 6, the metasemantics for a term can also be in flux and up for negoti-ation). Suppose you're not on board with any of this: you think you've got a good grasp of what the metasemantics for an expression E is, and you deny that the metasemantics can change. Then you need to know what counts as a successful implementation of a particular effort to effect change. That's a very significant further step and requires knowledge of very detailed empirical facts about usage in the past, dispositions, mental states of speakers, and so on. Again, gathering those facts and then using them to assess a particular instance is unlikely to be a matter of just implementing an algorithm—there will be judgment calls along the way. What counts as successful topic and lexical engineering is, if possible, even more amorphous. As I said above, it will depend in large part on the particular topic, the particular lexical effects, and the aims of the amelioration. Again, there's not going to be a set of informative necessary and sufficient conditions for success.

13.3 How Does a Theory of Conceptual Engineering Fit into an Overall Theory of Language and Communication?

Suppose the above is—in admittedly rough outline—a good framework for thinking about conceptual engineering. What does it tell us about language and communication generally? What, if anything, does it tell us about philosophy? The Austerity Framework is in part conservative and in part radical. I address these elements of the view in turn.

13.3.1 Conservative elements of the proposal

Most obviously, the Austerity Framework contains no new theoretical elements. The ingredients are all familiar. None of them are introduced specifically to account for conceptual engineering. Many alternative accounts introduce what I take to be mysterious and redundant theoretical entities (I discuss some of these in chapters 15 and 16). I don't rely on the assumption that speakers constantly make up micro-languages on the fly as Ludlow does (Ludlow 2014). Other views rely on assumptions that are inconsistent with even moderate forms of external-ism. The little dash of externalism that the Austerity Framework includes might be controversial in a few quarters, but it's far from radical or extreme. That samesaying and topic continuity are more coarse-grained than extensions and intensions should come as no surprise and is argued for based on data that is totally unrelated to conceptual engineering. Lexical effects haven't been much discussed, but the existence of this kind of effect should be fairly uncontroversial, and here too the arguments for lexical effects are unrelated to anything that has specifically to do with conceptual engineering. Plunkett, Sundell, and Ludlow all assume that the logical form of much of our speech is metalinguistic—that despite appearances and our lack of awareness, much ordinary non-linguistic discourse refers to the words being used, and talks about them (Ludlow 2014: 4, Plunkett and Sundell 2013). They assume that people who think they are talking about the non-linguistic world are really doing something very different. My view avoids making that assumption (and in the next chapter I explain why that's a good thing.) In sum: the Austerity Framework relies on fairly uncontroversial theoretical claims that are gathered from other domains, and can claim justification from those domains.

13.3.2 Radical elements of the proposal

On the other hand, the proposed framework is radical along two dimensions. *First*, according to the account given above, there's a real possibility that many or most of our representational devices are defective. It is hard to overemphasize the significance of this. It's a thought that, if you take it seriously, will change the way you approach all your talking and thinking. We tend to be complacent and trust in our representational devices. According to the view proposed here, that's a mistake: we should all be representational skeptics.

The recognition that there's likely to be widespread representational deficiencies makes it hard to get on with the real task of thinking: thinking constantly becomes self-reflective. When the representational non-sceptic reflects on a question, she just starts looking for an answer, compares alternative answers, looks for evidence, reasons, and arguments in favor of one answer over another. The representational sceptic, on the other hand, holds you back. She tells you: before you even start down that road, make sure the devices you use for articulating the question and the answers are up to the task.

Second, as a corollary of the first point there are some philosophical questions that come to the forefront: what are representational deficiencies? How can they be detected? How can such deficiencies be remedied? These are, at least from a certain perspective, the most fundamental questions of philosophy. Again, I find the passage from Rorty I quoted earlier suggestive of this point of view:

[P]hilosophy is the greatest game of all precisely because it is the game of "changing the rules." This game can be won by attending to the patterns by which these rules are changed, and formulating rules in terms of which to judge changes of rules. Those who take this view hold that philosophy in the old style—philosophy as "metaphysics, epistemology, and axiology"—needs to be replaced by metaphilosophy. Members of this school are, as it were, the metaphilosopher's metaphilosophers: since any metaphysical, epistemological, or axiological arguments can be defeated by redefinition, nothing remains but to make a virtue of necessity and to study this process of redefinition itself.

(Rorty 1961: 301)

Of course, Rorty didn't say this in the context of endorsing my theory of conceptual engineering—he went on to use these points for somewhat tangential purposes. That said, this passage is suggestive if you take his 'redefinition' to involve a kind of conceptual engineering. So understood, what Rorty says is that philosophy involves a continuous process of conceptual engineering and reflection on the nature of such engineering.[1]

---

[1] One point I would add to Rorty's characterization is that the process of redefinition itself is constantly being redefined—it isn't a stable process.

14

Objections, Replies, and Clarifications

That more or less completes the presentation of the Austerity Framework. Many aspects of that view will raise questions and in this chapter I briefly discuss seven objections or concerns that I have encountered while presenting this view:

  (i) The Old Problem Problem from Patrick Greenough
 (ii) Lack of precise articulation of externalism
(iii) The allegedly unified aversion of concepts
 (iv) Lack of a precise definition of 'control'
  (v) Lack of engagement of the implications of meaning holism
 (vi) How what I have said applies to thoughts
(vii) What to say about the possibility that our expressions are getting worse—that we are degenerating.

I should warn right away that I'm not quite sure what to say about some of these issues and my views are quite tentative.

14.1 The Old Problem Problem

Patrick Greenough (MS) raises what he calls 'The Old Problem Problem'. Suppose at time t we reflect on a question of the form: *Are Fs G?* Suppose 'F' undergoes revision/amelioration of the kind described in previous chapters and so now at t* (post-amelioration), we have a solution: *Fs are not Gs*. But is this statement an answer to the old question? On my view, there's topic continuity and the sentence post-amelioration expresses an answer to the question asked at t. I also say that those asking *Are Fs Gs?* at t* are asking the same question as those using that sentence at t. This is where the Old Problem Problem comes in. The semantic content of 'Are Fs Gs?' at t is not the same as it is at t*. And so there is a sense in which the answer at t* isn't an answer to the old question. We're just addressing what is in effect a new problem. We have made no progress.

Reply: It's true that we theorists can see that there's change in the semantic content of the question from t to t* and that the semantic content of the reply as expressed as t* might not be a reply to the semantic content as expressed at t. So there's a sense in which we haven't answered the semantic content of the original question. But just as an assertion says more than its semantic content, so there is more to a question than the semantic content of the sentence used to express it. What we have done is answer an improved version of that question—the right way to ask the question *Are Fs Gs?* We've answered an improved version of the question and left the old version behind, so to speak. And that's progress. If things have gone well—if the revision of *F* has been for the better—this is significant intellectual progress.

14.2 Externalism

One might worry that the externalist ideas developed above don't really constitute a theory—it's just a mishmash of fragments from different views—and there's not even a defense of those messy fragments. I have taken a bit from Kripke, a bit from Putnam, a bit from Burge, a bit from Williamson, and bits from Dorr and Hawthorne. I've argued for none this. I haven't defended it against familiar objections. I haven't put it together into a unified metasemantic theory. I haven't given you a set of necessary and sufficient conditions for anything so if that's what a theory is, I have no theory.

Reply: Guilty as charged, but I think it's okay. Arguments have to start somewhere and build on previous work. This book starts in an externalist neighborhood, but it doesn't matter much exactly where in that neighborhood it starts. Besides, this isn't an area where anyone comes up with necessary and sufficient conditions for anything. Kripke famously says he's not presenting a theory, that he doesn't believe in giving reductive necessary and sufficient metasemantic conditions. I agree that this is an illegitimate aim in this domain. If that were the standard for having a theory, then no one has a theory. Asking for that is asking too much. You can legitimately ask for more than what I have given you, but to include that in this book would have led us off topic and turned this book into a book on metasemantics. I don't think the details of how those fragments are incorporated will matter much for the points I've made.

14.3 Why This Aversion to Concepts?

There are lots of arguments for why we need concepts. There are familiar arguments for Fregean senses (arguments from opacity, informative identity statements, empty names, etc.). There are arguments for why an appeal to just extensions and intensions won't connect semantic content to action (and action motivation) in the right way. There's a plethora of other arguments for why we need some level of content in addition to just the bare minimum of extensions and intensions. I have not engaged with any of those arguments, but I still claim that a virtue of the Austerity Framework is that it can do without concepts. Why present that as a virtue when we need concepts anyway?

Reply: Twofold reply. (i) The first part of my reply is that I've made two assumptions throughout: (a) The cases of conceptual engineering that I aim to account for involve changes in extensions and intension; (b) Some version of an externalist metasemantics is true. If you're on board with (a) + (b), then it really doesn't matter much what other additional views you might have about concepts and their explanatory role. For example, Inscrutability and Lack of Control rely on those assumptions alone. What I say about topic continuity is largely untouched by additional views about concepts (though some of those views might be articulated differently by someone who thinks concepts play an important explanatory role). (ii) This second part of the reply is both programmatic and more substantive: I'm unmoved by any of the standard arguments for concepts. I don't think they perform any constructive theoretical work. There are very many different theories of what concepts are and each of these are deeply problematic in their own peculiar ways. As a corollary, any effort to place a particular theory of concepts at the center of a theory of conceptual engineering will make that theory parochial and hostage to a whole array of difficulties. To give a full-scale defense of what I just said would go beyond the scope of this book (though it's worth noting that others have done much of that work already, see e.g., Machery (2009)), but at least it gives a sense of some of the motivation behind the Austerity Framework.

14.4 No Precise Definition of 'Control'

A point that came up frequently when presenting this material is that I lack a precise definition of 'control'. I made a big point of criticizing conceptual engineers who think their talking and writing can in significant ways have an impact on semantic changes, but I didn't define 'impact' and said nothing about what I mean by 'control' when I say they lack control. I also made some provocative (and somewhat irrelevant) side-claims about how we are not in control (and don't understand the underlying mechanisms) of large-scale social changes. I say that while we love to reflect on how our social structures, for example, should and could be improved, these are not processes we have any significant degree of control over. Again, in saying that, I didn't define 'control', 'significant', or 'impact'.

Reply: So what? 'Significant', 'impact', and 'control' are all perfectly respectable English words. I trust readers to understand them. There are no doubt senses of 'control' different to that which I intend but those are not the ones that I use.

But shouldn't we be sheptical? And HC's "intended" meaning?

14.5 What about Meaning Holism?

The entire presentation so far has focused on single expressions and their extensions and intensions. There has been little focus on the interconnections between expressions. Won't changing 'woman' have implications for 'mother' and 'aunt' and 'sister' and 'family' and indefinitely many expressions? If the meaning of 'freedom' changes, what's the implication for 'responsible' and all other terms that in some significant sense rely on or are connected to 'freedom'? At a very general level it would be useful to know what these interconnections are.

Reply: Good point. There will no doubt be such interconnections. They will be many and complex. Your view of this will depend on your take on the atomism-molecularism-holism debate.[1] This book isn't the place to rehash that debate. Suffice it to say that this will add weight to my claims about the process being incomprehensible and inscrutable: if you were to succeed in changing the extension and intension of, say, 'woman', the implications for other parts of language would most likely be massive. They would also be not calculable or predictable.

14.6 What about Thoughts?

So far, this has been very language-focused. I've talked about expressions and avoided talk of concepts. What about *thought*? Shouldn't conceptual engineering also improve thought? When the focus is on thought, what are the categories analogous to the extension and intension of expressions?

Reply: This book is non-committal and neutral about the transition between language and thought. I hope that whatever view you have of thoughts can incorporate my view of conceptual engineering in language. This will be easiest if your view of thought is some version of the representational theory of the mind. However, there are a plethora of alternatives to this view and there are also many versions of the representational theory. This book is the beginning of a research project, not the end. For those sympathetic to a version of the view of conceptual engineering of language proposed here, the extension to pure thought is an important further research project.

---

[1] For an overview of this debate, see Fodor and Lepore 1992.

14.7 Why No Focus on Conceptual Degeneration?

Much of the literature I've used as my starting point has a kind of sanguine tone built into it: conceptual engineering is a process of amelioration. But do we have any reason to think these very same processes can't be used for evil? Couldn't engineering projects take us backwards? Given my insistence on inscrutability and lack of control, how would we ever know?

Reply: Throughout this book I try to abstain from making normative claims. I notice the authors I use as my starting point/data point make many normative claims and I've presented a framework to help make sense of that. My own view is one of agnosticism with respect to these various normative claims. Everything said in the imagined objection is right: conceptual engineering *could* be used for evil as well as for good—and it's extremely hard to tell them apart. The fact that conceptual engineering is inscrutable and out of our control means that it is also possible (sometimes I think even likely) that those who try to achieve good ends through conceptual engineering will end up causing harms they didn't intend. We have no prima facie reason to think the process is typically one that leads to amelioration rather than degeneration.

PART V

Compare and Contrast: Alternative Accounts of Conceptual Engineering

There are a plethora of alternative approaches to conceptual engineering. Many of these are embedded in different theories about language, concepts, semantics, pragmatics, and communication. In these remaining chapters I (too) briefly discuss some of these. In many cases, the overall theoretical frameworks are so different that comparison is hard, but I have tried to isolate various features that both illuminate aspects of my own theory and make at least partial comparison possible.

Here is the plan: I first discuss Ludlow, and Plunkett and Sundell, and Barker on micro-languages and metalinguistic negotiation (Chapter 15). I then consider Haslanger and others who think an appeal to the 'function' or 'purpose' or 'point' of concepts should play an important role when thinking about conceptual engineering (Chapter 16). Chapter 17 discusses the relation between Chalmers's subscript gambit and the Austerity Framework. Chapter 18 picks up some themes from Chalmers and Eklund on the limits of revision, revisiting some of the themes from Part III.

15

Metalinguistic Negotiation

This chapter brings together some themes from Ludlow's writings on what he calls the 'dynamic lexicon' (Ludlow 2014) and connects them with Plunkett and Sundell's work on metalinguistic negotiation (Plunkett and Sundell 2013). These authors present views on conceptual engineering that are either incompatible with aspects of the Austerity Framework or make claims about conceptual engineering that go beyond that framework. I'll argue that these proposals don't help us understand conceptual engineering.

15.1 Ludlow on Linguistic Negotiation over Micro-Languages

Peter Ludlow's book *Living Words* (Ludlow 2014) presents a view of language and communication that will strike many as congenial to the project of conceptual engineering. It's a book filled with engaging and instructive examples of what (at least look like) cases of conceptual engineering and an easy to grasp framework for understanding those cases. Here's a brief summary of some central and relevant aspects of Ludlow's picture.

Ludlow starts with observations of what he calls 'the extreme context sensitivity of language'. He rejects the idea that languages are stable abstract objects that we learn and then use. According to Ludlow, human languages are things that we build on a conversation-by-conversation basis—he calls them 'micro-languages'. He rejects the idea that words have stable and fixed meanings that we can come to learn. According to Ludlow, word meanings are dynamic and massively underdetermined. Shifts of meaning do not just occur between conversations, they also occur within conversations. At the core of Ludlow's view is a thesis he calls *Meaning Control*:

The doctrine of Meaning Control says that we (and our conversational partners) in principle have control over what our words mean. . . . If our conversational partners are willing to go with us, we can modulate word meanings as we see fit. (Ludlow 2014: 83)

As a matter of autobiography, Ludlow's book has been massively influential in my thinking about these issues. There's a great deal of positive things to be said about it, but this section will focus on some interconnected critical themes: (i) on the face of it, Ludlow's view seems to be inconsistent with my Lack of Control principle. If it is incompatible, then Ludlow's principle is wrong. There is, however, an important qualification to that critical point: I also argue that when Ludlow's view is properly interpreted, he should join me in rejecting the doctrine of Meaning Control. So interpreted, our views are more closely aligned. (ii) His theory of the dynamic lexicon and micro-languages sits uneasily with even moderate forms of externalism. (iii) Ludlow doesn't have enough to say about the continuity of interpretation and inquiry. (iv) The view falsely assumes that we have intentions (and other attitudes) towards micro-languages.

15.2 Comments and Objections

15.2.1 In or out of control?

According to Ludlow's Meaning Control principle, speakers and conversation partners are in joint control of the meaning of the words they use. The idea that we can intentionally control the meaning of our words in collaboration with our conversation partners is the central thesis of Ludlow's book. It's also, in part, what makes the book and the view inspiring and engaging: it gives the impression that meaning modulation is the kind of activity we can understand and get good at.

The doctrine of Meaning Control is either false or very poorly labeled (because properly understood it gives us no control whatsoever). Here are three ways to see that. The first and most obvious reason why Ludlow's view doesn't support Control is built into the very framework: you might be in control of your little momentary micro-language, but the next moment, when a new micro-language evolves, it's all up for grabs again. Even if you have control over the micro-language happening over your kitchen table, you don't have any influence on the conversation taking place next door. Any victory is at best both momentary and restricted (to you and your conversation partners). That's the whole point of what he calls 'Meaning Control': the conversation next door or in the next moment can, and typically will, be remodulated.

Second, note that Meaning Control makes meaning dependent on a group, those Ludlow calls 'conversation partners'. The extent to which any *one* of us is in control will depend on who is included in the group of conversation partners. When I write a book like this one, I'm thinking of people *in the past*, people *in the future*, people *existing now that I will never meet or know about*, and even *possible* people as my conversation partners. (I find that the process of writing a book in large part consists in having conversations with imaginary opponents.) According to the doctrine of Meaning Control, we have control over meaning modulations only insofar as we can get this diverse group to coordinate. That's unlikely to happen (since coordination with people in the past, the future, other possible worlds, and people in this world that you'll never meet is impossible). So even within Ludlow's framework, there's at least the potential for total *lack* of control over meaning modulation. Further, I think that this kind of broad audience is the norm, not the exception. This is especially so in cases where we care about things like meaning modulation. We don't intend for our conversations to be isolated linguistic events, disconnected from what has been said in the past, will be said in the future, or was said in disconnected conversations. Our speech is always continuous with speech in the past (it's a reply to or follow up on something someone said, or it presupposes parts of what has been said in the past)—it's intended for people to think about and talk in the future, it's intended to be passed along to other people, and it's intended for consumption in unpredictable ways. In slogan form: *There's no such thing as conversational solipsism.* With that in mind, the right way to understand 'conversation partners' is extremely broad, and so the doctrine of Meaning Control, properly interpreted, doesn't mean that *we* are in control, because the referent of 'we' is entirely open-ended.

Finally, as I point out in chapter 6, my Lack of Control principle springs out of the version of externalism I defend (where meanings of words depend a range of factors we don't know about and have no control over.) I also point out in that chapter that even internalism fails to secure Control: on most construals of internalism, it leads to Lack of Control at least as directly as externalism does (for this argument, see chapter 7, section 7.1). This last point is illustrated by Ludlow's view. Even if you buy into the picture where there are only micro-languages which are created anew in each context, it in no way follows that *the conversation partners* have control over what happens to their micro-language. The semantic features of a micro-language could supervene on facts about the speakers and their mental states (that, for the sake of argument, we can assume speakers are in control over) and it still wouldn't follow that the speakers are in control of the meaning of their expressions. Meaning Control follows only given certain additional assumptions about the determination relation. What Ludlow also needs is the assumption that speakers are in control over the determination relation, i.e., control over the move from the supervenience base to the semantic values. No argument for that is given in the book—it is asserted that they are in control, but no argument or evidence is given. This isn't to say arguments couldn't be given; I've just never seen any such arguments. So as things stand, Meaning Control is at best seen as a very tentative working hypothesis that needs lots of support to be established—no one has provided that support yet.

15.2.2 Externalism and the dynamic lexicon: uneasy bedfellows

Ludlow's view has a strong anti-externalist flavor. You don't have to be much of an externalist to think that what our words pick out (refer to) at a time, t, isn't determined by what we (the conversation partners) *want* them to pick out at a time t, nor what we think they pick out at t. The extension of 'water' or 'happiness' as Peter uses it at t isn't determined by what Peter wants it to mean at that time, or what he thinks it means. If we had that kind of control over extension and intensions, then even the (mild) versions of externalism I outlined in earlier chapters would have to be abandoned. So the simple objection is this: the Austerity Framework incorporates some plausible moderate externalist assumptions, and Ludlow's view is incompatible with those assumptions.

There's a bit more to say: Ludlow claims his view is *externalism friendly*. He says:

Meaning Control does not exclude the possibility of externalism about content—either environmental externalism or social externalism as in Burge (1979)—nor does it preclude the possibility of a division of linguistic labor as in Putnam (1975). The idea is that it is within our control to defer to others on elements of the meaning of our words (for example, a doctor on the meaning of 'arthritis' and a botanist on the referents of 'beech' and 'elm') and it is also within our control to be receptive to discoveries about the underlying physical structure of the things we refer to (for example, the discovery that 'water' refers to H2O and not XYZ).   (Ludlow 2014: 84)

Here is a way to understand Ludlow's position: his view appeals to a form of *meta*-metasemantic internalism: what makes it the case that externalism is true is that we, in a particular conversational setting, decide that it is. According to Ludlow, if a form of externalism is true for a conversation at a time (or: for a micro-language), that is because the conversational participants (the speakers of that micro-language) want it to be to be true at that time—because they choose (at that time) to defer to whatever external factors the relevant form of external-ism appeals to. It's a corollary of this view that if the speakers of a micro-language decide *not* to defer to any form of externalism, externalism is no longer true about their micro-language. They are free to change the meaning of their words at will. In principle, a group of speakers could be hardcore externalists at one moment and switch to the most radical form of internalism a moment later.

This, however, is not externalism. Externalism as I have understood it—and as it has been understood in the philosophical tradition that springs out of the work of Kripke, Burge, and Putnam—is not the view that conversational partners at any one point in time can just decide that externalist constraints on semantics don't apply. That makes a mockery of all the arguments for first-order external-ism. Consider the kinds of cases that Kripke discuss in *Naming and Necessity*, for example, the Gödel-Schmidt case (Kripke 1980: 83–92). According to Ludlow's form of externalism, Kripke's description of that case (viz., *the speaker is referring to Gödel and has the false belief that he proved incompleteness*) could be made false by the conversational partners deciding to ignore the externalist meta-constraints on meaning. We could, if we thought it convenient, decide on the spur of the moment that the externalist constraints were lifted and so 'Gödel' did refer to Schmidt. Then a moment later we could decide to reintroduce the externalist constraints and reference would switch back again (assuming you could get your conversational partners to go along). But that's not the view in *Naming and Necessity*. Similarly, the only way that Ludlow can work to accom-modate 'Anti-Creed' (see chapter 6, section 6.2) within his picture is by saying that we can decide for a particular conversational purpose to endorse it. We could equally well decide to reject it, if that suits our purpose. But that's not an endorsement of Anti-Creed.

15.2.3 The dynamic lexicon fails to explain communicative continuity and the continuity of inquiry

At several points in this book I have addressed the question of how conceptual engineering is compatible with the continuity of interpretation across contexts, the continuity of communication across contexts, and the continuity of inquiry across contexts (chapter 9 refers to this as 'the continuity data'). Ludlow's framework has no natural languages and no stable meanings. The core theoretical notion is that of micro-languages created on the fly for specific conversational purposes. Such a view has no good account of inter-contextual content stability. Ludlow's book has an almost demonstrative lack of engagement with those kinds of issues. If you are one of those who think explaining such continuity is one of the core tasks of a theory of meaning and of a theory of conceptual engineering, Ludlow's picture simply doesn't have much to offer. Here is an illustration of points made earlier (about continuity in context over time and across contexts):

> Question 1: Is a fetus a person? (see Ludlow 2014 56–64)
> Answer 1: A fetus is not a person. Answer 2: A fetus is a person.
> Question 2: Did Oswald kill Kennedy?
> Answer 1: Yes, Oswald did kill Kennedy. Answer 2: No, Oswald did not kill Kennedy.

People have asked these questions and presented these answers indefinitely many times all over the world in all kind of settings. That's a fact. You the reader can try to answer those questions now. You can understand the questions. You can understand those answers. You can agree with one answer and disagree with the other and in so doing agree or disagree with many other people. You have reasons for your view—reasons that have been presented by others and discussed extensively. I take these claims to be data points.

The crucial point—that is incompatible with Ludlow's view—is that you can do that without (much) knowledge of or reflection on the contexts in which others have asked that question or have given those answers. If Ludlow's view were correct, each utterance of these words has been made in a separate micro-language. There's no stability of extension and intension across contexts and so no prima facie reason to assume that the words mean the same—no prima facie reason to think that all those who ask, 'Is a fetus a person?' is asking the same question and no prima facie reason to assume that those answering, 'Yes, a fetus is a person' are agreeing with each other.

15.2.4 Against the idea that speakers have intentions towards micro-languages

For a moment, I'll put aside the worry from the previous sections and focus on another aspect of Ludlow's view. According to Ludlow, speakers are *intentionally* involved in the shaping of their micro-languages. We can adjust them, we negotiate over them, we build them, we engage in what Ludlow calls *lexical warfare* over them (see Ludlow 2014: C1). Here's an illustration concerning the word 'Hacktivist' (the book is filled with engaging examples like this one):

> There is a conflict between those who want to change the meaning of the word to denote immoral, sinister activities and those who want to defend the broader, more inclusive understanding of 'hacktivist'. (Ludlow 2014: 13)

I want to focus on the intentionalist terminology used to describe these activities. Ludlow aims to describe a kind of activity that people extensively engage in intentionally. Meaning negotiations are something we, according to Ludlow, care about—they matter massively to us. We passionately and reflectively engage in battles over what our words mean. I think this is *doubly false* (i.e., twice as false as just false). By this I mean that the descriptions are ambiguous and both readings are false. Here are the two ways to read Ludlow's descriptions of particular instances of meaning negotiation:

> *Reading 1:* This reading uses Ludlow's terminology to describe the activity ordinary speakers (allegedly) intend to engage in. In other words, speakers are described as caring about (battling over, etc.) the temporary meaning of an expression in a micro-language.

Reading 2:   This reading doesn't use Ludlow's theoretical framework for describing the activity ordinary speakers (allegedly) intend to engage in. Instead, it describes them as being interested in *the meaning of the English word 'hacktivist'*.

In this section I give reasons for thinking that Reading 1 is false and in the next section (the discussion of Plunkett and Sundell's view), I give arguments against Reading 2.

According to Reading 1, ordinary speakers passionately care about micro-languages. They intentionally go about building them, under that description (qua micro-languages), and have battles over them. This is not true because ordinary speakers have no idea that English doesn't exist; they don't know that they build a new micro-language every moment. They don't believe (or know) that they create meanings 'on the fly'. Ordinary speakers conceptualize their own speech as being 'in' natural language. English speakers think they speak *English*. They think 'hacktivist' is a word of English. The only people who believe in micro-languages are Ludlow and a few other philosophers and linguists. The notion of a micro-language plays no role in the intentional mental states of other speakers. A Ludlow-style view has to be accompanied by an error theory of how speakers conceptualize their own communicative abilities and knowledge. But such an error theory sits very poorly with the idea that speakers are passionate about meaning negotiation.

Someone attracted to a Ludlow-style view could try to say this:

Speakers are 'battling over micro-languages' and 'modulating meanings', but not under that description. They do something that has this effect—the effect of changing a micro-language—without being aware of doing it or of the effects of doing it. That description of the activity is compatible with such speakers thinking they are doing something entirely different.

Two comments on this. First, that construal doesn't sit well with Ludlow's intentionalist description of the activity (it's like describing someone who is trying to find Superman and who loves Superman as a person who is trying to find Clark Kent and loves Clark Kent; that's at best a very misleading description).

Second, if we were to make people aware of what they are doing (on analogy with telling them that Clark is Superman), they would lose interest in the activity (like someone who was told that Superman really just is Clark Kent could lose any interest in Superman). And they would be right to do so. It—the activity Ludlow describes—is pointless and something ordinary speakers wouldn't care much about at all. Who cares what a particular expression means in a micro-language when you know that this micro-language will go out of existence in a few seconds or a couple of minutes? Speakers might care about the process under Reading 2 above which has at least this going for it: the change you're trying to implement has a kind of permanence. However, even that reading is problematic, for reasons I go into below, in the discussion of Plunkett and Sundell.

15.3 Plunkett and Sundell on Metalinguistic Negotiation

15.3.1 The view and its relevance

Plunkett and Sundell present their view as building on Ludlow's view but claim to do so without relying on the most radical parts of Ludlow's view.

> Perhaps alone among the philosophers working in this area, Peter Ludlow argues that linguistic communication is pervasively metalinguistic. He argues that nearly all conversations proceed *via* a negotiation over how to use the relevant linguistic expressions. . . . Part of what Ludlow is arguing for is the thesis that metalinguistic disputes are capable of expressing genuine substantive disagreements and that philosophers of language need to pay more attention to these disputes in their construction of theories of the meaning of terms (including normative and evaluative ones). In this respect, Ludlow is arguing for much the same thesis that we are. However, there is an important difference between Ludlow and us. Ludlow reaches his conclusion by arguing for a view of language—a view he calls the *dynamic lexicon*—that will strike many philosophers as quite radical. On Ludlow's picture, almost all linguistic communication involves conversation-specific settling of antecedently *highly* underspecified meanings. We are sympathetic to Ludlow's view. *However, in this paper, we aim to demonstrate that the metalinguistic analysis of normative and evaluative disputes is consistent with, and indeed highly plausible on, entirely mainstream views of linguistic communication.* In this respect, our argumentative strategy marks a significant departure from the one that Ludlow is currently pursuing.
>
> (Plunkett and Sundell 2013: 4 n. 11, italics added)

So we can think of Plunkett and Sundell as a version of Ludlow without the heavy theoretical baggage. Since I have argued against that baggage, this sounds promising. If Plunkett and Sundell can make something like Ludlow's view compatible with 'entirely mainstream views of linguistic communication', at least some of the objections to Ludlow would be irrelevant.

One of the central ideas in Plunkett and Sundell 2013 and Plunkett 2015 is that a great deal of philosophical and non-philosophical talk concerns how words should be defined—they call that 'metalinguistic negotiation'. It is a natural thought that a theory of conceptual engineering should include an account of that phenomenon. The goal of this chapter is to explain why the Austerity Framework steers clear of it.

Plunkett and Sundell start by describing scenarios like the following: A utters 'Fa' and B utters 'not Fa'. They mean different things by 'F'. However, they still disagree and someone observing the conversation would rightly judge that they disagree. Plunkett and Sundell have an explanation for this disagreement: it is because A and B each pragmatically communicate another content which they disagree over. At first level, what A pragmatically communicates is that the word 'F' should have definition D, and what B pragmatically communicates is that word 'F' should not have definition D, but instead have definition D*. A and B have what Plunkett and Sundell call a 'metalinguistic disagreement'. They disagree about what words *should mean*. This in turn reflects another disagreement. According to Plunkett and Sundell the reason why A and B care about the definition of words is because they care about which words should play which functional roles.

Here is an illustration (Plunkett and Sundell 2013: 19, examples 6a and 6b):

A: waterboarding is not torture
B: waterboarding is torture

They imagine a scenario where A and B mean different things by the words 'torture'. According to Plunkett and Sundell, at the level of literal content there's no disagreement. However, there is a metalinguistic disagreement:

Even if we suppose that the speakers mean different things by the word 'torture', it is clear that we have not exhausted the normative and evaluative work to be done here. After all, in the context of discussions about the moral or legal issues surrounding the treatment of prisoners, there is a substantive question about which definition is better. By employing the word 'torture' in a way that excludes waterboarding, the speaker of B communicates (though not via literal expression) the view that such a usage is appropriate to those moral or legal discussions.

(Plunkett and Sundell 2013: 19)

They say that what motivates the disagreement over the definition of the English term is disagreement over "which concept is best suited to play a certain functional role in thought and practice" (Plunkett and Sundell 2013: 21). They describe this disagreement as follows:

There is the distinctive linguistic mechanism—metalinguistic usage—and a distinctive normative topic—a topic within what we have called 'conceptual ethics'. On our proposal, Bob and Chris's disagreement concerns which concept to express with the term 'morally right'. Our proposal is that they each advocate a view about which concept is best suited to play a certain functional role in thought and practice, a role that includes matters of how to treat others, what to hold each other responsible for doing, and how to live more generally.

(Plunkett and Sundell 2013: 3)

How does talking about the definitions of words help express that disagreement? Here is the closest I could get to an answer:

> One reason that Bob and Chris want their preferred concept to be the one expressed by the term 'morally right' is because they each believe (correctly) that whatever is called 'morally right' will likely play this role, and that people who think that 'morally right' should mean something different have a different view about what concept should play this functional role.   (Plunkett and Sundell 2013: 21)

In sum, Plunkett and Sundell imagine a series of scenarios in which there are three levels of content: the literal content (where there is no disagreement), the pragmatically communicated claim about how a specific word should be defined (here there is a disagreement), and finally another pragmatically communicated content about which functional role should be played by which concept (the conversation partners disagree also over this). *Disagree about def^n and which is best*

15.3.2 Comparison with the Austerity Framework

What follows will engage with Plunkett and Sundell only at a fairly high level of abstraction. The details of their view are hard to assess, in part because the view relies on a number of ideas that are not fully developed. In particular:

- We are not told what Plunkett and Sundell think concepts are;
- We are not told what it is for a concept to have a function (and we're given no arguments for the view that they have functions, we're not told how to pair functions with concepts, etc.);
- We are not told what pragmatic mechanisms get us from the literal content (where there's no disagreement) to the disagreement over how words should be used or defined;
- We are not told what communicative mechanism takes us from the pragmatically communicated disagreement over how words should be defined to another pragmatically communicated disagreement over which concepts should play which functional role.[1]

So there are a number of promissory notes in Plunkett and Sundell's work (I expect much of this will be elaborated on in their forthcoming book (Plunkett and Sundell forthcoming)). The goal in what follows is primarily to highlight various respects in which the Austerity Framework is significantly different from

---

[1] Another way to put this last point: we've not been told how to identify the content of this disagreement. Maybe it doesn't need to be communicated through pragmatic principles, but as theorists we need to be able describe the mechanism(s) that generate metalinguistic disagreement and that is more or less entirely missing from Plunkett and Sundell's account.

the Plunkett and Sundell framework and to point out what I see as advantages of my framework.

15.4 Against Metalinguistic Negotiation

15.4.1 Against metalinguistic negotiation (1): it's (something like) a category mistake

Can't we dispute them?
then.

It is something like a category mistake to think that word meanings are negotiated. We can no more negotiate meanings than we can negotiate overpopulation in India or starvation in Africa. Negotiation is the wrong category. Those are things we can think about and discuss, but they can't be negotiated. I take that to be a more or less direct corollary of the points about externalism made in Part II.

Another way to put this point is that the view inherits some of Ludlow's difficulties in accounting for externalism. Above I argued that externalists should be concerned about Ludlow's reliance on micro-languages. There are closely related concerns about the notion of 'meaning negotiation', as it is used by Plunkett and Sundell. Suppose you think metalinguistic negotiation is both real (it happens), it happens quite a bit (it's not a once-in-a-lifetime kind of thing), and it's genuinely significant: it has important effects. This combination of views is incompatible with externalism. The view presupposes that we have a level of control over meanings that we in fact do not have. They assume that a couple of people have power to change the meanings of the words they use. They don't. This talk of negotiation is reminiscent of Ludlow's appeal to micro-languages, and shows that the Ludlowian influence runs very deep in Plunkett and Sundell's work.[2] They haven't quite managed to develop a version of the view that is consistent with "entirely mainstream views of linguistic communication" (Plunkett and Sundell 2013: 4 n. 11).

There is a less ambitious version of their view that doesn't have this particular problem. Most people in the world haven't and never will read Part II of this book and they haven't thought about conceptual engineering. So maybe they're under the illusion that meanings can be negotiated. Maybe we can recast the talk of metalinguistic negotiation in an error-theoretic way: speakers *think* they can negotiate word meanings, they *want* to do it, and so they *try*. They'll never succeed, but that's a discovery and not something they're aware of. This version

---

[2] Note that this 'objection from externalism' is different from the one they discuss in section 6 of Plunkett and Sundell 2013. The objection they there consider is whether externalism undermines the claim that the conversation partners mean different things by, e.g., 'torture'. That's not what I'm questioning here.

of Plunkett and Sundell's view assumes that we care about the meanings of words. The next section raises some concerns about that assumption.

15.4.2 Against metalinguistic negotiation (2): people care about torture (and what it is or should be), not about the meaning of the concatenation of seven letters that make up 'torture'

Unlike Ludlow, Plunkett and Sundell don't take words to be in micro-languages. They think that what we care about are words in English, e.g., the English word 'torture'. Those who discuss whether waterboarding is torture, in the kinds of settings that Plunkett and Sundell describe, are, according to them, interested in how to define a specific English word. What follows are some reasons for doubting that:

Evidence that speakers don't care about the definition of specific English words: Speakers in the kinds of conversations Plunkett and Sundell use as their prime illustrations don't think their concerns and arguments are irrelevant to someone who speaks, say, Icelandic, Chinese, or Russian. One way to see this is to note that they will take themselves to be agreeing and disagreeing with those talking about the same issue in one of those other languages. Suppose a speaker of Icelandic says:

Waterboarding er ekki pyndingum.

As Plunkett and Sundell see it, this speaker is engaged in a discussion of the word 'pyndingum'. A Chinese speaker using a cognate sentence to engage in metalinguistic negotiation would be engaged in a discussion of:

拷打

and a Russian speaker would be talking about how to define:

Пытки.

So there should be no disagreement between the English, Icelandic, Chinese, and Russian speakers. They are, after all, talking about how to define different words. That's a misdescription of these situations: there is dis/agreement between speakers of different languages. It doesn't matter what language they speak. So disagreement over whether waterboarding is torture (in the relevant kinds of conversations) isn't best construed as disagreement over how to define a word in a particular language.

There's another way to see the point. Consider a passionate discussion of whether waterboarding is torture (in the kind of setting Plunkett and Sundell imagine). Suppose someone suggests that we stop using the string of letters 'torture'—and instead start using a new string, say, 'torrture**'. If Plunkett and Sundell were right, this would be a relevant proposal—one that would be of massive significance to the ongoing discussion. However, the proposal is completely irrelevant. In response to this suggestion, the participants would *not* respond:

Oh, very interesting. If we were to do that, we would be using a new word and I don't have strong views about how it should be defined. I was just talking about 'torture'—I have no view whatsoever about other strings, such as 'torrture**'.

The reason why they would not react like this is that their debate, and their disagreement, is independent of how particular words are used. It's about torture, not 'torture'.

A natural thought here is that Plunkett and Sundell could liberate their view from this focus on specific lexical items if it appealed to translations. Maybe an improved version of their view has it that what the speakers disagree over are *all* the lexical items that are translations of 'torture' into some language other than English. If the speakers make a claim about all those words, then we would guarantee disagreement between speakers of different languages and the objection above would be circumvented. However, this isn't a move available to Plunkett and Sundell. Recall that it's crucial that in their examples the speakers disagree about the meaning of the word and use the word with different meanings. In such settings it won't work to appeal to the idea of translation. We have to choose which meaning to translate from—if we pick two different meanings, then they won't be picking out the same set of expressions. If we pick the same one, we will bias the debate in favor of one speaker.

Note that the Austerity Framework gets these cases right. On the view I have proposed in the previous chapters, the speakers in Plunkett and Sundell's scenarios can be described as follows:

They disagree over whether waterboarding is torture.

How can they differ except metalinguistically.

This can be true even when the semantic values of 'torture' differ in their respective utterances. You get that result from incorporating an account of topic continuity and samesaying into the framework for thinking about conceptual engineering. The Austerity Framework can thus explain the data that Plunkett and Sundell aim to describe without assuming that some still to be specified pragmatic mechanism enables us to generate competing metalinguistic claims.

15.4.3 Why there is no disagreement over which concept should perform a certain function

As I mentioned above, there's a third level of content in Plunkett and Sundell's view. It concerns disagreement over which concept should perform a certain function. Here they use 'morally right' as their example:

There is the distinctive linguistic mechanism—metalinguistic usage—and a distinctive normative topic—a topic within what we have called 'conceptual ethics'. On our proposal, Bob and Chris's disagreement concerns which concept to express with the term 'morally right'. Our proposal is that *they each advocate a view about which concept is best suited to play a certain functional role in thought and practice,* a role that includes matters of how to treat others, what to hold each other responsible for doing, and how to live more generally.   (Plunkett and Sundell 2013: 21, italics added)

How do we get from a conversation about the definition of words to a discussion about concepts and functions? They say:

One reason that Bob and Chris want their preferred concept to be the one expressed by the term 'morally right' is because they each believe (correctly) that whatever is called 'morally right' will likely play this role, and that people who think that 'morally right' should mean something different have a different view about what concept should play this functional role.   (Plunkett and Sundell 2013: 21)

In order to assess this view and compare its virtues with those of the Austerity Framework it would help to be told what concepts are and what it is for them to have functions. It is an advantage of the Austerity Framework that it need not answer those questions. Plunkett and Sundell take on a burden that I'm free of. But for now, I'll put that aside. Suppose you believe in concepts and you think they can have functions. There's still a massive gap to fill here: how do two speakers in the kinds of conversations Plunkett and Sundell discuss manage to pragmatically communicate something *about the very same function*? They are not explicitly discussing functions. They are not, if they are normal speakers, thinking explicitly about the functions that concepts have and should have. So it's mysterious, to put it mildly, how the pragmatic mechanism manages to secure a focus on the same function for two conversation partners.

Plunkett and Sundell are not entirely silent on this. According to Plunkett and Sundell, speakers make the following assumption, which I'll call the Transitional Assumption:

Transitional Assumption (TA):   "they [the conversational participants] each believe (correctly) that whatever is called 'morally right' will likely play this role" (Plunkett and Sundell 2013: 21).

As Plunkett and Sundell see things, speakers assume that a certain string of letters, 'morally right', is likely to play a certain functional role. It's hard to assess that claim. We *could* change the meaning of 'morally right' so that means the same as 'more or less morally right'. Then it would not play the role that Plunkett and Sundell suppose is currently associated with it. But, say Plunkett and Sundell, that's not a likely development. But what are the likely developments and how do we assess their relative likelihood? Answering those questions (and so assessing TA) is particularly difficult in the context of the kinds of debates Plunkett and Sundell imagine the conversational participants being engaged in. This is a process where there's active negotiation over the meanings of words and one of the salient options in that kind of debate is linguistic innovation. In such settings it seems like question begging to assume that there will be stability in the functional role of particular strings of letters.

The point I just made can be illustrated by Chalmers' proposal (discussed in the next chapter) that in situations like this, the thing to do is to get rid of the old expression and introduce a series of new expressions with subscripts, for example: 'Morally right$_1$', and 'Morally right$_2$', each denoting different properties. If some version of that strategy wins out, then 'morally right' won't perform the relevant function. Is it unlikely that Chalmers's strategy wins and the string 'morally right' ends up being abandoned and useless? I have no idea. I guess it depends on which philosopher wins, or what linguistic developments happen for complex and largely unpredictable reasons. But in a context of where people are actively trying to change language and have different strategies for how to do it, it is particularly hard to know how likely it is for particular strings to end up with certain roles. In sum, it's simply unfounded, and potentially question-begging, to assume that one function (now assuming you believe in such things) is likely to be played by the string 'morally right'.[3]

15.4.4 Final remark on metalinguistic negotiation: why Barker's motivating example is misleading

Ludlow, Plunkett and Sundell, Sundell, and many others like to appeal to Barker's 2002 paper 'The Dynamics of Vagueness' in support of the view that we often engage in metalinguistic negotiation. When I present my objections to Ludlow, Plunkett, and Sundell, I often get the question of whether they can't just defer to Barker: hasn't he *proved* that metalinguistic discourse of the relevant kind is ubiquitous? The answer is that he did no such thing and that that paper provides no support for their views.

Here's the passage that's often cited by those who talk about metalinguistic negotiation:

Imagine that we are at a party. Perhaps Feynman stands before us a short distance away, . . . the exact degree to which Feynman is tall is common knowledge. You ask me what counts

---

[3] Chapter 11 discusses the significance of lexical effects and the connection between lexical effects and genuine conceptual engineering. The latter does and the former does not involve changes in extension and intension of an expression. I suspect that a great deal of what Plunkett and Sundell have in mind can be re-expressed by appealing to lexical effects.

as tall in my country. "Well," I say, around here...and I continue by uttering (1) [Feynman is tall]. This is not a descriptive use in the usual sense. I have not provided any new information about the world, or at least no new information about Feynman's height. In fact, assuming that *tall* means roughly 'having a maximal degree of height greater than a certain contextually-supplied standard', I haven't even provided you with any new information about the truth conditions of the word *tall*. All I have done is given you guidance concerning what the prevailing relevant standard for tallness happens to be in our community; in particular, that standard must be no greater than Feynman's maximal degree of height. The context update effect of accepting (1) would be to eliminate from further consideration some candidates for the standard of tallness. My purpose in uttering (1) under such circumstances would be nothing more than to communicate something about how to use a certain word appropriately—it would be a metalinguistic use.   (Barker 2002: 2)

Three comments on this passage.

1. Barker says that in uttering (1) he has provided no new information about the world—the utterance does nothing more than to communicate something about how to use certain words appropriately. That is wrong. There is new information. What's the information they already have? Maybe: *Feynman has that height* (watching him) or *F is 182cm*. Why should we go along with the claim that this is the same information as *that Feynman is above the cutoff of a scale that's supplied in context C*? Maybe the facts (the truth makers or whatever) are the same. I'm not sure they are, but even if we allow Barker that point, they are at least presented under a new mode of presentation. *It is new information in the sense that you can believe the one and not the other.* So things are going far too quickly in that passage. It's a bit like saying that if you know that Superman can fly, you already know that Clark Kent can fly, so any statement about Clark Kent would have to be metalinguistic, otherwise it would be pointless. That case itself shows no such thing and, as far as I can tell, is pretty neutral on those larger issues. So I think the deluge of reference to this paper, as if it had settled something about the ubiquity of metalinguistic information, is unfortunate.

2. The setup is unusual in that it is explicitly (close to) metalinguistic. The example is introduced as follows: "You ask me what counts as tall in my country." He imagines that he, Barker, is asked: *What counts as tall in the US?* That is (at least in certain contexts, see 3 below) naturally interpreted as a metalinguistic question. So the answer is also naturally so interpreted. However, the cases Ludlow, Plunkett, and Sundell are concerned with are not like this. They don't start out in this potentially metalinguistic way. So

even if what Barker says is right about this particular case, there is no good basis for the generalization.

3. Finally, I just said that it is natural to interpret the question Barker starts with as being about a word. I should modify that: there's another reading of the question, maybe as natural (at least for non-philosophers), where it's not metalinguistic and where the reply isn't either. On this reading, the question is about tallness. And the reply is about what counts as being tall. This is not information directly about the English word 'tall'. It implies something about 'tall', but it also implies something about 'høy' and 'hoch' and 'alto'. But it's not about any of those, it's about tallness. Even what's alleged to be a paradigm of metalinguistic communication lends itself to a worldly reading.

16

On Appeals to a Concept's Purpose or Function

16.1 Functions of Concepts

I turn now to a discussion of another strand in much of the literature on conceptual engineering. As illustrated by the discussion of Plunkett and Sundell in the previous chapter, many of those who write about conceptual engineering talk about concepts as things that have a 'purpose' or 'function', as doing a certain kind of 'work', or as 'having a point'.[1] Such authors make two assumptions:

1. They think concepts are things that have purposes (or points or aims or functions or jobs).
2. They think that *preservation* of purposes (or points or aims or functions or jobs) is important when thinking about conceptual revision.

The Austerity Framework doesn't appeal to purposes (or functions or points or anything like that). I don't think these appeals do any work and this chapter is an attempt to explain why. Of course, *people* have goals and aims and purposes when they use words on particular occasions. But I don't think concepts have purposes and certainly not words (or extensions or intensions).

I'll consider three versions of the view that an appeal to purposes is important:

- Haslanger's appeal to what she calls 'the central functions of a concept' (Haslanger 2000: 35)
- Brigandt's appeal to a concept's epistemic goal to characterize a concept's function (Brigandt 2010)
- Amie Thomasson's (forthcoming) appeal to natural functions.

---

[1] Terminological point: the literature I engage with here uses 'function', 'purpose', 'aim', 'job', and related terms for the most part interchangeably. I will adjust my choice of terminology to the author I am discussing.

16.2 Haslanger's Appeal to 'Central Functions' as the Limits of Revision

Haslanger, as we have seen, often engages with a version of Strawson's objection (though she doesn't call it that because she doesn't explicitly sees her own project as continuous with Carnap's). She raises the question of when it is appropriate to take on existing terminology—why, for example, use the word 'woman' in her ameliorative project? Why not use that for the old meaning and introduce a new term for the new? Put in terms I used in Part III, she's concerned with the limits of revision: how much change is too much? We can find at least two solutions to this in her work. One is an appeal to lexical effects. On this view, preservation of old terminology is justified when the lexical effects are such that it promotes the ameliorators' goals (and it doesn't matter whether the change is topic-preserving). I discussed this strategy in chapter 6 and I won't pursue the issue again here. Instead I focus on what Jennifer Saul helpfully describes as Haslanger's 'semantic condition' (Saul 2006: 126–7):

> *The Semantic Condition:* "[T]he proposed shift in meaning of the term would seem semantically warranted if central functions of the term remain the same, e.g., if it helps to organize or explain a core set of phenomena that the ordinary terms are used to identify or describe" (Haslanger 2000: 35).

Here is how I interpret this passage: One way to draw the limit between topic-preserving revisions and topic-abandoning revisions is by an appeal to a concept's central functions.[2] The thought is this: if the central functions are preserved, then we have topic preservation. If they are not preserved, then we have topic abandonment (a change of topic).

16.2.1 Objection to Haslanger's account

Haslanger's condition presupposes that concepts are the sorts of things that have 'central functions' and that these include 'organiz[ing] or explain[ing] a core set of phenomena'. I raise three questions:

1. What exactly are these 'functions' supposed to be and how do we distinguish between those that are central and those that are in the periphery?
2. Given a precise specification of the relevant notions of 'central' and 'function', is it true that concepts have them?
3. If it is true, does it help us understand the limits of revision?

---

[2] So in what follows I'm assuming that limits of revision go hand in hand with topic preservation. A proponent of Haslanger's position could deny this, but much of what I say in what follows is likely to be relevant to other ways of fleshing out the view.

16.2.2 *Contextualist vs. invariantist versions of the function reply*

In response to 1, it is useful to distinguish two rough categories of answers: *contextualist* and *invariantist*. According to the contextualist, the central function of F varies between contexts. More precisely:

- The contextualist thinks that even if the use of a concept F in a context C has a certain function, its use may have another function in context C*.
- The invariantist thinks the function doesn't vary: the point of talking about the function of concepts is to find something stable—the stable element that's there while it undergoes change in extension and intension.

With that distinction in mind, first note that the a contextualist version of the function theory isn't what Haslanger has in mind and shouldn't be. The semantic condition isn't relativized to contexts. Her view is not one in which, say, amelioration of 'women' is done for a particular context but then left unchanged in other contexts. This is good for a number of reasons. One important reason is that the very notion of 'contextually variable core functions' is hard or impossible to make sense of. Here are some contexts in which the expression 'women' is used:

1. There were three women on the flight
2. There are more women than men in my class
3. Women's shoes are more expensive than men's shoes
4. Women often do more housework than men
5. Women get breast cancer more often than men
6. Women smoke less than men.

What's the core function of 'women' in each of these? Of course, in each there's a stable function: 'women' is used to denote women. But what is the additional core function that varies? Without a very elaborate theory, that question simply has no answer. Of course, we can say that in 1 its function is to help the speaker say that there were three women on the flight, and in 2 its function is to say that there are more women than men in the class, etc. But that's not what Haslanger has in mind (and that kind of reply would be unhelpful).

So, a function theorist should be an *invariantist*. Here things get a bit more subtle. I don't think all versions of invariantism are false—I think there's a rather trivial and true version, but it's completely ineffective as an attempt to describe the limits of revision.

Trivial version of the function theory: According to this view the only *universal*, i.e., stable, function of a concept 'C' is to denote Cs. The function of the concept 'tiger' is to denote tigers. The function of the concept 'salad' is to denote salads, the function of the concept 'woman' is to denote women, and so on.

If someone is interested in the limits of revision, this kind of function will be of no help: We are in effect told that for a revision of 'C' to be topic-preserving, it has to still be about Cs (i.e., it has to denote Cs). Any revision of 'women' must, in order to be topic-preserving, still be about women. So understood, this is a version of the function theory that the Austerity Framework can incorporate. That said, this view doesn't provide much illumination. Someone interested in the limits of revision in effect asks: If the extension of 'C' changes, when do we still talk about Cs?[3] We start out with the concepts of 'tiger', 'woman', or 'salad'. We then revise their extensions and ask: *Why are you still talking about tigers, women, and salads?* What we have just considered is the following true but uninformative reply: *because the central function of the concept, i.e., to denote tigers, women, and salads, has been preserved.* Someone interested in the limits of revision will want more. She will want to know we can still be talking about those things after we have revised extensions.

Taking stock, the suggestion now under consideration is that in admissible revisions the ameliorated concept 'helps to organize or explain a core set of phenomena that the ordinary terms are used to identify or describe'. To assess this proposal, we need to identify the core set of phenomena that the ordinary concepts are supposed to identify or describe. What, for example, is the core set of phenomena that 'salmon' is supposed to identify and describe? I've argued that the *only non-controversial answer* to this is the disquotational one proposed above: 'salmon' is supposed to organize and describe salmon. That answer, however, is unhelpful for the reasons given above. If, however, that's not what Haslanger has in mind, it's very hard to see how the proposal is supposed to be helpful: it simply pushes us over to the question of how to identify 'the phenomena' and we're given no guidance for how to do that.

The kind of concerns that I have raised were made forcefully by Jennifer Saul (2006). In connection with the Haslanger's claim that "the proposed shift in meaning of the term would seem semantically warranted if central functions of the term remain the same, e.g., if it helps to organize or explain a core set of phenomena that the ordinary terms are used to identify or describe" (Haslanger 2000: 35 quoted in Saul 2006: 127), Saul says:

---

[3] This is on the assumption that she is not a lexical exploiter—for that option see chapter 11.

It seems to me that more work needs to be done to make the above condition really do what it needs to do. To see this, suppose that I were to propose an explicitly revisionary definition for 'woman' that was just like Haslanger's analysis of man ... I could defend this revisionary definition by arguing, 'The phenomenon that I am concerned to describe is that of inequalities between males and females. A term "woman", meaning what I suggest above, will be very useful to me in organizing and explaining this phenomenon.' Haslanger cannot deny that a term with this meaning would be useful for explaining the phenomenon at issue—after all, this is how she defines 'man'. This shift in meaning, then, would seem to meet Haslanger's semantic criterion. Most likely, the way to respond to this worry is to insist that the phenomenon specified above is not the right one. But it is far from obvious how the phenomenon in question should be specified.   (Saul 2006: 134–5)

I agree with Saul and would go somewhat further: What Haslanger's account needs, but doesn't provide, is a procedure for identifying 'the phenomena' that are being organized and explained. Haslanger has never responded to Saul's objection and my bold conjecture is this: there simply *isn't* a good way to identify 'the phenomenon' except disquotationally and the disquotational identification is unresponsive to the challenge of articulating the limits of revision.

16.3 Brigandt's Appeal to the Intended Epistemic Goal of a Concept

I turn now to an appeal to functions from a very different philosophical domain: the philosophy of biology. Brigandt (2010) is interested in the issue of how there can be continuity in a concept such as 'gene' when biologists' views of genes change over time. Despite being focused on a fairly specific field, I see this as in some ways continuous with issues that concerned Haslanger and that have been important in this book: how do we account for continuity through semantic changes?

Brigandt wants to account for how the gradual change in the extension of 'gene' as used by biologists can be rational. To provide such an account, he introduces the notion of an *epistemic goal of a concept* and this, he suggests, "accounts for the rationality of semantic change" (Brigandt 2010: 24). Here's one of his descriptions of epistemic goals:

[T]he concept's epistemic goal is the kinds of inferences and explanations that the concept is intended to support. A concept may be used to pursue certain theoretical, explanatory, or investigative goals, even though at the present time the concept—its inferential role reflecting current empirical beliefs—cannot adequately yield the intended epistemic product (inferences, explanations, discoveries), so that the concept's present inferential role does not fully meet its epistemic goal.   (Brigandt 2010: 24, italics added)

Two comments on this appeal to epistemic goals. First, note that Brigandt's claim is *severely limited*. He's only saying that *some* scientific concepts have epistemic goals. He is not claiming that all scientific concepts have epistemic goals and he certainly does not think that everyday notions such as 'salad', 'woman', 'belief', etc. do. This is important in the current context: his proposal would be helpful for the Haslanger-style strategy if an appeal to *intended* functions could be used to single out the core phenomenon that Haslanger appeals to. Here I'm aligned with Brigandt: even if you think this is true about a few scientific terms, *it simply doesn't generalize*. There are too many speakers with too many and too varied intentions. The relevant set of intentions will change between people in the group and it will change for each person over time. There simply isn't enough unity in the kinds of inferences and explanations that the concept of 'woman' is supposed to support. As a result, appealing to actual intentions of real speakers to fix the functions of concepts is unpromising as a *general* account of what 'the core function' of a concept is.

What I just said leaves open the possibility that Brigandt's account holds for a few scientific concepts. However, I think that too is dubious. It is in effect a speculative claim about what went on in the minds of certain people at a certain time. Brigandt provides no evidence that there is a set of inferences and explanations that a certain group of people intended for the concept to support. To provide evidence of that would require detailed specification of who these people are and what their intentions were at a certain point in time. My conjecture is that the set of intentions that biologists had will be too varied and conflicting for there to be any useful generalization available.

16.4 Thomasson and Millikan on the Proper Function of Linguistic Devices

Amie Thomasson (forthcoming) draws on work by Ruth Millikan to develop a notion of function that is useful for a theory of conceptual engineering. As she points out, Millikan "aims to identify functions of 'language devices' that are 'not found either by averaging over idiolects or by examining speaker intentions' (1984, 4)." She summarizes Millikan's view as follows:

On Millikan's view (roughly), a member of a 'reproductively established family' has as its proper function whatever its ancestors did that contributed to the reproductive success of the family, which contributes to explaining the existence of that member (1984, 28). Millikan explicitly applies the view to cultural products, including language, as much as to biological entities such as hearts and lungs. Meaningful linguistic devices, on her view, are also members of 'first-order reproductively established families' (1984, 29), and Millikan argues that "language devices must have direct proper functions at some level or levels. It must be because they correlate with functions that they proliferate" (1984, 31).

(Thomasson forthcoming)

This way of construing functions avoids the challenge to Brigandt above. The proper function need not be intended by any speakers.

So far, so good, but how do we, in particular cases, identify proper functions? Thomasson recognizes that this is hard, but we can get a 'set of clues' by asking: *What makes the linguistic items in question useful for us?* In particular, we should ask "what we can do better with such a vocabulary than if we lacked it" (Thomasson forthcoming). She provides three illustrations:

- "Stephen Yablo's (2005) view according to which 'introducing noun terms for numbers enables us to simplify our statements of laws in certain effective ways—so that we can state in finite form laws that otherwise would take an infinite series of infinitely long sentences'."
- "The expressivist's analysis of the point of moral discourse, as enabling us to express and coordinate our attitudes in ways that put pressure on certain forms of agreement that thereby enable us to better live together."
- "Paul Horwich's (1999) view of the role that the truth predicate serves as a device of generalization can also be understood in this light." (Thomasson forthcoming)

What is crucial about each of these cases is that they "purport to identify something that this range of vocabulary *does* or (better) *enables us to do,* that we couldn't do (or couldn't do as effectively or efficiently) without it":

Analyses like these can serve as clues to proper function analyses: to why it would have been useful to have terms like this, why they might have been perpetuated and continued in our culture. And these are functional analyses that remain separate from discussions of what anyone *intends* or *believes* the function to be, or even what individuals, on various occasions, *use* the relevant terms to do, and so avoid Cappelen's objections.[4]

(Thomasson forthcoming)

Thomasson asks us to identify something that "this range of vocabulary *does* or (better) *enables us to do,* that we couldn't do (or couldn't do as effectively or efficiently) without it." Much here will depend on what is meant by 'vocabulary'.

---

[4] To clarify, Thomasson is here referring and responding to an earlier version of this book—a version of the book that did not include this section discussing her view.

Suppose that this refers to the words. We then have to ask whether it is true that there is something that, say, the expression '1' enables us to do that we couldn't do without it. On one construal at least, the answer seems to be obviously 'no'. It is not true that denoting 1 is something '1' does that couldn't be done (or couldn't be done as effectively) without '1'. We could have had a different symbol—say '2'—and as long as *it* was used to denote 1, the job '1' is doing would have been done just as well. We really don't need '1'. It is hard to see that there's anything '1' can do that '2' couldn't have done just as well. So, there's nothing that '1' does that we couldn't have done just as well without '1'.

It might be felt that this criticism misses Thomasson's central point. The central suggestion is that we try to find the functions of terminologies by looking for what makes them useful for us (and hence perpetuated in our culture). If the point is put just like that, then in some sense I think there might be functions of the relevant kinds. These are, however, the philosophically unhelpful functions mentioned in the discussion of Haslanger. The reason 'salmon' is useful for us is that it can be used to talk about salmons (or denote salmons). The reason 'freedom' is useful is that it can be used to talk about freedom. We care about salmons and freedom and so we have words that enable us to talk about them. (Of course, all of this could have been done by other words—so we don't need any of those terms to perform that function.) However—and this is the key point—beyond these disquotationally specified functions, there's variability. We can use 'freedom' in speech acts that have as their aim to undermine freedom or promote it or discuss it or disparage or make fun of it or . . . There's no limit to what we can go on to do with this term. These activities will vary wildly between contexts and over time. If the goal is to find functions that are more substantive and informative than the disquotationally specified functions, then it will be unsuccessful. For example, one of the things we can do with noun words for numbers is simplify our statements of laws, but communities can have a practice of using words like 'one' and 'two' just as we do (to denote one and two), without using them for that purpose.

That ends my brief discussion of appeal to functions, points, and purposes. There are of course entire frameworks that could be discussed here: functionalism about content, versions of inferentialism, and the so-called Canberra plan all spring to mind. In none of those traditions has there been a sustained effort to address the questions in this book and in particular there has been little effort to use those frameworks to describe the limits of revision. They are for the most part static frameworks and they're not constructed to account for constant evolution and revision. A full discussion of, e.g., inferentialism and the Canberra plan would go beyond the scope of this book (and bring in a range of issues irrelevant to its central concerns.) Versions of the objections raised in this chapter will, I predict, be challenges for any effort to use those frameworks to answer the central questions in this book, but that prediction is a promissory note (and I hope to get an opportunity to say more about it when proponents of those theories develop competing accounts of conceptual engineering).

17

Chalmers's Subscript Gambit, the Importance of Topics, and Lack of Control

17.1 Chalmers on the Method of Elimination and the Subscript Gambit

In section 2.1.12 of chapter 2 I described Chalmers's view. This view is similar to the Austerity Framework along one important dimension: Chalmers agrees that there's a range of properties philosophical terms could denote. We have different beliefs about which property is expressed by an expression and so we talk past one another. S1 thinks 'freedom' denotes property P1, thinks being P1 leads to being F, and on that basis says: 'Freedom is F', while speaker S2 thinks 'freedom' denotes property P2 and thinks being P2 leads to being not F and so says 'Freedom is not F'. It looks like they are disagreeing, but they are not. There need be no real disagreement here. I want to focus on Chalmers's proposed solution—his suggestion for what to do when we face a situation where a debate is stuck because of the kind of miscommunication he describes. He calls his proposal 'the method of elimination' (Chalmers 2011: 526).

Here is what Chalmers suggests we do when we are faced with a dispute concerning a sentence, S, that might be a verbal, non-substantive, dispute centered on the meaning of the term T:

- First: one bars the use (and the mention) of term T.
- Second: one tries to find a sentence S' in the newly restricted vocabulary such that the parties disagree nonverbally over S' and such that the disagreement over S' is part of the dispute over S.
- Third: if there is such an S', the dispute over S is not wholly verbal, or at least there is a substantive dispute in the vicinity.
- Fourth: if there is no such S' then the dispute over S is wholly verbal (except in the special case of vocabulary exhaustion, discussed below).

Here are three illustrations of the method at work. The first is applied to the question of whether O.J. Simpson is a murderer:

[T]o adjudicate a dispute over whether O.J. Simpson is a murderer is verbal with respect to 'murderer', one may bar the use of the term. In this case, it is likely that we will find various sentences S' such that nonverbal dispute over S' is part of the original dispute: for example, did Simpson slash his wife's neck with a knife? If so, the original dispute is not wholly verbal.   (Chalmers 2011: 523)

Here is how we can use this method to clarify the dispute over whether Pluto is a planet:

In the case of 'Pluto is a planet', one may bar the use of 'planet'. Here it may be hard to find any nonverbal dispute not involving the term 'planet' that is part of the original dispute. If there is no such dispute, then the dispute is verbal.   (Chalmers 2011: 527)

In philosophy, Chalmers's advice is that when "faced with a dispute that is potentially verbal with respect to a term T, one can simply ask the parties: can you state what you are disagreeing about without using (or mentioning) T?" (Chalmers 2011: 529). In the case of many philosophical disputes, he suggests that we can apply a special case of the method of elimination that he calls 'the subscript gambit'. So, for example, in the case of debates over free will we should proceed as follows:

[O]ne party might say "Freedom is the ability to do what one wants", while the other says "Freedom is the ability to ultimately originate one's choices". We can then introduce "freedom$_1$" and "freedom$_2$" for the two right-hand sides here, and ask: do the parties differ over freedom$_1$ and freedom$_2$? Perhaps they will disagree over "Freedom$_2$ is required for moral responsibility", or over "Freedom$_1$ is what we truly value". If so, this clarifies the debate. On the other hand, perhaps they will agree that freedom$_1$ conveys a certain watered-down moral responsibility, that freedom$_2$ would be really valuable but that freedom$_1$ is somewhat valuable, and so on. If so, this is a sign that the apparent disagreement over the nature of free will is merely verbal.   (Chalmers 2011: 532)

A comparison with Plunkett and Sundell and Ludlow is helpful: according to Chalmers, the best way to proceed when the conversational participants have different views about what meaning a particular string of letters does or should have is to stop using that string of letters and instead start using two new strings—one for each candidate meaning. This isn't to say that Chalmers thinks each meaning is necessarily as good as the other. One might be better for various reasons (i.e., he can agree with Plunkett and Sundell and Ludlow that assessing meanings can be a complicated and interesting task). What he is not on board with is the idea that we should waste time fighting over which string gets to express which meaning.

Plunkett + Sundell don't either

17.2 The Importance of Topics and Topic Continuity

To make things a bit simple, I'll focus on a Chalmers-like view.[1] Core philosophical terms—'freedom', 'causation', 'goodness', 'beauty', 'truth', 'consciousness', 'reference', 'belief', 'knowledge', 'justification', 'perception', etc.—might in fact pick out one particular property, but in the neighborhood of each of those properties are indefinitely many other properties and which property our term happens to pick out has no particular significance. What we need to do is get clear on the range of properties, label them ('justification$_1$', justification$_2$'...etc., 'freedom$_1$', 'freedom$_2$'...etc.), and then talk about and investigate each of these—the focus on what freedom really is doesn't matter. What we discover when doing philosophy is the plurality of properties in a neighborhood and our task is to figure out truths about each of these.

While this is a massively useful perspective—and one with important practical implications—it leaves out a lot of what I've been trying to focus on in this book. The rest of this chapter briefly sketches what I take to be some important limitations of Chalmers's view.

17.3 Chalmers on Fetishistic Value Systems

According to Chalmers, once we have all the truths about, say freedom$_1$, freedom$_2$, . . . etc., there's no other interesting further question to ask. In particular, Chalmers scorns those interested in the question: But what is freedom? He says that those who care about that question have a 'fetishistic' value system. Here is a passage from Chalmers where he discusses a similar issue. He's imagining someone asking whether physicalism is physicalism$_1$, or physicalism$_2$, or . . . About this 'residual' question, he says it's a purely linguistic question, and brings out no important first-order facts.

> Perhaps there could be an intellectual value system that gave true beliefs about flying or roundness or physicalism significant nonderivative value, over and above the value of the other true beliefs in question. But such a value system would seem fetishistic.
>
> (Chalmers 2011: 536–7)

Note that, if that's a fetishistic interest, then an interest in the Haslanger-style question is also fetishistic. For Chalmers, the question of what gender (without a subscript) *ought to be* is of no more interest than the question what gender *really*

---

[1] I say 'Chalmers-like' because it glosses over some of the subtlety in Chalmers's view. To articulate my objections using all of Chalmers's terminology would make the presentation more convoluted, but not affect the argument.

is. An interest in either would, according to Chalmers, exhibit a fetishistic value system. The Chalmers-style philosopher, when faced with the question *What should gender be?*, simply replies: *There's just a bunch of properties, gender₁, gender₂, etc. We state the truth about each of these and that's the end of the story.* There's nothing more that's interesting. It is of course possible that talking about gender₁ is more useful for certain political or practical purposes than talking about gender₂, but that's the way to describe it. What gender (simpliciter) ought to be isn't worth asking. The claim *that gender ought to be, say, gender₁* is exactly the sort of thing his method is an effort to move us away from.[2] For Chalmers the questions about what gender (without a subscript) really is (independently of the questions of what gender₁, gender₂, etc. are) is simply the question of what 'gender' happens to refer to—it's a linguistic issue with no intrinsic interest (or an interest only to those with a certain fetish). That view threatens to undermine the central project of this book. I've been concerned with how our current concepts can be improved—how 'freedom', for example, can be improved. That's a concern that Chalmers rejects.

Not only should Chalmers's characterization of these issues as fetishistic be rejected, but it comes very close to generating an internal inconsistency in Chalmers's view. Here is why: The Chalmers subscripts—freedom₁, freedom₂, etc.—presuppose that they are versions of freedom (simpliciter). If instead of subscripts we introduced unrelated names for various properties—'Nora', 'Emilia', 'Mie', etc.—for the various properties, we would miss an essential connection between them: They are all ways to ameliorate freedom (simpliciter). That's why they are not part of the cluster: responsibility₁, responsibility₂, etc. So someone sympathetic to the subscript gambit should not also dismiss an interest in what we can call 'the simpliciter property', e.g., freedom without a subscript. The subscript strategy presupposes that there is a freedom cluster (all the freedom₁, freedom₂ properties). It presupposes that some properties are within the freedom cluster and other properties are not. For example, the property of being one of my eyes isn't in the freedom cluster. Why not? Because it's not a candidate amelioration of freedom. The appeal to what I just called 'the simpliciter property' is in effect an appeal to what I've called topics and the

---

[2] I'm not here concerned with the lexical effects of terms like 'gender'—Chalmers rightly dismisses that concern as one that would only afflict non-ideal agents: "Ideal agents might be unaffected by which terms are used for which concepts, but for nonideal agents such as ourselves, the accepted meaning for a key term will make a difference to which concepts are highlighted, which questions can easily be raised, and which associations and inferences are naturally made" (Chalmers 2011: 542). I take this to be a point about how nonideal agents are affected by lexical effects. That's not what I'm focused on here.

argument just given shows that an interest in them isn't fetishistic. They're theoretically indispensable. We can't even articulate the subscript view without presupposing them.

17.4 Chalmers's Ahistorical Internalism

There's a second feature of Chalmers's view that contrasts sharply with the Austerity Framework. Someone enamored by the subscript gambit is thinking that she is very much in control of the meaning of her words. The outlook is one in which we can proceed as follows:

The inquirer discovers different properties in a domain, she then labels them with new expressions, say 'gender$_1$', 'gender$_2$', etc., then she tries to state the truths about each of those.

But that isn't how language works. That picture assumes that we are in control— that we can sit in the privacy of our offices, choose which labels to put on which properties, and then our words just stick to them. If you're sympathetic to the view I have defended in this book (even if you don't buy the rather strong version of it that I advocate), you will reject Chalmers's description of how verbal disputes can be resolved. The subscript gambit assumes we are in control of the meaning of the words we use when we specify the meaning of the subscripts, but we are not: what those words mean depends on the past, other people, and patterns of use that we know nothing about and have no control over. As I said in chapter 7, this applies also to these efforts to stipulate meanings in the privacy of your own office or even paper. Applied to a proponent of the subscript gambit: the meanings of 'freedom$_1$', 'freedom$_2$', . . . 'gender$_1$', 'gender$_2$', etc. will be as much hostage to the external factors as the originals, 'freedom' and 'gender'. Once that is taken on board, the subscript gambit isn't even an option any more: its entire rationale was that there were contents we had no access to—the semantic referents of 'freedom' or 'gender'. Speakers have different beliefs about what they refer to (that's why they engage in broadly verbal disputes), and we (or they) then label the properties they think they refer to. As soon as that labeling process is problematized—when there's no guarantee that we end up having transparent access to the meanings of the subscripted expressions (i.e., if they are as opaque to us as the referents of the original expressions), then the subscripting process can't do the work Chalmers wants it to.

18

Conceptual Engineering without Bedrock and without Fixed Points

18.1 The Limits of Conceptual Engineering?

Are some terms so basic that they cannot be engineered? Are some terms so fundamental that we are stuck with them—so basic that evolution, revision, and amelioration are impossible? that evolution, revision, and amelioration are impossible? You could argue for such views in various ways. One line of thought has it that, as a matter of empirical fact, there are certain meanings that we're born with and just can't get rid of—they're stuck in our brains and however much we try, they remain there. Another line of thought has it that there are specific features of specific meanings that make the idea of evolution problematic. In what follows I will focus on this second line of thought and I'll consider two arguments—one from Chalmers and one from Eklund. My conclusion will be that we should stick with the working hypothesis that *everything is in flux—that all representational devices can be revised, and there's no natural end point to conceptual engineering.*

18.2 Chalmers on Bedrock Concepts

Chalmers believes in something he calls bedrock concepts—in my terminology, these are expressions that cannot be engineered. They are conceptual foundations where there's no option of moving to a neighboring property—the property pluralism Chalmers endorses doesn't apply here. He lists some candidates for bedrock concepts:

Some candidates for bedrock concepts include: phenomenal concepts (consciousness, specific phenomenal qualities?); normative concepts (certain moral and epistemic oughts?); some logical or mathematical concepts (negation, existential quantification?); some nomic or modal concepts (nomological necessity?); spatiotemporal concepts (relative location, temporal order?); some indexical concepts (I, now?); and just possibly, the concept of explanation (it is striking that many philosophical disputes resolve themselves into disputes over what explains what). Other philosophers will add other concepts: those of secondary qualities, intentional states, freedom?   (Chalmers 2011: 552)

His diagnostic for how to find bedrock concepts involves an appeal to what he calls the 'asymmetrical structure among the space of disputes':

In effect, the notion of a bedrock dispute requires a sort of asymmetrical structure among the space of disputes, such that (for example) disputes over 'conscious' are more basic than disputes over 'see' and disputes over 'ought' are more basic than disputes over 'murder'. This asymmetrical structure does not fall out of the very notion of a verbal dispute. Instead, it is suggested by the character of the relations among disputes that we find on examination. . . . Of course an opponent might hold that any apparent structure here is a mere artifact of our psychology or our attitudes. *But I will adopt the idea that there is some privileged structure among disputes, at least as a promising working hypothesis.*   (my emphasis)(Chalmers 2011: 548–9)

I think that working hypothesis is very implausible. What I have to say here is really just a plea for replacing one conjecture with another, but I think it's worth getting clear on just what we are making the conjecture about. The claim about an asymmetry in the 'space of disputes' is an empirical conjecture. It's an empirical guess about how philosophical disputes have evolved and will evolve over time. In particular, I suppose, a claim about how they *end* (with the bedrock concepts) and where they tend to start (not with the bedrock concepts). Showing that there is such an asymmetry would require detailed empirical investigation into philosophical disputes throughout the history of philosophy and then provide evidence that (i) these disputes tend to 'bottom out' with a certain subset of concepts and (ii) those concepts are not themselves subject to the same degree of disputes. Here is my alternative conjecture: the actual history of philosophy will provide no such patterns. I suspect that the history of philosophy will turn out to be an extreme mess, with different patterns in different time periods, and in different communities. The only way to provide a structure to it will be to insist on a restriction of the domain (i.e., focus on a few people over a brief period), but any such restriction will be ad hoc, question begging, and undermine the universal claim about bedrock status for certain concepts. It would at most show that for some people in a certain place at a certain time, some concepts played a certain role. So construed, bedrock status would be an indexed property of concepts. That is not what Chalmers has in mind. So if we put aside this indexing strategy, I will suggest that a far more plausible working hypothesis is that what we would find after such a monumental undertaking was no structure and instead historically variable patterns. Moreover, the very notions of *the structure of a debate* and of *bottoming out* would themselves be up for dispute. If this is right, we should replace Chalmers' suggested working hypothesis with the following: It's conceptual engineering all the way down.

18.3 Eklund on Normative Limits

That said, I will end by considering one argument to the effect that a specific concept is immune to engineering—it is an argument due to Matti Eklund and it concerns the role of normative concepts in conceptual engineering. Eklund argues that there's a kind of internal inconsistency in thinking that the normative concepts that we use when assessing conceptual change could themselves be subject to engineering. According to Eklund, this shows that "there must be important limits to conceptual engineering: that certain in some sense basic concepts cannot be replaced" (Eklund 2015: 378). Here is how Eklund sets up the problem:

[C]an there be words non-coextensive with our 'good', 'right', etc. but with the same evaluative and normative roles? If not, then a certain kind of conceptual engineering isn't possible: that of finding alternative concepts with the same normative roles as our actual concepts but different in extension. (Eklund 2015: 381)

Eklund asks us to imagine the following scenario:

There is a linguistic community speaking a language much like English, except for the following differences (and whatever differences are directly entailed). While their words 'good', 'right' and 'ought' have the same evaluative and normative roles as our words 'good', 'right' and 'ought' have, their words aren't coextensive with our 'good', 'right' and 'ought'. So even if they are exactly right about what is 'good' and 'right' and what 'ought' to be done, in their sense, and they seek to promote and to do what is 'good' and 'right' and what 'ought' to be done in their sense, they do not seek to promote what is good and right and what ought to be done. (Eklund 2015: 380–1)

For the purposes of the current discussion, we can think of the following as a decision to be made by a conceptual engineer: Should she use 'ought' with its current extension or a new extension? (and of course, one important question will be how to interpret the 'should' in the previous sentence). Eklund says:

If the sort of scenario sketched is indeed possible, then, a first thought may be, there is a question of which normative concepts are the *best* ones, the ones we employ or the ones employed by a community like this. And once that thought arises, a certain skeptical thought suggests itself: maybe our concepts aren't the ones that ought to be used? (And how can we even know which concepts ought to be used?) (Eklund 2015: 381)

According to Eklund, "there is something that seems very peculiar about these thoughts." And the peculiar thing is that we have to choose which normative concepts to use when we ask these normative questions:

[I]t is reasonable to assume that "the concepts that ought to be used are 'good', 'ought', etc." is a true sentence of our language even while "the concepts that ought* to be used are 'good*', 'ought*', etc." is a true sentence of their language (where I use asterisks to indicate the counterpart expressions they use). In other words when we try to ask the supposed further questions that arise, we end up asking questions that are answered in our favor, and when they try to ask the supposed further questions that arise they end up asking questions that are answered in their favor. This means that we and they fail to ask the question sought. That question threatens to be ineffable.   (Eklund 2015: 381)

Eklund presents us with a dilemma: Either there is this further ineffable question or we end up embracing a conclusion that is "antithetical to the spirit of realism":

Suppose there is a given action that would be deemed right* but not right. Suppose, for example, that their concepts are utilitarian and ours are deontological, and what's deemed right* is sacrificing someone innocent for the greater good of the majority. As they are about to sacrifice this someone, we think this is something they ought not to do. We say "Stop it! You ought not do that!". They say "Yes. We know. We ought not do that. But we ought* to do this!". We persist, "But you ought to do what you ought to do!". They say "Yes again. But also, we ought* to do what we ought* to do". And if there is no further question there—some further fact that we and they disagree about—there is no disagreement over facts here, as they go about sacrificing the innocent. Certain antirealists are happy to embrace such a conclusion, but the conclusion is antithetical to the spirit of realism.   (Eklund 2015: 381–2) ? Just sounds like a metalinguistic dispute?

Eklund concludes that there is a certain sense in which our thinnest normative concepts are irreplaceable.

This is an important line of thought and what I say in what follows will only be the beginning of an exploration of these deep and subtle issues (see Eklund 2017 for extended discussion). First, and this is something Eklund would agree with, the moral realists shouldn't think that their position is undermined by the second horn of the dilemma After all, this is a realist who gets to say that it is true—in the most robust sense you'd like—that we ought to not do that (e.g., sacrifice someone for the sake of the greater good of the majority). She also gets to say *that the others use moral concepts that they ought not to use.* That claim too is true in the most robust sense. You can't, of course, stop them from acting and you can't make them have the concepts they ought to have or act on the concepts they ought to act on (at least not through argumentation). But any realist who hopes her realism will deliver that has fundamentally misguided expectations.

Eklund would agree with what I just said, but add that the description I just gave leaves something out. There's a disagreement between the two groups, but we're not able to articulate it—there's an unresolved issue that can't be articulated using either their or our language. I share Eklund's sense that there's something missing, and I think the theory presented above enables us to capture it. For someone convinced of the evidence presented in chapter 10 (according to which what we say is more coarse-grained than the semantic values (extensions and intensions) of our words) there is room to say what Eklund describes as ineffable. Here is why: Consider two utterances of 'Ought you to F?' that differ in the way Eklund envisions with respect to the extension of 'ought'. What Eklund assumes is that they have asked different questions. He then goes on to indicate the difference by introducing a new expression 'ought*'—and uses that expression to say what the other group is saying. That move makes it hard to see one of the options for how to describe the situation. According to the view proposed in this book, they can both ask the same question: *Ought you to F?* And they can give diverging answers: One group says you ought to F and the other that it's not the case that you ought to F. Eklund's reason for denying this is that their respective uses of 'ought' have different extensions, and so they can't both say the same. That assumption, I have suggested, is mistaken.

I haven't told you what the semantic value of 'ought' is as it occurs in my description of what they both ask. So when I said: "They can both ask the same question: *Ought you to F?*" I didn't tell you the semantics for 'ought' as it occurred there. You might think it's hard to answer that question: either I use it to mean what just one community means or what neither of them means—both seem problematic. But I bypass that dilemma because on the view I propose, what I say when I say, "They can both ask the same question: *Ought you to F?*" goes beyond the semantics of the words used to say it: What has been said in saying that is, in part, that there is continuity of topic between the two groups of speakers. Maybe the elusiveness of what it is they both say—the elusiveness of topics—captures some of what Eklund has in mind when talking about ineffability. Sharing topics, as I construe it, is not the sharing of a new level of contents (a content neither of the two groups expressed semantically). For there to be topic continuity is for the groups to be treated as samesayers for certain purposes. So construed, the foundation is 'ineffable' in that it's not a new saying or a new content. What creates unity in topic are acts of treating them as samesayers.

Concluding Remarks and the Limits of the Intellect

Calling the topic of this book 'conceptual engineering' wasn't an easy choice and arguably it wasn't a good one. At the end of the day—looking at the positive proposal as a whole—there aren't any concepts involved and there's hardly any engineering. I've given you a theory of conceptual engineering without concepts and without engineering. The things most philosophers and psychologists call 'concepts' play no role. And there's very little engineering because the changes that happen are the result of inscrutable external factors that we lack control over. So why use the expression 'conceptual engineering' when it turns out to be so misleading?

I mentioned a few of reasons earlier and it's worth revisiting them here at the end. The most important reason is that this label best captures the self-image of the various philosophers that I describe in Part I. The work of these philosophers is, so to speak, my initial data point. I'm interested in the kind of activity they are engaged in. So it makes sense then to use a label that they would recognize, at least tentatively identify with, and endorse. Some of them also have theories about what they are doing and in those theories 'concept-like' entities often play a role. They are also sanguine about what they're doing: they tend to think (or at least they hold out hope) that their conceptual activism can have significant effects. So that's one reason for choosing a label that's ultimately misleading: it's familiar to the people and the traditions that the book theorizes about.

There's a second and related reason: my view helps bring out that many conceptual engineers have been mistaken about what they've been doing, mistaken about how to go about doing what they want to do, and also about the very possibility of doing what they want to do. This, again, isn't unusual: people are often pretty bad at describing what they are doing and we tend to wildly exaggerate our own significance and effectiveness. In particular, people who spend big chunks of their lives thinking, writing, and talking tend to think that those activities are important and have significant impact. For the most part that is not so.

A third reason for using the label 'conceptual engineering' is that I hope this book will encourage others to provide competing frameworks. In particular, it would be useful if those who believe in concepts and the engineering of them could come up with theoretical frameworks. Such philosophers will, as we have seen, often appeal to *clusters of beliefs* or to *platitudes* or to *functions* or to *jobs* or to *roles*. Their challenge is twofold:

(i) Find ways to identify the proper subset of such things—there are infinitely many platitudes, functions, jobs, and roles so how can you single out the relevant subset? (This is often as hard as (or the same as) the task of defining analyticity.)

(ii) Having identified this conceptual core, they need to show how it can be engineered.

It would be wonderful if in a few years time there were a wide range of such theories on offer. Note that part of that task (ii) will be to say something about the limits of revision. I suspect that with respect to that issue, the competing theories will be able to find common ground with mine.

Finally, it is worth revisiting another issue that came up earlier. I started the book by saying that a critical and constructive attitude to one's representational tools is essential for any serious thinker or talker. I also suggested that representational defects are widespread. Then, when my view is on the table, I told you: Sorry, there's little or nothing you can do about these representational defects. Isn't that all a bit bleak and pessimistic? On the view I defend, the tools we think with are often defective, but there's very little we can do about it. We can talk and think about it. We can articulate theories about what would be better. But doing so just contributes to what I have called the metasemantic superstructure and has little or no effect on the metasemantic base. It's like me talking to you about crime in Baltimore or poverty in Bangladesh. On the face of it, it's a bit hard to see how I can advocate for and be enthusiastic about such a project. How can this book be a defense of conceptual engineering? Isn't it, after all, just a disguised debunking project?

As mentioned earlier, I sympathize with this concern, but I also think that it is deeply misguided. It fails to take into account that what I've just described is an almost universal aspect of large-scale normative reflections. Anyone who spends time thinking and talking about large-scale normative matters should do so without holding out too much hope that their talking and thinking will have significant or predictable effects on the relevant aspect of the world. If you think your views and theories about crime in Baltimore or poverty in Bangladesh will have a significant or predictable effect on either, you're extremely likely to be disappointed (and to end up feeling you've wasted the part of your life that has been devoted to these issues). There are of course small-scale local issues where normative reflections will have a direct effect. If I think my daughter shouldn't have an ice cream, then, at least in a few cases, the result will be that she eats no ice cream. Moving to slightly larger-scale issues—say speed bumps in the street where I live—my opinions, views, and pleadings will have *tiny* effects, but already these effects will be fairly marginal, unsystematic, and unpredictable (as I've discovered). On the view proposed in this book, changes in extensions and intensions are far over on the large-scale and unpredictable side. Much closer to crime in Baltimore than to speed bumps in Sofies Gate. So, in sum, the worry that I've painted too bleak a picture of the prospects of conceptual engineering simply fails to take into account the relevant comparison class. What I say about conceptual engineering shouldn't be surprising and doesn't make the activity of trying to engineer concepts much different from a wide range of other human efforts to think about how things should be.

That said, the analogy goes only so far. The limitations on our ability to improve our representational devices are perhaps more painful and cut deeper than the other limitations I've mentioned. We are animals who pride ourselves on our rationality. The ability to think and represent is at the core of that rationality. That ability enables us to recognize both that our own representational devices are defective and that there isn't much we can do about it. We can observe these defects, describe them, reflect on them, and think of ameliorative strategies. But careful thinking also reveals that such reflection is ineffective. Amelioration might happen, but if it does, it has little to do with our intentional efforts. Our intellect can diagnose itself, figure out a cure, but is impotent when it comes to doing anything. Emphasizing this highlights an important limitation on human rationality and intellect.

Bibliography

[Note: this is a fast-moving field, and many of the works referenced in the book are not yet published.]

Appiah, Kwame Anthony (1992). *In My Father's House: Africa in the Philosophy of Culture*. Oxford University Press.

Appiah, Kwame Anthony (1996). Race, culture, identity: misunderstood connections. In Peterson, Grethe B., *The Tanner Lectures on Human Values XVII*. University of Utah Press, 51–136.

Austin, John (1956). A plea for excuses. *Proceedings of the Aristotelian Society* 57: 1–30.

Ball, Derek (forthcoming). Relativism, metasemantics, and the future. *Inquiry*.

Barker, Chris (2002). The dynamics of vagueness. *Linguistics and Philosophy* 25 (1): 1–36.

Beall, Jc, Glanzberg, Michael, and Ripley, David (2016). Liar paradox. In Edward N. Zalta (ed.), *The Stanford Encyclopedia of Philosophy* (Winter 2016 edition), https://plato.stanford.edu/archives/win2016/entries/liar-paradox/.

Belnap, Nuel (1993). On rigorous definitions. *Philosophical Studies* 72 (2–3): 115–46.

Biko, Stephen Bantu (1971). The definition of black consciousness. Paper produced for a South African student organization leadership training course in December 1971, available at http://www.sahistory.org.za/archive/definition-black-consciousness-bantu-stephen-biko-december-1971-south-africa [accessed August 9, 2016].

Blackburn, Simon (1999). *Think: A Compelling Introduction to Philosophy*. Oxford University Press.

Boghossian, Paul (2011). Williamson on the a priori and the analytic. *Philosophy and Phenomenological Research* 82 (2): 488–97.

Brigandt, Ingo (2010). The epistemic goal of a concept: accounting for the rationality of semantic change and variation. *Synthese* 177 (1): 19–40.

Brun, Georg (2016). Explication as a method of conceptual re-engineering. *Erkenntnis* 81 (6): 1211–41.

Burge, Tyler (1979). Individualism and the mental. *Midwest Studies in Philosophy* 4 (1): 73–122.

Burgess, Alexis, Cappelen, Herman, and Plunkett, David (eds.) (forthcoming). *Conceptual Ethics and Conceptual Engineering*. Oxford University Press.

Burgess, Alexis, and Plunkett, David (2013a). Conceptual ethics I. *Philosophy Compass* 8 (12): 1091–101.

Burgess, Alexis, and Plunkett, David (2013b). Conceptual ethics II. *Philosophy Compass* 8 (12): 1102–10.

Burgess, Alexis, and Sherman, Brett (eds.) (2014). *Metasemantics: New Essays on the Foundations of Meaning*. Oxford University Press.

Cappelen, Herman (1999). Intentions in words. *Noûs* 33: 92–102.

Cappelen, Herman (2008a). Content relativism. In M. Kolbel and M. Garcia-Carpintero (eds.), *Relative Truth*. Oxford University Press, 265–86.

Cappelen, Herman (2008b). The creative interpreter: content relativism and assertion. *Noûs* 42 (1): 23–46.

Cappelen, Herman (2012). *Philosophy without Intuitions*. Oxford University Press.

Cappelen, Herman (2013). Nonsense and illusions of thought. *Philosophical Perspectives* 27 (1): 22–50.

Cappelen, Herman (2017). Why philosophers shouldn't do semantics. *Review of Philosophy and Psychology* 8 (4): 743–62.

Cappelen, Herman, and Dever, Josh (2013). *The Inessential Indexical: On the Philosophical Insignificance of Perspective and the First Person*. Oxford University Press.

Cappelen, Herman, and Dever, Josh (2016). *Context and Communication*. Oxford University Press.

Cappelen, Herman, and Dever, Josh (2018). *Puzzles about Reference*. Oxford University Press.

Cappelen, Herman, and Hawthorne, John (2009). *Relativism and Monadic Truth*. Oxford University Press.

Cappelen, Herman, and Lepore, Ernest (1997). *Liberating Content*. Oxford University Press.

Cappelen, Herman, and Lepore, Ernest (2005). *Insensitive Semantics: A Defense of Semantic Minimalism and Speech Act Pluralism*. Wiley-Blackwell.

Cappelen, Herman, and Lepore, Ernest (2007). *Language Turned on Itself: The Semantics and Pragmatics of Metalinguistic Discourse*. Oxford University Press.

Carey, Susan (2009). *The Origin of Concepts*. Oxford University Press.

Carnap, R. (1963). P. F. Strawson on linguistic naturalism. In P. A. Schilpp (ed.), *The Philosophy of Rudolf Carnap*, volume XI of The Library of Living Philosophers. Open Court, 933–40.

Carnap, Rudolf (1950). *The Logical Foundations of Probability*. University of Chicago Press.

Carnap, Rudolf (1959). The elimination of metaphysics through the logical analysis of language, trans. Arthur Pap. In A. J. Ayer (ed.), *Logical Positivism*. The Free Press, 60–8.

Carston, Robyn, and Seiji, Uchida (eds.) (1998). *Relevance Theory: Applications and Implications*. Benjamins.

Chalmers, D., Manley, D., and Wasserman, R. (eds.) (2009). *Metametaphysics: New Essays on the Foundations of Ontology*. Oxford University Press.

Chalmers, David J. (2011). Verbal disputes. *Philosophical Review* 120 (4): 515–66.

Chignell, Andrew (ed.) (forthcoming). *Evil*. Oxford University Press.

Chihara, Charles (1979). The semantic paradoxes: a diagnostic investigation. *Philosophical Review* 88 (4): 590–618.

Clark, Andy, and Chalmers, David J. (1998). The extended mind. *Analysis* 58 (1): 7–19.

Carston, Robyn (2004). Explicature and semantics. In Steven Davis and Brendan S. Gillon (eds.), *Semantics: A Reader*. Oxford University Press, 817–45.

Davidson, Donald (1978). What metaphors mean. *Critical Inquiry* 5(1): 31–47. Reprinted in *Inquiries into Truth and Interpretation*. Oxford University Press, 1984, 245–64.

Davidson, Donald (1986). A coherence theory of truth and knowledge. In Ernest Lepore (ed.), *Truth and Interpretation: Perspectives on the Philosophy of Donald Davidson*. Basil Blackwell, 307–19.

Devitt, Michael (1981). *Designation*. Columbia University Press.

Dorr, Cian, and Hawthorne, John (2014). Semantic plasticity and speech reports. *Philosophical Review* 123 (3): 281–338.

Dummett, Michael (1973). *Frege: Philosophy of Language*. Duckworth.

Dummett, Michael (1978). *Truth and Other Enigmas*. Harvard University Press.

Egan, Andy (2007). Epistemic modals, relativism and assertion. *Philosophical Studies* 133 (1): 1–22.

Eklund, Matti (2002). Inconsistent languages. *Philosophy and Phenomenological Research* 64 (2): 251–75.

Eklund, Matti (2014). Replacing truth? In Alexis Burgess and Brett Sherman (eds.), *Metasemantics: New Essays on the Foundations of Meaning*. Oxford University Press, 293–310.

Eklund, Matti (2015). Intuitions, conceptual engineering, and conceptual fixed points. In Chris Daly (ed.), *The Palgrave Handbook of Philosophical Methods*. Palgrave Macmillan, 363–85.

Eklund, Matti (2017). *Choosing Normative Concepts*. Oxford University Press.

Epstein, Brian (2015). *The Ant Trap: Rebuilding the Foundations of the Social Sciences*. Oxford University Press.

Evans, Gareth (1973). The causal theory of names. *Aristotelian Society Supplementary Volume* 47 (1): 187–208.

Fassio, Davide, and McKenna, Robin (2015). Revisionary epistemology. *Inquiry* 58 (7–8): 755–79.

FBI Criminal Justice Information Services Division (2014). Rape definition. Available at: https://ucr.fbi.gov/crime-in-the-u.s/2014/crime-in-the-u.s.-2014/offenses-known-to-law-enforcement/rape [accessed September 12, 2016].

Fodor, Jerry A., and Lepore, Ernest (1992). *Holism: A Shopper's Guide*. Blackwell.

Frege, Gottlob (1879). *Begriffsschrift: Eine der arithmetischen nachgebildete Formelsprache des reinen Denkens*. Verlag L. Nebert. English translation by S. Bauer-Mengelberg in van Heijenoort (1967), 1–82; and by T. W. Bynum in Frege (1972).

Frege, Gottlob (1972). *Conceptual Notation and Related Articles*. Translated and edited by T. W. Bynum. Clarendon Press.

Gallie, W. B. (1955). Essentially contested concepts. *Proceedings of the Aristotelian Society* 56 (1): 167–98.

Gettier, Edmund (1963). Is justified true belief knowledge? *Analysis* 23 (6): 121–3.

Greenough, Patrick (MS) Against conceptual engineering.

Gupta, Anil (2015). Definitions. In Edward N. Zalta (ed.), *The Stanford Encyclopedia of Philosophy* (Summer 2015 edition), <http://plato.stanford.edu/archives/sum2015/entries/definitions/>.

Hacking, Ian (1999). *The Social Construction of What?* Harvard University Press.

Haslanger, Sally (1995). Ontology and social construction. *Philosophical Topics* 23 (2): 95–125.

Haslanger, Sally (1999). What knowledge is and what it ought to be: feminist values and normative epistemology. *Noûs* 33 (13): 459–80.

Haslanger, Sally (2000). Gender and race: (what) are they? (what) do we want them to be? *Noûs* 34 (1): 31–55.

Haslanger, Sally (2004). Future genders? Future races? *Philosophic Exchange* 34 (2003–4): 4–27.

Haslanger, Sally (2005). What are we talking about? The semantics and politics of social kinds. *Hypatia* 20 (4): 10–26.

Haslanger, Sally (2006). What good are our intuitions? Philosophical analysis and social kinds. *Aristotelian Society Supplementary Volume* 80 (1): 89–118.

Haslanger, Sally (2008). A Social constructionist analysis of race. In B. Koenig, S. Lee, and S. Richardson (eds.), *Revisiting Race in the Genomic Age*. Rutgers University Press, 56–69.

Haslanger, Sally (2009). Exploring race in life, in speech, and in philosophy: comments on Joshua Glasgow's "A Theory of Race." *Symposia on Gender, Race and Philosophy* 5 (2): 1–7.

Haslanger, Sally (2010). Language, politics, and "the folk": looking for "the meaning" of 'race'. *The Monist* 93 (2): 169–87.

Haslanger, Sally (2012). *Resisting Reality: Social Construction and Social Critique*. Oxford University Press.

Haslanger, Sally (2016). Theorizing with a purpose: the many kinds of sex. In Catherine Kendig (ed.), *Natural Kinds and Classification in Scientific Practice*. Routledge, 129–44.

Horwich, Paul (1999). The minimalist conception of truth. In Simon Blackburn and Keith Simmons (eds.), *Truth*. Oxford University Press, 239–63.

Jackman, Henry (1999). We live forwards but understand backwards: linguistic practices and future behavior. *Pacific Philosophical Quarterly* 80 (2): 157–77.

Jackman, Henry (2005). Temporal externalism, deference, and our ordinary linguistic practice. *Pacific Philosophical Quarterly* 86 (3): 365–80.

Jackson, Frank (1998). *From Metaphysics to Ethics: A Defence of Conceptual Analysis*. Oxford University Press.

Janiak, Andrew (ed.) (forthcoming). *Space*. Oxford University Press.

Joyce, Richard (2005). *The Myth of Morality*. Cambridge University Press.

Justus, James (2012). Carnap on concept determination: methodology for philosophy of science. *European Journal for Philosophy of Science* 2 (2): 161–79.

Kaplan, David (1977/1989). Demonstratives. In Joseph Almog, John Perry, and Howard Wettstein (eds.), *Themes from Kaplan*. Oxford University Press, 481–563.

Kaplan, David (1990). Words. *Proceedings of the Aristotelian Society, Supplementary Volumes* 64: 93–119.

Kauppinen, Antti (2007). The rise and fall of experimental philosophy. *Philosophical Explorations* 10 (2): 95–118.

Kearns, Stephen, and Magidor, Ofra (2008). Epistemicism about vagueness and meta-linguistic safety. *Philosophical Perspectives* 22 (1): 277–304.

Kekes, John (1977). Essentially contested concepts: a reconsideration. *Philosophy and Rhetoric* 10 (2): 71–89.

Kölbel, Max (2002). *Truth without Objectivity*. Routledge.

Kölbel, Max (2009). The evidence for relativism. *Synthese* 166 (2): 375–95.

Kornblith, Hilary (2002). *Knowledge and its Place in Nature*. Oxford University Press.

Korta, Kepa, and Perry, John (2015). Pragmatics. In *The Stanford Encyclopedia of Philosophy* (Winter 2015 edition), https://plato.stanford.edu/archives/win2015/entries/pragmatics.

Kripke, Saul A. (1980). *Naming and Necessity*. Harvard University Press.

Kripke, Saul A. (1982). *Wittgenstein on Rules and Private Language*. Harvard University Press.

Lakoff, George (2004). *Don't Think of an Elephant: Know Your Values and Frame the Debate*. Chelsea Green Publishing.

Lasersohn, Peter (2013). Non-world indices and assessment-sensitivity. *Inquiry* 56 (2–3): 122–48.

Lepore, Ernest, and Cappelen, Herman (2005). *Insensitive Semantics: A Defense of Semantic Minimalism and Speech Act Pluralism*. Blackwell.

Leslie, Sarah-Jane (2017). The original sin of cognition: fear, prejudice, and generalization. *Journal of Philosophy*.

Leslie, Sarah-Jane, and Lerner, Adam (2016). Generic generalizations. In *The Stanford Encyclopedia of Philosophy* (Winter 2016 edition), https://plato.stanford.edu/archives/win2016/entries/generics/.

Lewis, David (1969). *Convention: A Philosophical Study*. Harvard University Press.

Lewis, David (1996). Elusive knowledge. *Australasian Journal of Philosophy* 74 (4): 549–67.

Ludlow, Peter (2005). Contextualism and the new linguistic turn in epistemology. In Gerhard Preyer and Georg Peter (eds.), *Contextualism in Philosophy: Knowledge, Meaning, and Truth*. Oxford University Press, 11–50.

Ludlow, Peter (2014). *Living Words: Meaning Underdetermination and the Dynamic Lexicon*. Oxford University Press.

MacFarlane, John (2014). *Assessment Sensitivity: Relative Truth and its Applications*. Oxford University Press.

Machery, Edouard (2009). *Doing without Concepts*. Oxford University Press.

MacIntyre, Alasdair (1973). The essential contestability of some social concepts. *Ethics* 84 (1): 1–9.

Maher, Patrick (2007). Explication defended. *Studia Logica* 86 (2): 331–41.

Mallon, Ron (2004). Passing, traveling and reality: social constructionism and the metaphysics of race. *Noûs* 38 (4): 644–73.

Mallon, Ron (2006). 'Race': normative, not metaphysical or semantic. *Ethics* 116 (3): 525–51.

Melamed, Yitzhak Y. (ed.) (2016). *Eternity: A History*. Oxford University Press.

Millikan, Ruth (1984). *Language, Thought and Other Biological Categories*. MIT Press.

Neale, Stephen (2001). Implicature and colouring. In G. Cosenza (ed.), *Paul Grice's Heritage*. Brepols, 135–80.

Nikulin, Dmitri (ed.) (2015). *Memory: A History*. Oxford University Press.

Olsson, Erik (2015). Gettier and the method of explication: a 60 year old solution to a 50 year old problem. *Philosophical Studies* 172 (1): 57–72.

Pasnau, R. (2013). Epistemology idealized. *Mind* 122 (488): 987–1021.

Plunkett, David (2015). Which concepts should we use? Metalinguistic negotiations and the methodology of philosophy. *Inquiry: An Interdisciplinary Journal of Philosophy* 58 (7–8): 828–74.

Plunkett, David, and Sundell, Timothy (2013). Disagreement and the semantics of normative and evaluative terms. *Philosophers' Imprint* 13 (23): 1–37.

Plunkett, David, and Sundell, Timothy (forthcoming). Title to be determined.

Preyer, Gerhard, and Peter, Georg (eds.) (2005). *Contextualism in Philosophy: Knowledge, Meaning, and Truth*. Oxford University Press.

Priest, Graham (2005). *Doubt Truth to Be a Liar*. Oxford University Press.

Priest, Graham (2006). *In Contradiction: A Study of the Transconsistent*. Oxford University Press.

Putnam, Hilary (1975). The meaning of 'meaning'. *Minnesota Studies in the Philosophy of Science* 7: 131–93.

Quine, W. V. (1960). *Word and Object*. MIT Press.

Railton, Peter (1989). Naturalism and prescriptivity. *Social Philosophy and Policy* 7 (1): 151.

Railton, Peter (1993). Noncognitivism about rationality: benefits, costs, and an alternative. *Philosophical Issues* 4: 36–51.

Recanati, François (1997). Can we believe what we do not understand? *Mind and Language* 12 (1): 84–100.

Recanati, François (2004). *Literal Meaning*. Cambridge University Press.

Richard, Mark (2014). Analysis, concepts, and intuitions. *Analytic Philosophy* 55 (4): 394–406.

Richard, Mark (forthcoming). *Meaning as Species*.

Rorty, Richard (1961). Recent metaphilosophy. *Review of Metaphysics* 15 (2): 299–318.

Saul, Jennifer (2006). Gender and race. *Aristotelian Society Supplementary Volume* 80 (1): 119–43.

Scharp, Kevin (2007). Replacing truth. *Inquiry* 50 (6): 606–21.

Scharp, Kevin (2013a). *Replacing Truth*. Oxford University Press.

Scharp, Kevin (2013b). Truth, the liar, and relativism. *Philosophical Review* 122 (3): 427–510.

Schupbach, Jonah N. (2015). Experimental explication. *Philosophy and Phenomenological Research* 91 (2): 672–710.

Searle, John (1980). The background of meaning. In J. R. Searle, F. Kiefer, and M. Bierwisch (eds.), *Speech Act Theory and Pragmatics*. Reidel, 221–32.

Searle, John (1995). *The Construction of Social Reality*. Free Press.

Soames, Scott (2002). *Beyond Rigidity: The Unfinished Semantic Agenda of Naming and Necessity*. Oxford University Press.

Soames, Scott (2003a). *Philosophical Analysis in the Twentieth Century*, Volume 1: *The Dawn of Analysis*. Princeton University Press.

Soames, Scott (2003b). *Philosophical Analysis in the Twentieth Century*, Volume 2: *The Age of Meaning*. Princeton University Press.

Sperber, Dan, and Deirdre Wilson (1995). *Relevance*. Second edition. Blackwell.

Spicer, Finn (2008). Are there any conceptual truths about knowledge? *Proceedings of the Aristotelian Society* 108 (1part1): 43–60.

Sterken, Rachel (forthcoming). Transformative communicative disruptions. In Burgess, Cappelen, and Plunkett (eds.), *Conceptual Ethics and Conceptual Engineering*. Oxford University Press.

Strawson, P. F. (1959). *Individuals*. Routledge.

Strawson, Peter F. (1963). Carnap's views on conceptual systems versus natural languages in analytic philosophy. In Paul Arthur Schilpp (ed.), *The Philosophy of Rudolf Carnap*. Open Court, 503–18.

Swanton, Christine (1985). On the 'essential contestedness' of political concepts. *Ethics* 95 (4): 811–27.

Tarski, Alfred (1933). The concept of truth in formalized languages. Trans. J. H. Woodger. Reprinted in *Logic, Semantics, Metamathematics*, ed. J. Corcoran. Hackett Publishing Company, 1983, 152–278.

Tarski, Alfred (1944). The semantic conception of truth. *Philosophy and Phenomenological Research* 4: 341–76.

Tarski, Alfred (1979). The semantic paradoxes: a diagnostic investigation. *The Philosophical Review* 88: 590–618.

Tarski, Alfred (1984). The semantic paradoxes: some second thoughts. *Philosophical Studies* 45: 223–9.

Thomasson, Amie (forthcoming). A pragmatic method for conceptual ethics. In Burgess, Cappelen, and Plunkett (eds.), *Conceptual Ethics and Conceptual Engineering*. Oxford University Press.

Travis, Charles (1996). Meaning's role in truth. *Mind* 105 (419): 451–66.

van Heijenoort, Jean (ed.) (1967). *From Frege to Gödel: A Source Book in Mathematical Logic, 1879–1931*. Harvard University Press.

van Inwagen, Peter (2008). How to think about the problem of free will. *Journal of Ethics* 12 (3/4): 327–41.

Väyrynen, Pekka (2014). Essential contestability and evaluation. *Australasian Journal of Philosophy* 3: 1–18.

Weiner, Matt (2009). The (mostly harmless) inconsistency of knowledge ascriptions. *Philosophers' Imprint* 9 (1): 1–25.

Williamson, Timothy (1994). *Vagueness*. Routledge.

Williamson, Timothy (2000). *Knowledge and its Limits*. Oxford University Press.

Williamson, Timothy (2007). *The Philosophy of Philosophy*. Blackwell.

Williamson, Timothy (2009). Reference, inference, and the semantics of pejoratives. In Joseph Almog and Paolo Leonardi (eds.), *The Philosophy of David Kaplan*. Oxford University Press, 137–59.

Williamson, Timothy (2011). Williamson on the a priori and the analytic reply. *Philosophy and Phenomenological Research* 82 (2): 498–506.

Williamson, Timothy (2013). How deep is the distinction between a priori and a posteriori knowledge? In Albert Casullo and Joshua C. Thurow (eds.), *The A Priori in Philosophy*. Oxford University Press, 291–312.

Wilson, M. (1982). Predicate meets property. *The Philosophical Review* 91 (4): 549–89.

Wittgenstein, Ludwig (2001/1921). *Tractatus Logico-Philosophicus*, trans. D. F. Pears and B. F. McGuinness. Routledge.

Wittgenstein, Ludwig (2009/1953). *Philosophical Investigations*. 4th edition, trans. P. Hacker and J. Schulte. Wiley-Blackwell.

Yablo, Stephen (2005). The myth of seven. In Mark Eli Kalderon (ed.), *Fictionalism in Metaphysics*. Oxford University Press, 88–115.

Index